FORKNER SHORTHAND

Fifth Edition

HAMDEN L. FORKNER, JR., ED.D.

FRANCES A. BROWN, M.A.
Professor of Education
University of Washington

Forkner Publishing Corporation

A SUBSIDIARY OF CANADA PUBLISHING CORPORATION

ISBN 0-912036-31-1

Library of Congress Catalog Card No. 81-65399

2 3 4 5 K 9 8 7 6

Printed and Bound in the United States of America

TO THE TEACHER

FORKNER SHORTHAND was introduced in 1952 after ten years of research. Today, it is taught in thousands of high school and college classrooms throughout the world.

FORKNER SHORTHAND students succeed in business because they can write at high speeds and transcribe accurately. They consistently win awards for writing speeds and transcription accuracy in contests sponsored by national organizations.

FORKNER PROGRAMS succeed in secondary schools and colleges because the system is easy to learn to write. It combines 19 letters of the alphabet with a few symbols. Because **FORKNER SHORTHAND** is based on what students already know—how to read and write longhand—they need not learn a whole new language to become competent in shorthand. Consequently, many high school students acquire a marketable shorthand skill in one year.

Motivation is high in Forkner programs because shorthand writing begins the first class period. Students make speedy progress toward their goals. Shorthand enrollments go up. These new materials are designed to equip the student to meet the current challenge of entry-level jobs in business and government.

This New Edition

Those who have taught **FORKNER SHORTHAND** over the years will feel at home with this new generation of Forkner materials. We have retained the "rule discovery" approach in which students figure out the writing rules themselves. All materials are self-keyed, providing immediate reinforcement to the learner. Every fourth chapter provides a review and applies previously-learned theory through the medium of business letters. The **STUDY GUIDE** includes a self-test on each new writing rule and on transcription skills, so that both student and instructor can monitor progress.

New Features of the Fifth Edition

The textbook. The new first-semester text features the following improvements over earlier editions:

1. A new sequence of theory presentation gives students a more gradual introduction to shorthand theory.
2. The number of theory principles has been reduced. This reduction cuts even further the time required to learn Forkner theory. More class time is available for building speed and for teaching essential transcription skills. The new text has 32 rather than 37 chapters.
3. The number of abbreviated words has been reduced by some 40 percent, thus lessening the memory burden.
4. Heavy emphasis is placed on transcription and on English skills. Many chapters provide a special section, "Building Transcription Skills."
5. Over 20 percent more dictation material is provided.
6. The STUDY GUIDE exercises are perforated so that out-of-class work may be checked periodically.

The Study Guide. Correlated chapter-by-chapter with the textbook, the STUDY GUIDE gives students additional practice in applying each writing principle. It consists of 32 units of self-tests, and is completely self-keyed. Designed for out-of-class work, each unit requires about 30 minutes to complete.

The examinations. After each four chapters, an examination is provided to test students' ability to write, transcribe, and deal with English skills. The examinations are bound in the back of the STUDY GUIDE for self-testing by students. At the instructor's discretion, they may be removed before books are distributed to students.

Dictation tapes. THEORY AND SPEED-BUILDING TAPES IN FORKNER SHORTHAND are correlated with the text and STUDY GUIDE. Sixteen cassettes give students additional practice on all material presented in the 32 text chapters and STUDY GUIDE units. A variety of speed-forcing dictation plans is used. Two additional cassettes provide compact reviews for use periodically during the course. There are almost 18 hours of dictation practice for classroom use and for make-up work for students who are absent from class.

Other teaching aids for beginning classes. A complete range of materials is available for teaching beginning shorthand. These include the following: FORKNER SHORTHAND DICTIONARY FOR BEGINNERS—a dictionary that includes outlines for all words appearing in the first-year Forkner texts and workbooks, as well as additional words that appear in business correspondence.

ACKNOWLEDGEMENTS

The authors and publisher of this edition of FORKNER SHORTHAND are indebted to the late Dr. Hamden L. Forkner, Sr., who invented the system and was an author of previous editions.

We are grateful to schools, colleges, universities, and educators everywhere who have used the four previous editions of FORKNER SHORTHAND and who continue to hold workshops and conferences to acquaint teachers with the benefits of the FORKNER SHORTHAND system.

H. L. F., Jr.
F. A. B.

Second Semester — Dictation and Transcription

FORKNER SHORTHAND, Fifth Edition, is designed to be completed in one semester of classroom study. Most students, however, should take a second-semester course in FORKNER SHORTHAND to increase dictation and transcription skills, and to improve language arts skills.

CORRELATED DICTATION AND TRANSCRIPTION, Third Edition, has been prepared for second-semester courses in FORKNER SHORTHAND. This program, consisting of textbook, study guide, and tape library, provides ample dictation and transcription material to assist the student in the refinement of grammar, punctuation, spelling, and word usage skills, and to develop faster writing and transcription speeds.

CONTENTS

CONTENTS

CONTENTS

TO THE STUDENT

As you begin your study of FORKNER SHORTHAND, you join thousands of other students throughout the world who are learning either the English- or French-language version of this scientific shorthand system. As you probably know, there is a strong demand for shorthand writers today, and employment experts say there will be a greater demand for people with shorthand skills in the future.

Recent studies show that *there will be a greater need for secretaries in the next 10 years than for any other occupational skill*.

Why study shorthand? Because a shorthand skill will *help you to*:

- *Land the job you want*. With a shorthand skill, beginning office workers can often select a stimulating job rather than settle for routine tasks.
- *Increase the size of your paycheck*. Beginning and advanced-level office workers who are good at shorthand get better pay than those who do not have that skill.
- *Increase your chances for promotions and raises*. If you have good shorthand skills and show a willingness to work, you will probably find yourself at the top of the list for promotions and raises.

Developing writing speed

In order to write shorthand rapidly, you must be able to move your hand quickly. How fast can you write longhand?

To find out, write the following speed sentence in longhand as many times as you can in ten seconds (one-sixth of a minute). Your instructor will time you. Then multiply the total number of words you write by 6 to get your longhand writing rate. Try writing this sentence a number of times to see whether you can double your longhand writing rate.

Speed sentence: THEY WILL MAKE SURE EACH PAGE WILL LOOK VERY GOOD.

FORKNER SHORTHAND is easy to learn because it blends letters of the alphabet with a few symbols. If you follow your instructor's directions, you will soon have a skill that will give you an excellent start in your business career.

WRITING IN YOUR SHORTHAND NOTEBOOK

As a student of **FORKNER SHORTHAND**, you will need a shorthand notebook in which to practice and to take shorthand dictation for transcription. Note that each page in your shorthand notebook has a line down the center. When writing shorthand, begin at the top left edge of the page and write to the center line. When you have completed the left column, begin at the top of the right column and write until all lines are filled. (See illustration below).

As you complete the right column, use your left hand to flip the left corner, ready to turn quickly to the next sheet. Turn the page and write *on the next sheet* (not on the back of the page just completed). Thus, you will write through an entire notebook in one direction and then turn the notebook over and write in the other direction. Write the current date at the bottom of each notebook page.

For efficiency, attach an elastic band to the cover of your notebook so that as shorthand is transcribed, pages are slipped under the band.

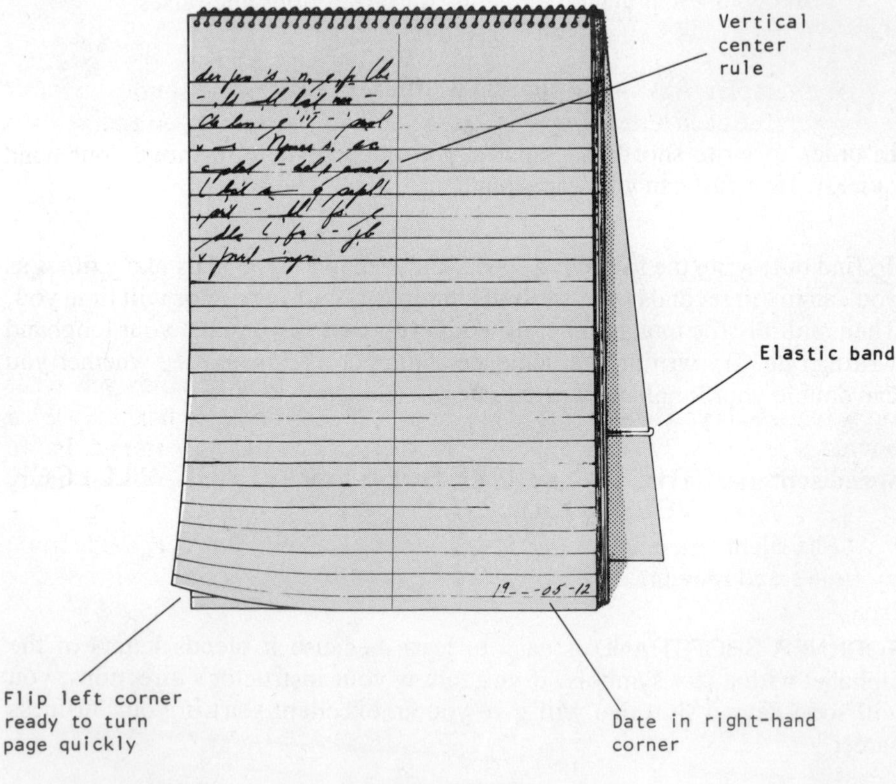

CHAPTER 1

WRITING SOUNDS OF LONG AND SHORT **E** AND LONG **I**

Assignment 1 — **Saving writing strokes**. Write the letters as they are written below until you can write them quickly and without hesitation. The samples below show how to eliminate unneeded strokes when letters are written *at the beginning of a word*.

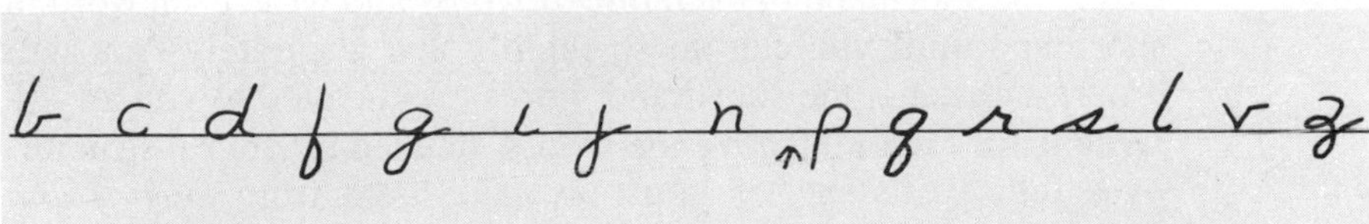

Learning tips:

1. Note that the usual beginning stroke is omitted from letters that begin a word or that stand alone.
2. When the letter *b* or *f* begins a word or stands alone, start at the top of the letter.
3. When *p* begins a word or stands alone, start below the line and make an upward stroke with the loop on the line.

The samples below show how to omit unneeded strokes in *letters that end a word*. Write each letter several times, remembering to omit the ending loop or stroke.

Assignment 2 — **Writing by sound**. When writing shorthand, you write only the sounds you hear. For example, in the word *leave*, you hear only three sounds, *l*, *e*, and *v*. Those are the sounds you would write in shorthand. In the word *light*, you do not hear the *g* or *h*; therefore, you write *l-i-t* in shorthand.

The silent letters in the words below have been crossed out. Study these examples and remember to write only what you hear when you write shorthand.

leave	day	goal	know
might	free	pay	scene
slow	own	sign	bright

Assignment 3 — **Rule discovery**. Follow the steps below to learn each writing principle.

Step 1. Examine both the shorthand and the print of the first group of words under the heading, Sounds of Long and Short E. Try to discover the rule for writing that group of words. When you think you have discovered the rule, check the writing principles that follow to see if you have made the correct discovery.

Step 2. Cover the print of each line of shorthand words and read the shorthand until you can read each line as rapidly as you can read the print. Use an index card as a shield.

Step 3. Cover the shorthand of each line of words and write each word in shorthand until you can do so rapidly and accurately. You will progress faster if the shorthand words are dictated to you as you write them. You may have the words dictated by your instructor, by a fellow student, or you may take them from *Theory and Speed-Building Tapes in Forkner Shorthand*.

SOUNDS OF LONG AND SHORT **E**

fe	del	feld	evn	se	ledr	pepl
fee	deal	field	even	see-sea	leader	people
ner	nvr	brd	srv	sd	sl	fl
near	never	bread	serve	said	sell	fell
ls	dd	eg	ern	rde	vre	ned
less	dead	egg	earn	ready	very	need
ded	les	sel	fel			
deed	lease	seal	feel			

Learning tips:

1. When you hear the *name* of the letter *e* in a word, you have a long *e* sound. For example, you hear the name of the letter *e* in *fee*; therefore, *fee* has a long *e*.

2. The final *y* in many words has a long *e* sound. See the words *very* and *ready* above.

3. Note that both *long* and *short* sounds of *e* are written at the beginning of a word. See *even*, *earn*, and *egg* above. You need the beginning sounds of all words in order to read them accurately.

4. When an outline stands for more than one word, as in *see-sea*, the meaning of the sentence tells you the correct word. When reading a shorthand outline, you should say all words which are represented by that outline.

SOUND OF LONG I

lif	lin	driv	sin	fin	rid	bi	i
life	line	drive	sign	fine	ride	buy	I-eye

idl	fil	fibr	finr	piplin	sirn
idle	file	fiber	finer	pipeline	siren

Learning tips:

1. Note that *i* is written with a short downward stroke when beginning a word or when it stands alone as in *idle* and *I*.
2. The final *y* in words such as *buy*, *fly*, and *cry* has a long *i* sound.

WRITING PRINCIPLES

LONG AND SHORT E — Write *e* for long *e* sounds. Omit *e* when the short sound of *e* occurs in the *body* of a word.

The letter *e* has two basic sounds: a long sound, as in *fee* and *deal*, and a short sound, as in *never* and *bread*. Note that the *e* is written when the short sound of *e* begins a word. See *earn* and *egg* on page 2.

LONG I — Write an undotted *i* for all long sounds of *i*.

The letter *i* has two basic sounds: a long sound, as in *sign* and *life*, and a short sound, as in *big* and *bill*. The short sound of *i* is presented in the next chapter.

Assignment 4 — **New vocabulary**. Some words that occur often are abbreviated in shorthand. These words are called *abbreviated words*. You must memorize abbreviated words so that you can read and write each one quickly and easily. The abbreviated words come first in each "New Vocabulary" section. They are also shown in italics and underlined with a solid line in color so you will know which words must be memorized.

Follow these steps to learn abbreviated words:

Step 1. Memorize the shorthand abbreviation for each word.

Step 2. Cover the print of each line of abbreviated words and read the outlines until you can read them as rapidly as you can read the print.

Step 3. Cover the shorthand of each line of words and write the outlines for each abbreviated word several times, saying the word to yourself each time you write it.

c	f	g	e	s	–
can	for	go-good	he	is-his-us	the

Learning tip: The outline for *the* is the cross of the letter *t* and is written above the line when it stands alone.

Assignment 5 — **Speed-building reading and writing**. Follow the steps below:

Step 1. Read each sentence from the shorthand until you can read it as rapidly as you can read from print. (These sentences are printed at the end of this chapter).
Write each sentence in shorthand until you can write each one rapidly and accurately.

1. – brd s vre g.
2. i c bi – brd f – ledr.
3. i c ern ern – vre g fe f – del.
4. e c nvr sl – feld.
5. s les f – fin feld s rde.
6. – ledr c sin – vre g les f s.
7. – pepl c se – ned f – fe.
8. i sd i nvr g ner – se.
9. e sd e s rde f – red.

Learning tips:

1. You do not begin a sentence with a capital letter when writing shorthand. Of course, you will capitalize the first word of a sentence when you transcribe.

2. To build your writing speed, place a sheet of notebook paper directly under the shorthand sentence you wish to practice. Then dictate the sentence to yourself as you write the shorthand, making your outlines like those in the book. When you can write the sentence rapidly and without hesitation, move on to the next sentence.

3. Note that sentences ending in a period are punctuated with a period in shorthand.

STUDY GUIDE ASSIGNMENT

Turn to Unit 1 of the *Study Guide* and complete the self-tests before you proceed with the rest of this chapter.

TAKING TAPE DICTATION

To write from dictation the words and sentences in this chapter, use Cassette 1 Side A of the *Theory and Speed-Building Tapes*. Your instructor will show you how to use the playback equipment.

IN-CLASS DICTATION AND TRANSCRIPTION

Assignment 6 — **Transcription**. Transcribe the shorthand sentences in Assignment 5 at your best typing or longhand writing rate. Do not number the sentences.

Assignment 7 — **Dictation**. Write from dictation the sentences in Assignment 5. Your instructor will dictate each group of 20 words to you at various speeds. In order to build speed, your instructor will often dictate at a rate faster than you can write comfortably. Taking dictation at speeds that "force" you to write faster is the best way to build your writing speed.

Note that the printed sentences at the end of this chapter include numbers in parentheses after certain sentences. These numbers indicate the number of standard words in the sentences up to that point. The numbers make it possible to dictate the sentences at a desired speed.

The table on page 6 gives a cumulative count of seconds for dictating 20-word groups at various speeds. For example, to dictate a passage at 70 words a minute the dictator should finish reading the first 20-word group in 17 seconds; the second 20-word group in 34 seconds; and the third 20-word group in 51 seconds. The fourth group should be completed when the stop watch reaches 1 minute and 8 seconds, and so on.

Speed of Dictation										
	50	60	70	80	90	100	110	120	130	140
Seconds Elapsed										
First	24	20	17	15	13	12	11	10	09	08
Minute	48	40	34	30	26	24	22	20	18	17
Second	12	60	51	45	40	36	33	30	27	25
Minute	36	20	08	60	53	48	44	40	37	34
	60	40	25	15	06	60	55	50	46	42
		60	42	30	20	12	06	60	55	51
			60	45	33	24	17	10	04	60
				60	47	36	28	20	14	08
					60	47	39	30	23	17
						60	50	40	32	25
							60	50	41	34
								60	51	42
									60	51
										60

To dictate for more than two minutes, simply repeat the cycle.

50 wpm--20 words every 24 seconds	100 wpm--20 words every 12 seconds
60 wpm--20 words every 20 seconds	110 wpm--20 words every 11 seconds
70 wpm--20 words every 17 seconds	120 wpm--20 words every 10 seconds
80 wpm--20 words every 15 seconds	130 wpm--20 words every 9 seconds
90 wpm--20 words every 13 seconds	140 wpm--20 words every 8 seconds

Assignment 8 — **Own-note transcription**. After you have taken the sentences in shorthand, select your best set of notes and transcribe them at your best typing or longhand writing rate. Do not number the sentences.

TRANSCRIPT OF SHORTHAND SENTENCES

1. The bread is very good.
2. I can buy the bread for the leader.
3. I can even earn the very good fee for the deal. (20)
4. He can never sell the field.
5. His lease for the fine field is ready.
6. The leader can sign the very good lease for us. (40)
7. The people can see the need for the fee.
8. I said I never go near the sea.
9. He said he is ready for the ride. (60)

CHAPTER 2

WRITING SOUNDS OF **A**, **T**, AND SHORT **I**

Assignment 1 – **Rule discovery**. Follow the steps below to learn each writing principle.

Step 1. Examine the shorthand and the print of the first group of words. Try to discover the rule for writing that group of words. When you think you have discovered the rule, check the appropriate writing principle in your text to see if you have made the correct discovery.

Step 2. Cover the print of each line of shorthand words and read the shorthand until you can read each line as rapidly as you can read the print. Remember to say all the words each shorthand outline stands for.

Step 3. Cover the shorthand of each line of words and write each word in shorthand until you can do so rapidly and accurately. You will progress faster if the shorthand words are dictated to you as you write them.

SOUNDS OF **A**

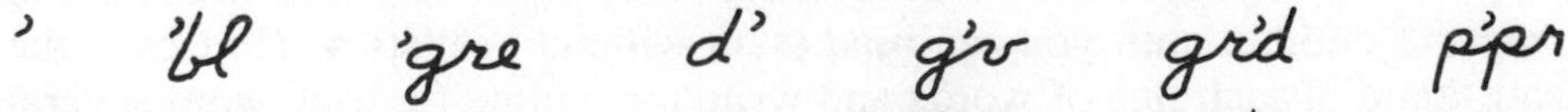

a   able   agree   day   gave   grade   paper

fall-fail   pay   sale-sail   plan-plain-plane   fair-fare-far

Learning tips:

1. In shorthand, a symbol is sometimes used to increase writing speed.
2. Write the *a* symbol first when it comes first in a word. Write it last at all other times.

SOUND OF **T**

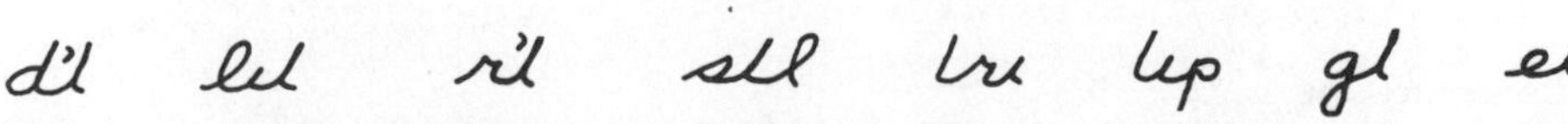

date   light   rate-rat   settle   try   type   get   eat

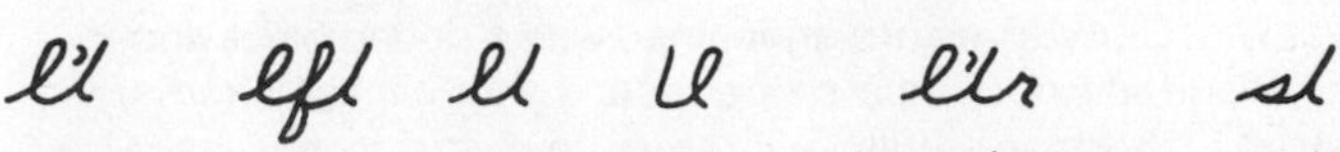

late   left   let   tell   later-latter   set

Learning tip: Note that *t* is written with a downward stroke when it stands alone or when it begins a word, as in *try* and *type* on page 7.

SOUND OF SHORT I

big bill did give if trip little fill

WRITING PRINCIPLES

A Write an apostrophe for all sounds of *a*.

Write the *a* first when an *a* sound comes first in a word; write the *a* last at all other times.

The *a* is written like an apostrophe because it can be written much more quickly than the longhand letter *a*.

T Write the *t* without a cross.

SHORT I Where the sound of short *i* occurs, write a dot above the line.

Assignment 2 — **New vocabulary**. Follow these steps in learning new vocabulary words: (1) Study the print and the shorthand until you know the shorthand outline for each word. (2) Cover the print of each line of words and read the outlines until you can read them without hesitation. (3) Cover the shorthand of each line of words and write the outline for each word several times, saying the word to yourself each time you write it.

Remember, the abbreviated words that must be memorized are shown in italics and underlined in color.

all *be-but-by-bye* *it-at-to* *of* *your* today idea

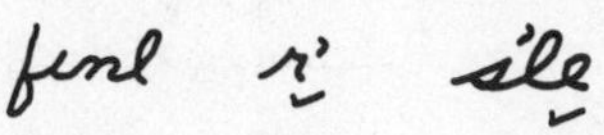

final Ray Sally

Learning tips:

1. Note that the word *today* is made up of two words—the abbreviated word *to* and the word *day*. Words that are made up of an abbreviated word and another word or syllable are called *derivatives*. Derivatives are underlined with a dotted black line.

2. When writing shorthand, do not begin proper nouns with capital letters. Put a small check mark under the shorthand outline to show that it is to be capitalized when you transcribe the shorthand outline. It is not necessary to put a check mark

under the first word in the sentence because you know that word must be capitalized.

3. The *a* in *final* does not have an *a* sound. It has an indistinct neutral sound. Several longhand letters sometimes express this same indistinct sound. For example, the *i* in *possible*, the *o* in *method*, and the *u* in *butter* all have the same indistinct sound. To save writing time, we do not use a symbol or letter to express the neutral sounds in the body of a word. However, neutral vowel sounds must be expressed at the beginning and ending of a word.

Examples: above 'bv ; data d'l'

Assignment 3 — **Phrases**. Joining two or more words when writing shorthand is called *phrasing*. Phrasing saves writing time. Cover the print of the following phrases and read them until you can do so rapidly. Then cover the shorthand and write the phrases from print, saying the phrase to yourself as you write it.

ic	v	lq	lsll	esd	f
I can	of the	to go	to settle	he said	for the
lgv	ec	lpl'n	lb	ls	
to give	he can	to plan	to be	it is	

Learning tip: The outline for the phrase *it is* can also stand for *to us*, *to his*, *at his*, and *at us*. The meaning of the sentence will tell you the correct phrase.

Assignment 4 — **Reading and writing shorthand**. Read each sentence from shorthand until you can read it as rapidly as you can read from print. Write each sentence in shorthand until you can write each one rapidly and accurately.

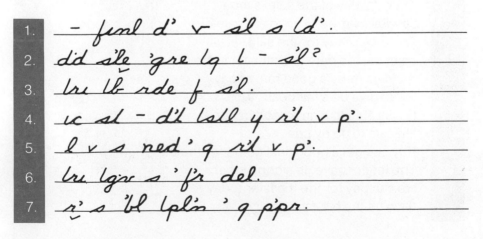

1. - finl d' v s'l s ld'.
2. did s'le 'gre lq l - s'l?
3. bre lb rde f s'l.
4. ic sl - d'l lsll y r'l v p'.
5. l v s ned' q r'l v p'.
6. bre lgv s 'fr del.
7. r' s 'bl lpl'n ' q ppr.

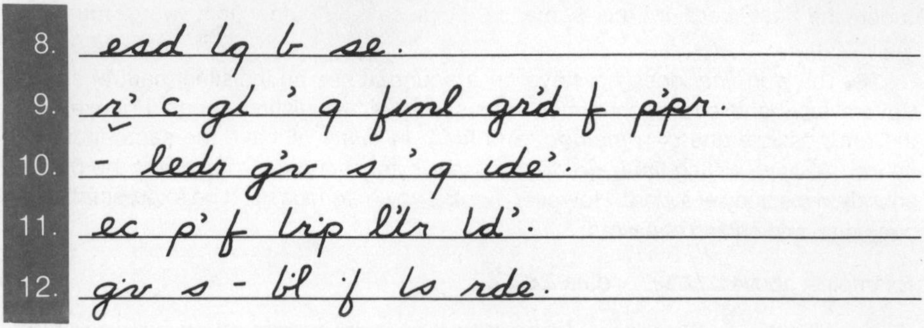

BUILDING SHORTHAND SPEED AND TRANSCRIPTION ACCURACY

Assignment 5 — **Self-testing**. Complete Unit 2 in your *Study Guide* before you proceed with the rest of this chapter.

Assignment 6 — **Taking tape dictation**. To write from dictation the new words and sentences in this chapter, use Cassette 2 Side A from *Theory and Speed-Building Tapes*.

Assignment 7 — **Taking live dictation**. Write from dictation the sentences which are printed at the end of this chapter. Your instructor will dictate each group of 20 words to you at various speeds.

Assignment 8 — **Own-note transcription**. After you have taken the sentences in shorthand, select your best set of notes and transcribe them at your best typing rate. Do not number the sentences.

TRANSCRIPT OF SHORTHAND SENTENCES

1. The final day of the sale is today.
2. Did Sally agree to go to the sale?
3. Try to be ready for the sale. (20)
4. I can set the date to settle your rate of pay.
5. All of us need a good rate of pay.
6. Try to give us a fair deal. (40)
7. Ray is able to plan a good paper.
8. He said to go by sea.
9. Ray can get a good final grade for the paper. (60)
10. The leader gave us a good idea.
11. He can pay for the trip later today.
12. Give us the bill if it is ready. (80)

CHAPTER 3

WRITING SOUNDS OF HARD **C** AND **K**, **O**, AND SOFT **C**

Assignment 1 — **Rule discovery**. Follow the steps below to learn each writing principle.

Step 1. Examine the shorthand and the print of the first group of words. Try to discover the rule for writing that group of words. When you think you have discovered the rule, check the appropriate writing principle in your text to see if you have made the correct discovery.

Step 2. Cover the print of each line of shorthand words and read the shorthand until you can read each line as rapidly as you can read the print.

Step 3. Cover the shorthand of each line of words and write each word in shorthand until you can do so rapidly and accurately. You will progress faster if the shorthand words are dictated to you as you write them.

SOUND OF HARD **C** AND **K**

clear   key   back-bake   ask   take-talk-tack   car-care

keep   attack   carry   seek

SOUNDS OF **O**

no-know   old   lower   loan-lone   follow   copy

offer   open   operate   possible   sold   locate

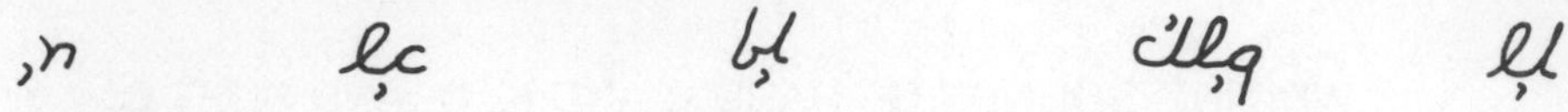

on-own lock bought-boat catalog lot

factory course-coarse got sorry

SOUND OF SOFT **C**

face nice price office service notice policy

WRITING PRINCIPLES

HARD **C** AND **K** — Write the longhand *c* to express the sound of hard *c* and *k*. The longhand *c* is used because it is much easier to write than *k*.

O — Write a small curved stroke like a comma on or below the line of writing for all sounds of *o*.

SOFT **C** — Write a longhand *s* when *c* has an *s* sound. When you write shorthand, you write what you hear.

Assignment 2 — **New vocabulary**. Follow these steps in learning new vocabulary words: (1) Study the print and the shorthand until you know the shorthand outline for each word. (2) Cover the print of each line of words and read the outlines until you can read them without hesitation. (3) Cover the shorthand of each line of words and write the outline for each word several times, saying the word to yourself each time you write it.

Remember, the abbreviated words that must be memorized are shown in italics and underlined in color.

n	nx	⌒	d	cn	den	nt
not	next	and	do	cannot	dean	note

icn	idid	in,	tp'	tsin	,n
I cannot	I did	I know	to pay	to sign	on the

Learning tip: Note how the *x* is written in *next* to save strokes. Simply add a tail to the *n* and cross the tail to form the *x*.

Assignment 3 — **Reading and writing shorthand**. Read each sentence from shorthand until you can read it as rapidly as you can read from print. Write each sentence in shorthand until you can write each one rapidly and accurately.

1. icn lct y cpe v ,ld plse.
2. i d 'gre tp' - cllg prus f cr.
3. r' c ,prl - ce ⌒ ,pn - ,ld lc.
4. in, ec gl vre q srvs l - fclre.
5. ls psbl l ,fr - crs l y ,fs.
6. - den sd - cllg c gv nts v crs.
7. - fclre srvs pln s ,pn l l pepl.
8. ic 'sc - fclre l ,fr ' lr prus.
9. sle sn rde l sin ' nt f ' ln l - ,fs.
10. - rl ,n nx nt s lr ld'.

VOWELS IN FORKNER SHORTHAND

All vowel symbols should be inserted when writing isolated words.

However, some writers find they can omit many vowel symbols in words that *appear in a sentence* and still transcribe their notes accurately. Others find that they must insert most vowels. In the shorthand passages in this and later chapters, some vowel symbols have been omitted because the writer felt the passage could be accurately transcribed without them. In some cases, the writer has inserted a vowel in a word and later in the passage may have omitted the vowel in that same word. This was done because the writer felt the need for the vowel in some sentences and not in others.

The flexibility in the use of vowel symbols is an important feature of *Forkner Shorthand*. The more vowel symbols you can omit and still read your writing, the faster you will be able to take dictation.

BUILDING SHORTHAND SPEED AND TRANSCRIPTION ACCURACY

Assignment 4 — **Self-testing**. Complete Unit 3 in your *Study Guide* before you proceed with the rest of this chapter.

Assignment 5 — **Taking tape dictation**. To write from dictation the new words and sentences in this chapter, use Cassette 3 Side A from *Theory and Speed-Building Tapes*.

Assignment 6 — **Taking live dictation**. Write from dictation the sentences which are printed at the end of this chapter. Your instructor will dictate each group of 20 words to you at various speeds.

Assignment 7 — **Own-note transcription**. After you have taken the sentences in shorthand, select your best set of notes and transcribe them at your best typing rate. Do not number the sentences.

TRANSCRIPT OF SHORTHAND SENTENCES

1. I cannot locate your copy of the old policy.
2. I do agree to pay the catalog price for the car. (20)
3. Ray can operate the key and open the old lock.
4. I know he can get very good service at the factory. (40)
5. It is possible to offer the course at your office.
6. The dean said the catalog can give notice of the course. (60)
7. The factory service plan is open to all people.
8. I can ask the factory to offer a lower price. (80)
9. Sally is not ready to sign a note for a loan at the office.
10. The rate on the next note is lower today. (100).

CHAPTER 4

BUSINESS LETTER DICTATION AND TRANSCRIPTION

No new writing principles are presented in this chapter. Instead, you will be taking business letters in shorthand and transcribing them. Because these letters *review* the writing principles you have already learned, you should concentrate on building your writing speed and transcription skills.

TRANSCRIBING BUSINESS LETTERS

Business letters are set up and typed according to certain guidelines. These guidelines will not be presented now because you should concentrate at this time on building speed in taking dictation and in transcribing your notes accurately. Therefore, do not type the letters in regular letter form until you are instructed to do so.

When you are ready to transcribe from the shorthand letters in the book or from your own notes, simply set your typewriter margins as directed and type the letters in the form shown under the heading, "Transcripts of Letters 1 and 2."

BUILDING TRANSCRIPTION SKILLS

Assignment 1 — **Correspondence Forms**. The *salutation* in a letter is the greeting that comes before the body of a letter. Some salutations are given below. Note that the salutation begins with a capital letter, usually includes the person's title (Mr., Mrs., Ms., Miss, Dr., etc.), and usually ends with a colon.

Dear Mrs. Jones:	Dear Miss Conti:	Ladies:
Dear Mr. Smith:	Dear Madam:	Ladies and Gentlemen:
Dear Ms. Taylor:	Gentlemen:	Mesdames:

The *complimentary close* comes after the body of a letter. Common complimentary closes include:

Yours truly,	Sincerely yours,	Yours sincerely,
Yours very truly,	Cordially yours,	

The first word in a complimentary close begins with a capital. A comma comes after the complimentary close if a colon is used after the salutation.

Assignment 2 — **Capitalization preview**. When transcribing, always capitalize days of the week, months, and names of holidays. Do not abbreviate days of the week or months when transcribing.

1. She will visit us the last Friday in August.
2. I believe that New Year's Day is on Sunday this year.
3. I will report for work on Monday.

Assignment 3 — **Using standard abbreviations**. Words that are commonly abbreviated in longhand are called *standard abbreviations*. To increase your writing speed, you should use these abbreviations. As you can see from the examples that follow, you apply the shorthand writing principles in writing standard abbreviations. Note that standard abbreviations are underlined with a dotted line in color.

Read and write the following standard abbreviations until you can do so rapidly and accurately.

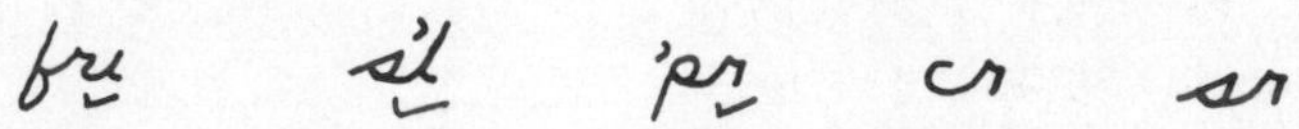

Friday Saturday April credit senior

BUSINESS LETTERS

Assignment 4 — **Letter 1**. Read and write each of the new words and phrases for Letter 1 until you can read and write each one rapidly and accurately. Then read and write the shorthand for Letter 1 until you can read and write it rapidly and accurately.

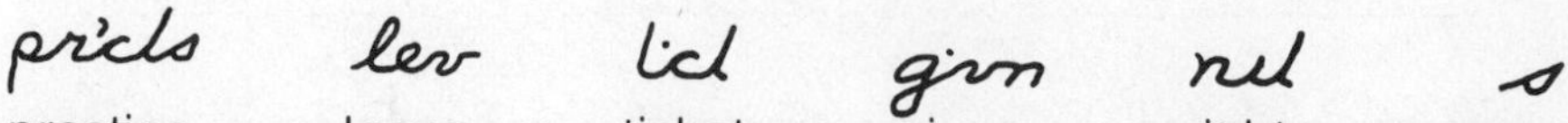

practice leave ticket given night say-saw

dear Debby play also class or-oar-ore

Yours truly paid-pad

Learning tip: *Yours truly* is an example of a *correspondence form*. Abbreviations for other complimentary closes and salutations will be introduced as they are used in the business letters. A list of correspondence forms is on page 15.

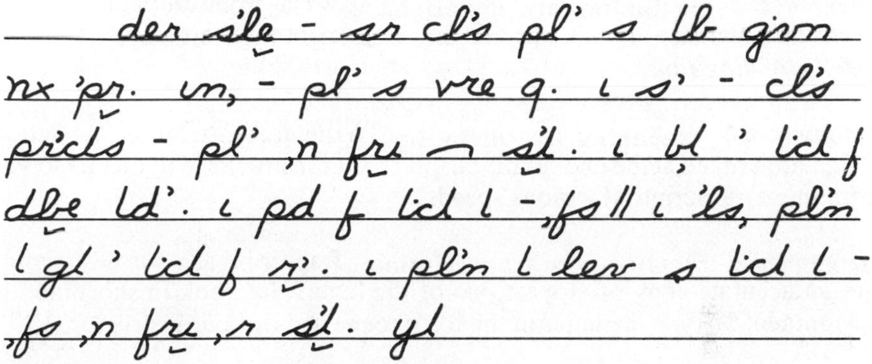

Learning tip: When taking dictation, indicate a paragraph in your notes with two parallel diagonal lines as shown in the letter above.

Assignment 5 — **Letter 2**. Read and write each new word and phrase for Letter 2 until you can read and write each one rapidly and accurately. Then read and write the shorthand for Letter 2 until you can read and write it rapidly and accurately.

lcl	pnl	brcn	cbnt	fx	dr	lre
local	panel	broken	cabinet	fix	door	Larry

eddn
he did not

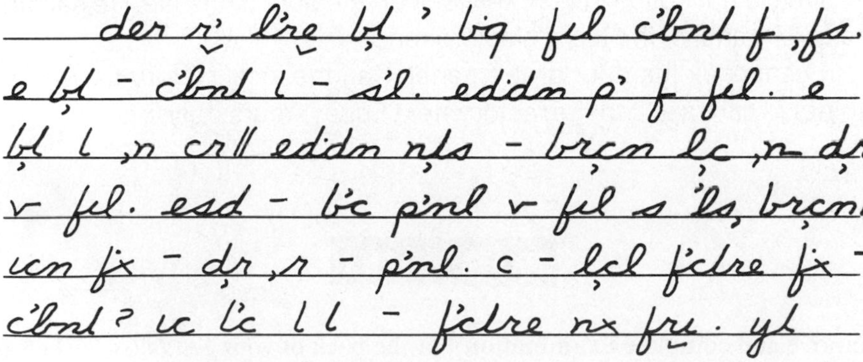

BUILDING SHORTHAND SPEED AND TRANSCRIPTION ACCURACY

Assignment 6 — **Self-testing**. Complete Unit 4 in your *Study Guide* before you proceed with the rest of this chapter.

Assignment 7 — **Taking tape dictation**. To write from dictation the new words and sentences in this chapter, use Cassette 4 Side A from *Theory and Speed-Building Tapes*.

Assignment 8 — **Taking live dictation**. Write from dictation the letters which are printed at the end of this chapter. Your instructor will dictate to you from these transcripts at various speeds.

Assignment 9 — **Own-note transcription**. Transcribe at your best typing rate an accurate copy of at least one of the letters you took in shorthand in Assignment 8. Type the letter in the form requested by your instructor.

TRANSCRIPTS OF LETTERS 1 AND 2

Letter 1 Dear Sally: The senior class play is to be given next April. I know the play is very good. I saw the class (20) practice the play on Friday and Saturday. I bought a ticket for Debby today. I paid for the ticket at (40) the office.

I also plan to get a ticket for Ray. I plan to leave his ticket at the office on Friday (60) or Saturday. Yours truly, (65)

Letter 2 Dear Ray: Larry bought a big file cabinet for the office. He bought the cabinet at the sale. He did not pay (20) for the file. He bought it on credit.

He did not notice the broken lock on the door of the file. He said the back (40) panel of the file is also broken.

I cannot fix the door or the panel. Can the local factory fix (60) the cabinet? I can take it to the factory next Friday. Yours truly, (73)

EXAMINATION I

Remove and complete Examination 1 at the back of your *Study Guide* before proceeding to Chapter 5 of your textbook.

CHAPTER 5

WRITING SOUNDS OF **U-OO**, **M**, AND **MENT**

Assignment 1 – **Rule discovery**. Follow the three-step plan to learn the new writing principles: (1) Discover the rule for each group of words. (2) Read the shorthand outlines until you can read them rapidly. (3) Cover the shorthand and write each word until you can do so rapidly and accurately.

SOUNDS OF **U-OO**

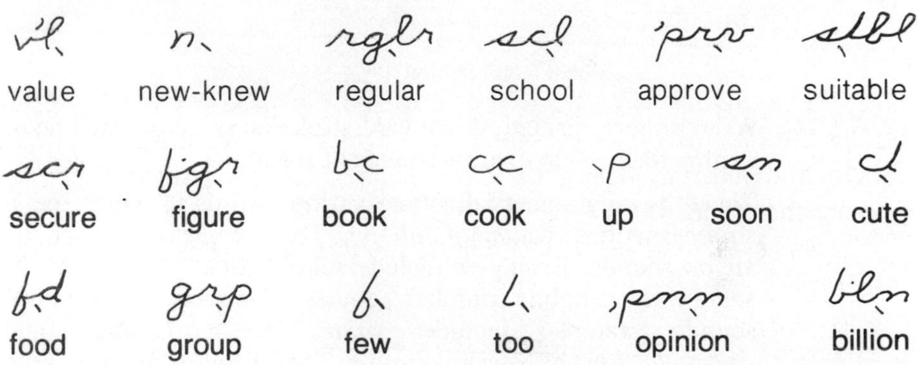

SOUND OF **M**

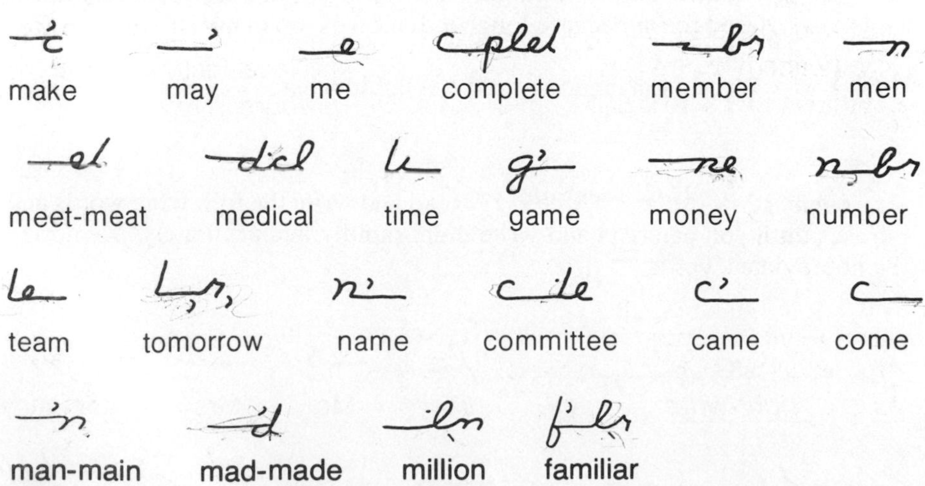

Learning tip: Note that the *m*'s in *member* are joined with a slight jog so that the two *m*'s can be easily recognized. Make the jog very small so it will not be mistaken for an *i*.

SYLLABLE **MENT**

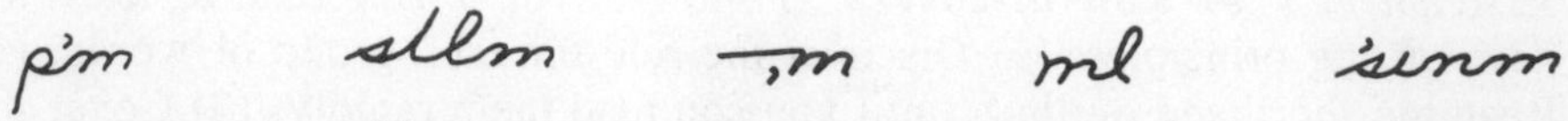

payment settlement moment mental assignment

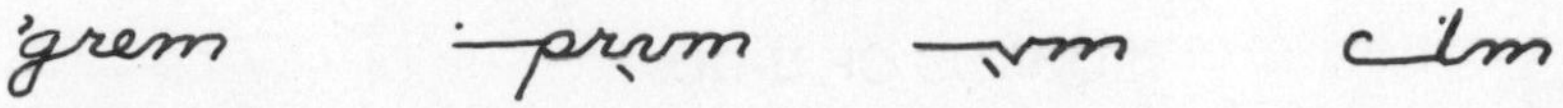

agreement improvement movement commitment

WRITING PRINCIPLES

U-OO Write a short, slanted, downward stroke on or below the line of writing thus ` to express sounds of *u* and *oo*.

The following sounds illustrate various words in which the *u* stroke is written: *value, up, full, few.* The *u* stroke is also used for all *oo* sounds. Examples include sch*oo*l, b*oo*k, and st*oo*d. In some words a lightly sounded *y* comes before a *u* or other vowel sound. Examples include: *value, secure, familiar*, and *ammonia*. In such words, omit the lightly sounded *y* and write the *u* stroke.

M Write a long, straight line to express *m*. The long, straight line is used for *m* because longhand *m* takes too many strokes to write.

MENT Write a longhand *m* for the syllable *ment*.

Assignment 2 — **New vocabulary**. Read and write the following words and phrases until you can read and write them rapidly and accurately. Memorize the abbreviated words.

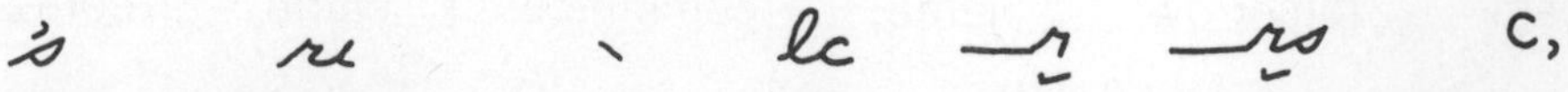

as right-write you like Mr. Mrs. company

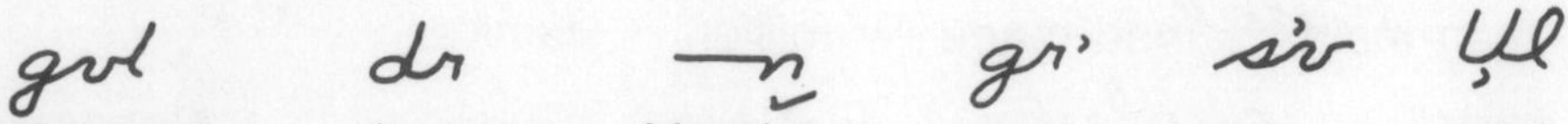

government doctor Monday gray save total

sn	cl	sple	pl's	l,	lsn
sun-son	cut	supply	place	low	it is not
—bbl	'ssns	Lel	f		
may be able	as soon as	to meet	if you		

Learning tip: Note that the *w* in *write* is silent. The *w* is silent in many other words. Examples include: *grow*, *sew*, *wrong*, and *wreck*.

Assignment 3 —**Reading and writing shorthand**. Read each sentence from shorthand until you can read it as rapidly as you can read from print. Write each sentence in shorthand until you can write each one rapidly and accurately.

1. - rglr feld —' n b rde f g—.
2. c - le— scr 'slbl pl's b nx sl?
3. - cr ,fs —' —c 'sllm v ,ld bl.
4. - n —br c —c - lll pm ld'.
5. —r gr' —' sun - 'grem f - fgr s ru.
6. - 'grem c sv —ne f c,.
7. lsn psbl f —rs cc Lel s Lr,.
8. - c'le c —el ,n —n f lc.
9. - gvl —' 'prv' n —dcl pln sn.
10. y dr —'bbl lgv - n pln l.
11. - scl bc sple s l l, l - —m.
12. ic cplel - 'sunm 'ssns - bc s rde.

BUILDING SHORTHAND SPEED AND TRANSCRIPTION ACCURACY

Assignment 4 — **Self-testing**. Complete Unit 5 in your *Study Guide* before you proceed with the rest of this chapter.

Assignment 5 — **Taking tape dictation**. To write from dictation the new words and sentences in this chapter, use Cassette 5 Side A from *Theory and Speed-Building Tapes*.

Assignment 6 — **Taking live dictation**. Write from dictation the sentences which are printed at the end of this chapter. Your instructor will dictate each group of 20 words to you at various speeds.

Assignment 7 — **Own-note transcription**. After you have taken the sentences in shorthand, select your best set of notes and transcribe them at your best typing rate. Do not number the sentences.

TRANSCRIPT OF SHORTHAND SENTENCES

1. The regular field may not be ready for the game.
2. Can the team secure a suitable place by next Saturday? (20)
3. The credit office may make a settlement of the old bill.
4. The new member can make the total payment today. (40)
5. Mr. Gray may sign the agreement if the figure is right.
6. The agreement can save money for the company. (60)
7. It is not possible for Mrs. Cook to meet us tomorrow.
8. The committee can meet on Monday if you like. (80)
9. The government may approve a new medical plan soon.
10. Your doctor may be able to give the new plan to you. (100)
11. The school book supply is too low at the moment.
12. I can complete the assignment as soon as the book is ready. (120)

CHAPTER 6

WRITING SOUNDS OF SOFT **G** AND **J**, **IN-EN-UN**, AND **D** OR **ED** ADDED TO A ROOT WORD

Assignment 1 — **Rule discovery**. Follow the three-step plan to learn the new writing principles: (1) Discover the rule for each group of words. (2) Read the shorthand outlines until you can read them rapidly. (3) Cover the shorthand and write each word until you can do so rapidly and accurately.

SOUND OF SOFT **G** AND **J**

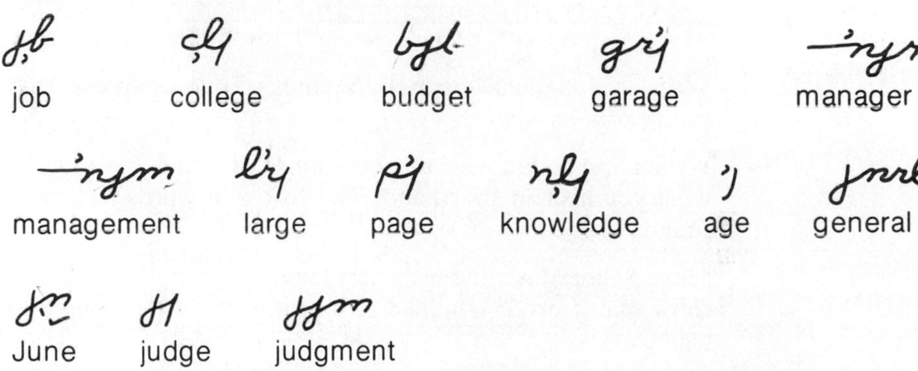

Learning tip: Remember to save time by omitting the final upward stroke in words ending in *j* or *g* (see *college* and *garage* above).

PREFIXES **IN-EN-UN**

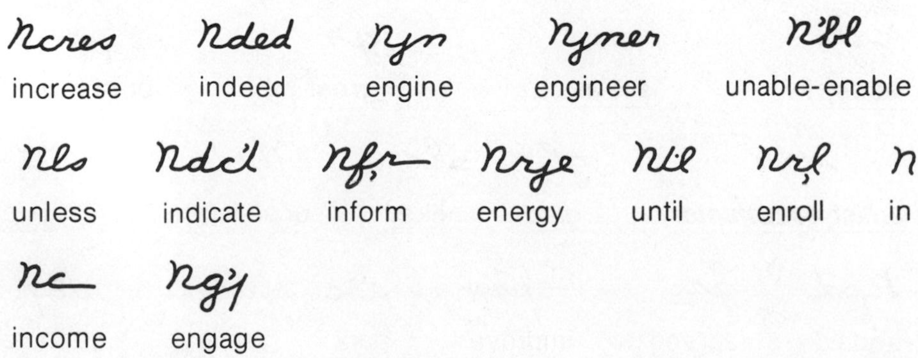

D OR **ED** ADDED TO A ROOT WORD

pln	sbt	cnsl	dj	-plt	
planned	submitted	canceled	damaged	completed	
sc	cl	Nvt	lct	Nfr-	pl
asked	called	invited	located	informed	played

Learning tip: Note that the short dash is written directly under the *a* in *played*.

WRITING PRINCIPLES

IN-EN-UN Write a longhand capital *N* thus N to express the prefixes *in-en-un*.

SOFT **G** AND **J** Write an undotted *j* for all soft sounds of *g* and *j*. You write what you hear in shorthand. The soft *g* in words like *edge* sounds like *j*.

PAST TENSE Make a short dash under the last letter or symbol in a word to show that *d* or *ed* is added to a root word to form the past tense.

This method of indicating past tense will help you transcribe accurately words that sound alike. An example: build bld billed bl

Assignment 2 — **New vocabulary**. Read and write the following words and phrases until you can read and write them rapidly. Memorize the abbreviated words.

csp	—	gr	pr
accept	*am-more*	*great*	*opportunity*

sts	gl	lc	Nsts	Nl
satisfy-satisfactory	*glad*	liked	unsatisfactory	into

Npd	gre	-prv	prc	slre	dj
unpaid	agreed	improve	park	salary	damage

football my I am to talk-take Dear Madam

to your for me in the

Assignment 3 — **Reading and writing shorthand**. Read each sentence from shorthand until you can read it as rapidly as you can read from print. Write each sentence in shorthand until you can write each one rapidly and accurately.

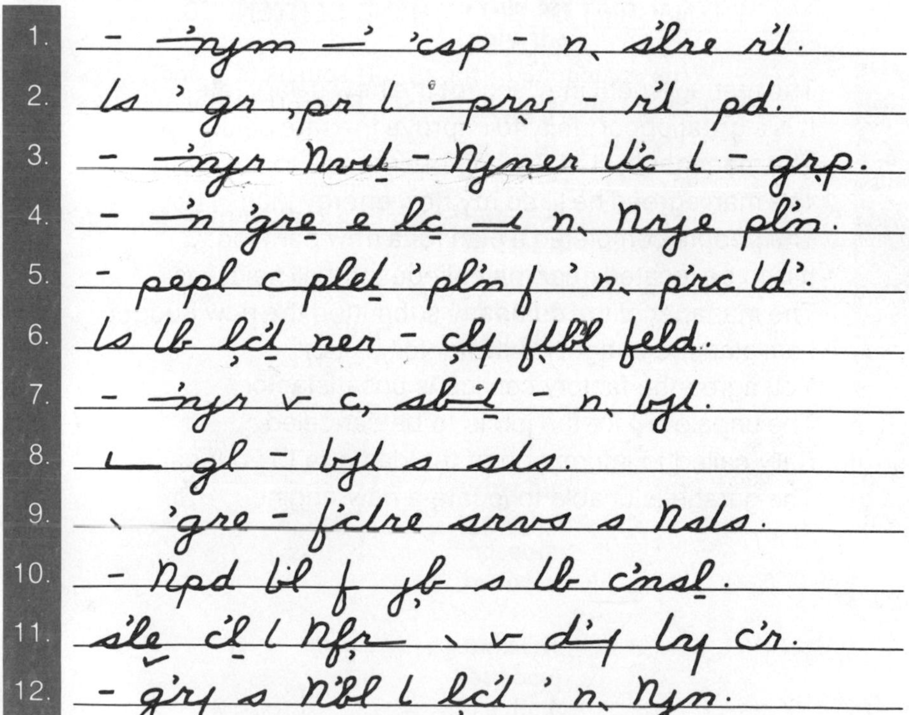

BUILDING SHORTHAND SPEED AND TRANSCRIPTION ACCURACY

Assignment 4 — **Self-testing**. Complete Unit 6 in your *Study Guide* before you proceed with the rest of this chapter.

Assignment 5 — **Taking tape dictation**. To write from dictation the new words and sentences in this chapter, use Cassette 6 Side A from *Theory and Speed-Building Tapes*.

Assignment 6 — **Taking live dictation**. Write from dictation the sentences which are printed at the end of this chapter. Your instructor will dictate each group of 20 words to you at various speeds.

Assignment 7 — **Own-note transcription**. After you have taken the sentences in shorthand, select your best set of notes and transcribe them at your best typing rate. Do not number the sentences.

Assignment 8 — **Supplemental business letters.** If instructed to do so, read and write the additional business letter for this chapter found in "Supplemental Letters for Dictation" at the back of this book.

TRANSCRIPT OF SHORTHAND SENTENCES

1. The management may accept the new salary rate.
2. It is a great opportunity to improve the rate paid. (20)
3. The manager invited the engineer to talk to the group.
4. The man agreed he liked my new energy plan. (40)
5. The people completed a plan for a new park today.
6. It is to be located near the college football field. (60)
7. The manager of the company submitted the new budget.
8. I am glad the budget is satisfactory. (80)
9. You agree the factory service is unsatisfactory.
10. The unpaid bill for the job is to be canceled. (100)
11. Sally called to inform you of the damage to your car.
12. The garage is unable to locate a new engine. (120)

CHAPTER 7

WRITING SOUNDS OF **W-WH**, **AWA-AWAY**, AND **CON-COUN-COUNT**

Assignment 1 — **Rule discovery**. Follow the three-step plan to learn the new writing principles: (1) Discover the rule for each group of words. (2) Read the shorthand outlines until you can read them rapidly. (3) Cover the shorthand and write each word until you can do so rapidly and accurately.

SOUNDS OF **W-WH**

we week-weak warm warmer water-waiter when

way-weigh where-were why woman women wide

one-won white win work what-wait-weight

would-wood while wheel wire twice somewhere

Learning tip: When the *w-wh* stroke comes first in a word, begin the stroke below the line so the next letter rests on the line.

AWA-AWAY

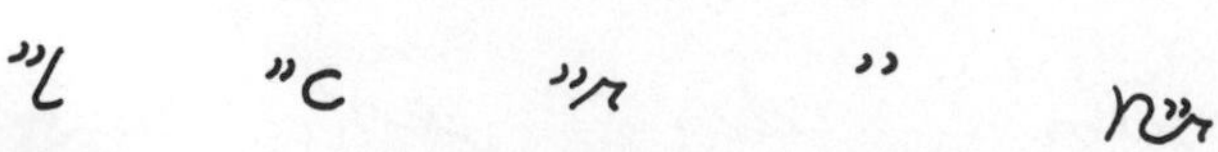

await awake aware away unaware

PREFIXES **CON-COUN-COUNT**

Csrn	Csrn̲	Csidr	Cl'n	Csll̲
concern	concerned	consider	contain	consulted
Csl	Ce	Csidr̲	Cln	Cre
council-counsel	county	considered	continue	country

WRITING PRINCIPLES

W-WH — Write a long, upward, slanted line thus / for the sounds of *w* and *wh*.

AWA — Write two *a* symbols thus ” for the combination *awa* and *away*.

CON-COUN-COUNT — Write a capital C to express the prefixes *con, coun,* and *count*.

Assignment 2 — **New vocabulary**. Read and write the following words and phrases until you can read and write them rapidly. Memorize the abbreviated words.

'f	ne	r	/	'r	clb	cd
after	any	are	will-well	arm	club	could
enf	nn	nlfi	p'cj	Nvi	Njr̲	
enough	noon	notify	package	invite	injured	
yl	'tr	tp	leg	fl̲	s	
yellow	matter	top	league	followed	some-sum	
fre	nn	cdn	idn	er	didn	
free	none	could not	I do not	we are	did not	
ec	db	ds				
we can	would be	Dear Sir				

Assignment 3 — **Reading and writing shorthand**. Read each sentence from shorthand until you can read it as rapidly as you can read from print. Write each sentence in shorthand until you can write each one rapidly and accurately.

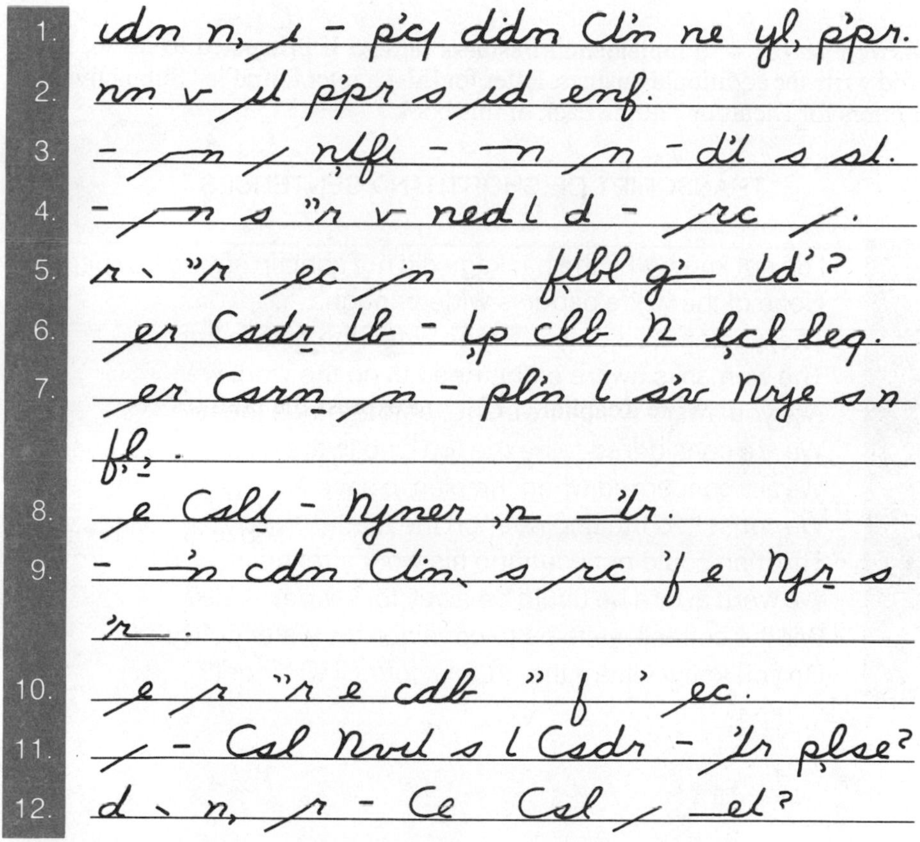

BUILDING SHORTHAND SPEED AND TRANSCRIPTION ACCURACY

Assignment 4 — **Self-testing**. Complete Unit 7 in your *Study Guide* before you proceed with the rest of this chapter.

Assignment 5 — **Taking tape dictation**. To write from dictation the new words and sentences in this chapter, use Cassette 7 Side A from *Theory and Speed-Building Tapes*.

Assignment 6 — **Taking live dictation**. Write from dictation the sentences which are printed at the end of this chapter. Your instructor will dictate each group of 20 words to you at various speeds.

Assignment 7 — **Own-note transcription**. After you have taken the sentences in shorthand, select your best set of notes and transcribe them at your best typing rate. Do not number the sentences.

Assignment 8 — **Supplemental business letters.** If instructed to do so, read and write the additional business letter for this chapter found in "Supplemental Letters for Dictation" at the back of this book.

TRANSCRIPT OF SHORTHAND SENTENCES

1. I do not know why the package did not contain any yellow paper.
2. None of the white paper is wide enough. (20)
3. The women will notify the men when the date is set.
4. The woman is aware of the need to do the work well. (40)
5. Are you aware we can win the football game today?
6. We are considered to be the top club in the local league. (60)
7. We are concerned when the plan to save energy is not followed.
8. We consulted the engineer on the matter. (80)
9. The man could not continue his work after he injured his arm.
10. We were aware he could be away for a week. (100)
11. Will the council invite us to consider the water policy?
12. Do you know where the county council will meet? (120)

CHAPTER 8

BUSINESS LETTER DICTATION AND TRANSCRIPTION

BUILDING TRANSCRIPTION SKILLS

Assignment 1 — **Punctuating introductory words, phrases, and clauses.** An introductory word or expression introduces the reader to the rest of the sentence. Place a comma after an introductory word, phrase, or clause.

The most common introductory words and expressions include: *therefore, however, nevertheless, even so, furthermore,* and *for example*. Introductory phrases and clauses usually begin with one of the following words: *if, since, when, after, although, as, because, in, unless, upon, whenever,* and *while*.

The letters in this chapter include introductory expressions that are set off by commas. Note how the punctuation rule for introductory expressions is applied in the following examples. Apply the rule when transcribing the letters.

1. If you accept the offer, we will make you a partner.
2. When you visit me in August, we can go to the lake.
3. While I was on vacation, my new car arrived.
4. Unless your paper is completed in time, you will get an incomplete.
5. However, exceptions will be made in case of illness.
6. Therefore, make every effort to get your paper in on time.
7. Furthermore, the term paper should be typed.
8. As you know, my car ran out of gas last night.

Assignment 2 — **Punctuating shorthand notes.** If time permits, you may insert commas and other punctuation during dictation. Circle the punctuation marks within a sentence so you can distinguish them easily when transcribing. Because periods and question marks do not come within a sentence, they need not be circled. Note how the commas are circled in Letters 1 and 2.

Assignment 3 — **Spelling review.** To transcribe accurately, a secretary must be able to spell correctly. When in doubt about the spelling of a word when transcribing, always look up the word in a dictionary.

This and later spelling reviews cover common words that are often misspelled when transcribing. Use the following steps to check your ability to spell these words correctly:

Step 1. Pronounce each word slowly, one syllable at a time, as you note how each word is spelled.

Step 2. Then write the shorthand outline for each spelling word in a column on the left side of your shorthand notebook. The outlines for all the words have been presented in previous chapters in your textbook.

Step 3. Close your textbook and write the transcript of each outline you have written in your notebook.

Step 4. Check your spelling of each word with the spelling in your textbook. Study any words you may have misspelled.

1. accept
2. budget
3. catalog
4. committee
5. complete
6. damage
7. energy
8. engineer
9. follow
10. general
11. government
12. increase
13. knowledge
14. management
15. office
16. operate
17. people
18. policy
19. possible
20. ready
21. service
22. until

BUSINESS LETTERS

Assignment 4 — **Letter 1**. Read and write each new word and phrase for Letter 1 until you can read and write each one rapidly and accurately. Then read and write the shorthand for Letter 1 to build your writing speed.

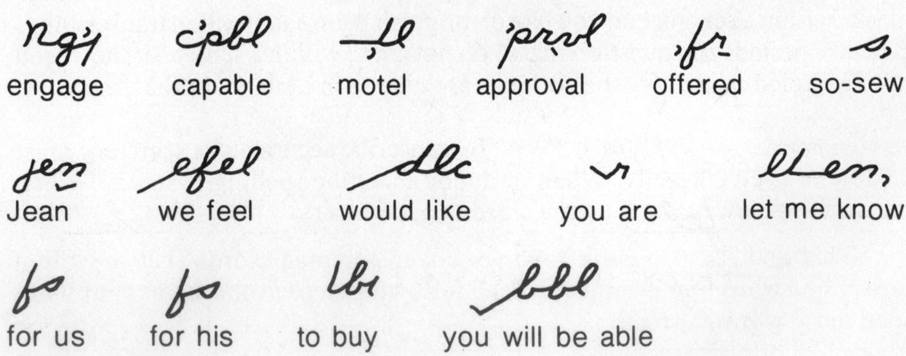

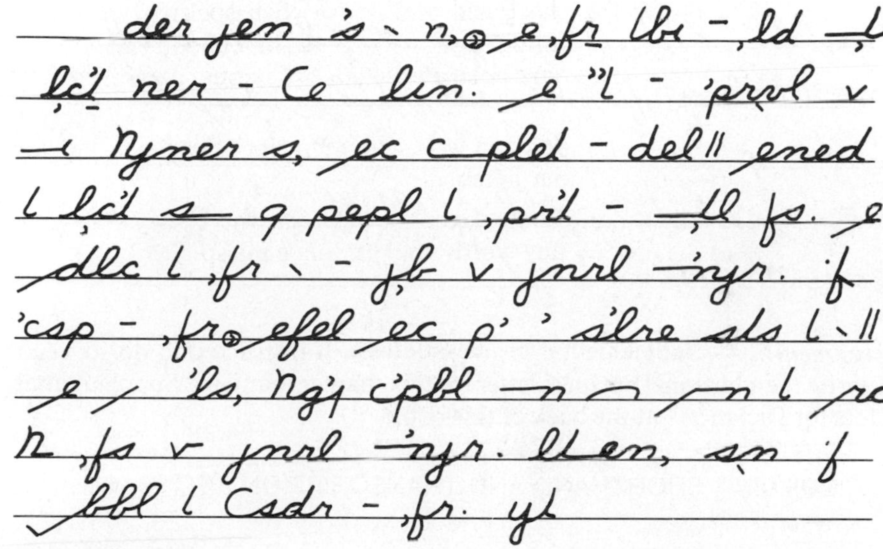

Assignment 5 — **Letter 2**. Read and write each new word and phrase for Letter 2 until you can read and write each one rapidly and accurately. Then read and write the shorthand for Letter 2 to build your writing speed.

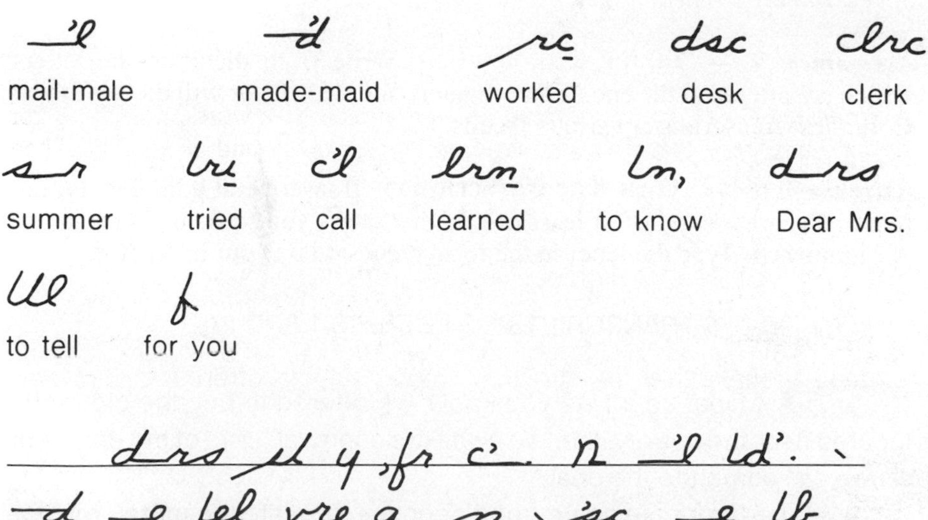

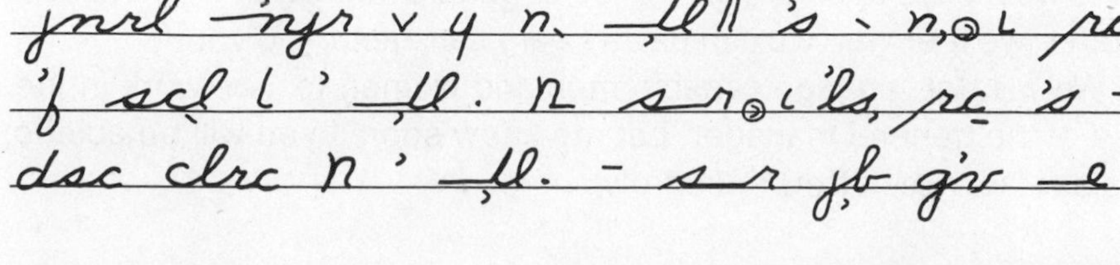

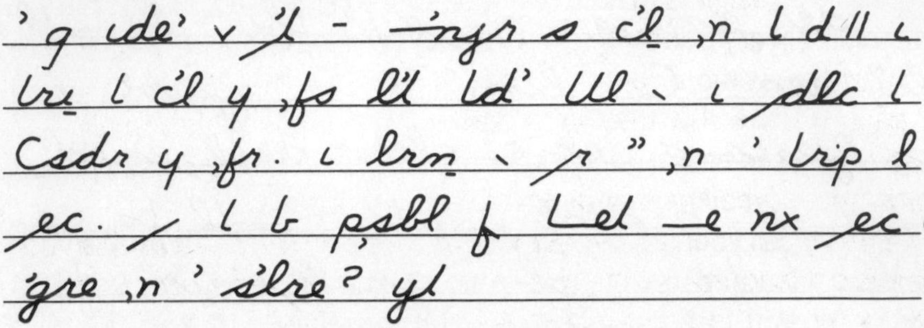

Assignment 6 — **Supplemental business letters.** If instructed to do so, read and write the additional business letter for this chapter found in "Supplemental Letters for Dictation" at the back of this book.

BUILDING SHORTHAND AND TRANSCRIPTION ACCURACY

Assignment 7 — **Self-testing**. Complete Unit 8 in your *Study Guide* before you proceed with the rest of this chapter.

Assignment 8 — **Taking tape dictation**. To write from dictation the new words and letters in this chapter, use Cassette 8 Side A from *Theory and Speed-Building Tapes*.

Assignment 9 — **Taking live dictation**. Write from dictation the letters which are printed at the end of this chapter. Your instructor will dictate to you from these transcripts at various speeds.

Assignment 10 — **Own-note transcription**. Transcribe at your best typing rate an accurate copy of at least one of the letters you took in shorthand in Assignment 9. Type the letter in the form requested by your instructor.

TRANSCRIPTS OF LETTERS 1 AND 2

Letter 1 Dear Jean: As you know, we offered to buy the old motel located near the county line. We await the approval (20) of my engineer so we can complete the deal.

We need to locate some good people to operate the motel (40) for us. We would like to offer you the job of general manager. If you accept the offer, we feel (60) we can pay a salary satisfactory to you.

We will also engage capable men and women to (80) work in the office of the general manager. Let me know soon if you will be able to consider the (100) offer. Yours truly, (104)

Letter 2 Dear Mrs. White: Your offer came in the mail today. You made me feel very good when you asked me to be general (20) manager of your new motel.

As you know, I worked after school at a motel. In the summer, I also (40) worked as the desk clerk in a motel. The summer job gave me a good idea of what the manager is called (60) on to do.

I tried to call your office late today to tell you I would like to consider your offer. I learned (80) you were away on a trip all week. Will it be possible for you to meet me next week to agree on a (100) salary? Yours truly, (103)

REVIEWING THE WRITING PRINCIPLES

All the writing principles, abbreviated words, and standard abbreviations you have learned in Chapters 1 through 8 are reviewed on Tape 17 Side A of the *Theory and Speed-Building Tapes*. Take dictation from this tape before completing Examination 2.

EXAMINATION 2

Remove and complete Examination 2 at the back of your *Study Guide* before proceeding to Chapter 9 of your textbook.

CHAPTER 9

WRITING SOUNDS OF **H**, **SH**, AND **BE-DE-RE**

Assignment 1 – **Rule discovery**. Follow the three-step plan to learn the new writing principles: (1) Discover the rule for each group of words. (2) Read the shorthand outlines until you can read them rapidly. (3) Cover the shorthand and write each word until you can do so rapidly and accurately.

SOUND OF **H**

her help had hold high him home hot

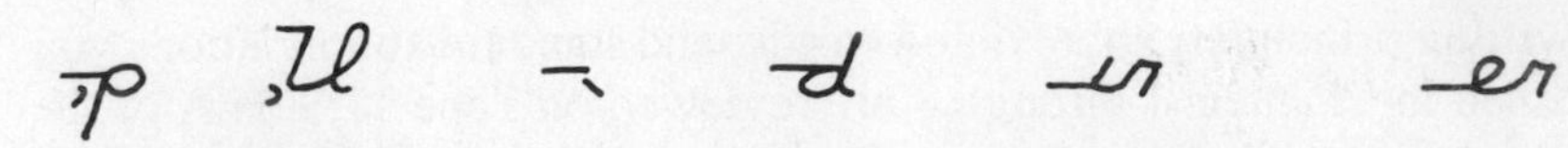

hope hotel who head hire-higher hear-here

Learning tips:

1. Make the *h* dash short so you will not confuse it with the long line for *m*.
2. Note that *h* is joined to *m* in *him* and *home* with a very slight jog.
3. The *h* dash may be written on the line, as in *her*, or above the line, as in *hot*.

SOUND OF **SH**

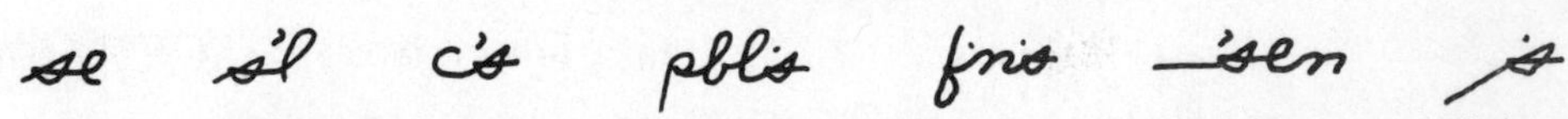

she shall cash publish finish machine wish

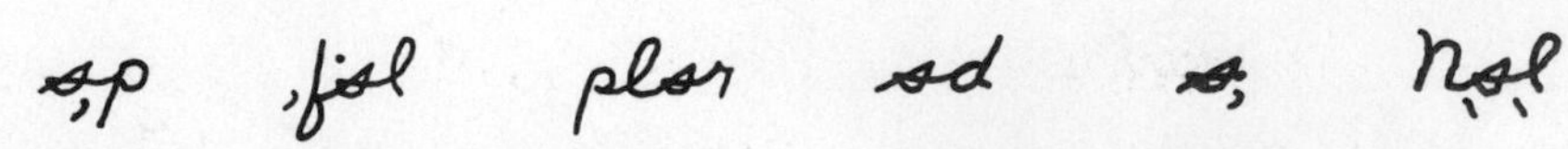

shop official pleasure should show unusual

PREFIXES **BE-DE-RE**

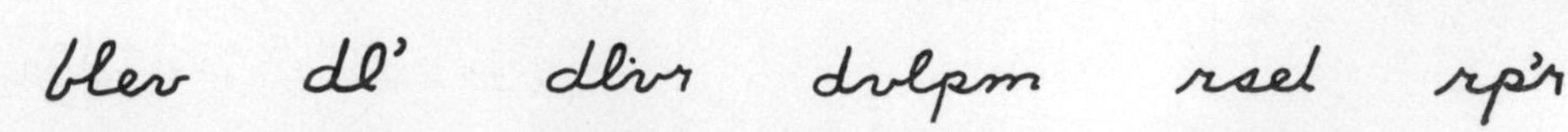

believe delay deliver development receipt repair

return release become begin

WRITING PRINCIPLES

H	Write a short dash thus — to express the sound of *h*.
SH	Write an *h* dash through the *s* to express *sh*.
BE-DE-RE	Omit the *e* in the prefixes *be*, *de*, and *re*.

Assignment 2 — **New vocabulary**. Read and write the following words and phrases until you can read and write them rapidly. Memorize the abbreviated words.

appreciate	have	put-please	receive	ship-short
side	Wednesday	decide	before	decided
received	shipment	from	firm	bulletin
signed	cover	below-blow	should not	should be
we should	we shall	we believe	to see	to receive
I hope	we received			

Assignment 3 — **Reading and writing shorthand**. Read each sentence from shorthand until you can read it as rapidly as you can read from print. Write each sentence in shorthand until you can write each one rapidly and accurately.

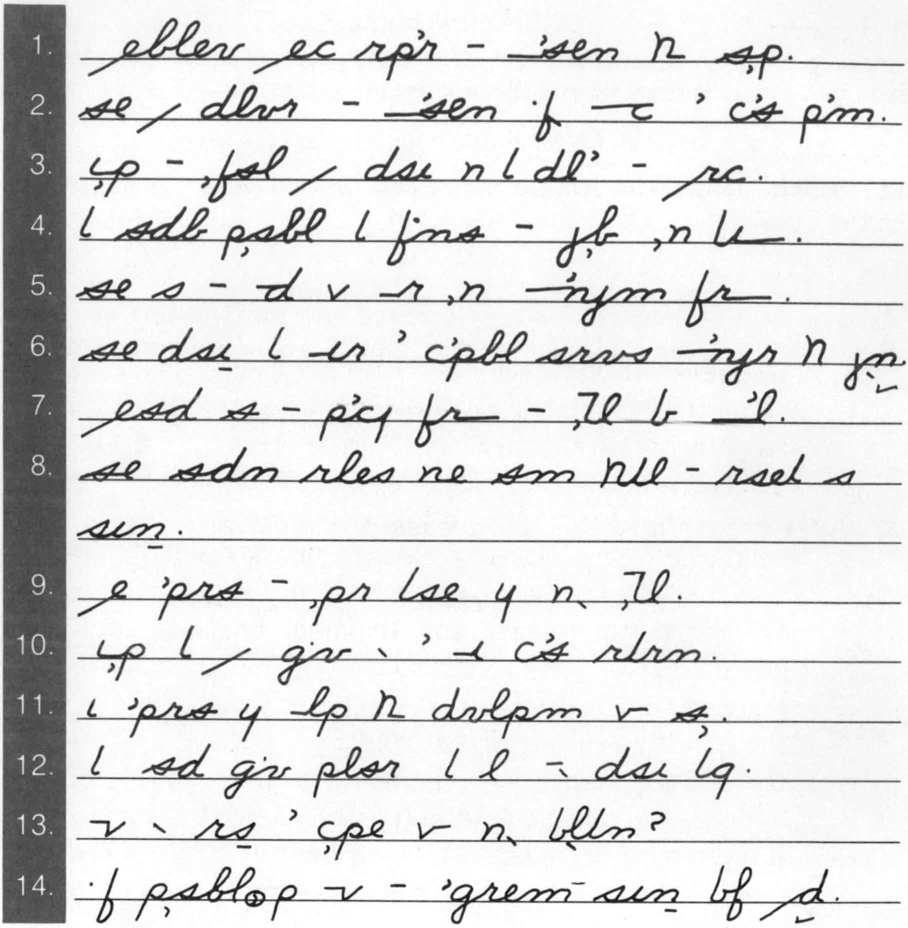

BUILDING SHORTHAND SPEED AND TRANSCRIPTION ACCURACY

Assignment 4 — **Self-testing**. Complete Unit 9 in your *Study Guide* before you proceed with the rest of this chapter.

Assignment 5 — **Taking tape dictation**. To write from dictation the new words and sentences in this chapter, use Cassette 9 Side A from *Theory and Speed-Building Tapes*.

Assignment 6 — **Taking live dictation**. Write from dictation the sentences which are printed at the end of this chapter. Your instructor will dictate each group of 20 words to you at various speeds.

Assignment 7 — **Own-note transcription**. After you have taken the sentences in shorthand, select your best set of notes and transcribe them at your best typing rate. Do not number the sentences.

Assignment 8 — **Supplemental business letters.** If instructed to do so, read and write the additional business letter for this chapter found in "Supplemental Letters for Dictation" at the back of this book.

TRANSCRIPT OF SHORTHAND SENTENCES

1. We believe we can repair the machine in the shop.
2. She will deliver the machine if you make a cash payment. (20)
3. I hope the official will decide not to delay the work.
4. It should be possible to finish the job on time. (40)
5. She is the head of her own management firm.
6. She decided to hire a capable service manager in June. (60)
7. We should ship the package from the hotel by mail.
8. She should not release any shipment until the receipt is signed. (80)
9. We appreciate the opportunity to see your new hotel.
10. I hope it will give you a high cash return. (100)
11. I appreciate your help in the development of the show.
12. It should give pleasure to all who decide to go. (120)
13. Have you received a copy of the new bulletin?
14. If possible, please have the agreement signed before Wednesday. (140)

CHAPTER 10

WRITING SOUNDS OF **CH**, **TH**, AND HARD **S** AND **Z**

Assignment 1 — **Rule discovery**. Follow the three-step plan to learn the new writing principles: (1) Discover the rule for each group of words. (2) Read the shorthand outlines until you can read them rapidly. (3) Cover the shorthand and write each word until you can do so rapidly and accurately.

SOUND OF **CH**

chair charge check chapter child children

teach much which such attach reach church

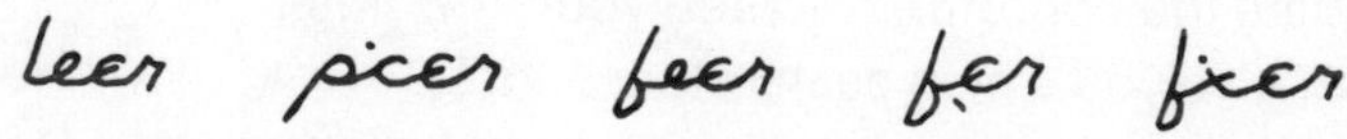

teacher picture feature future fixture

Learning tips:

1. Be sure to write the *ch* sound as shown above. The word *church* illustrates the two ways that the *ch* sound is written.

2. Note that some words have a *ch* sound but do not have the letters *ch* in them. Examples: *feature*, *future*, *picture*. Remember to write what you hear.

SOUND OF **TH**

than then them their-there either rather

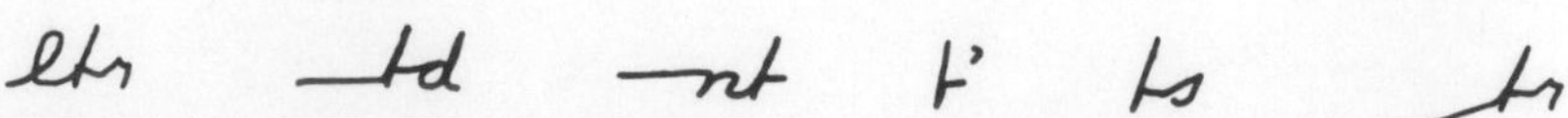

leather method month they this weather-whether

SOUND OF HARD **S** AND **Z**

busy — choose — close (v) — deposit — desire — visit

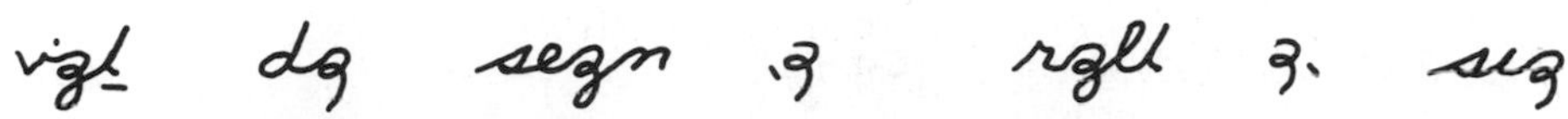

visited — does — season — use (v) — result — zoo — size

was — reason — these — those — cause

Learning tip: The *(v)* after *close* and *use* indicates that these are verb forms of the words.

WRITING PRINCIPLES

CH Write an *h* dash through the *c* to express *ch*.

When writing *ch* at the beginning of a word, write the *c* first. Then write the dash through the *c*, joining the *h* dash to the next letter, as in the words *chair* and *charge*. When *ch* occurs in the body or at the end of a word, make the *h* dash *an extension* of the preceding letter. Then write the *c* through the *h* dash, as in the word *feature*.

TH Join an *h* dash to the *t* to express *th*.

Most writers find it is easier to join the *h* to *t* by retracing the *t* part way up and then writing the *h* dash. Some writers prefer to write *th* thus  . Either way is correct.

HARD S AND Z Write a small longhand *z* to express the hard sound of *s*. This rule follows the principle of writing the sound you *hear* when you write shorthand.

Assignment 2 — **New vocabulary**. Read and write the following words and phrases until you can read and write them rapidly. Memorize the abbreviated words.

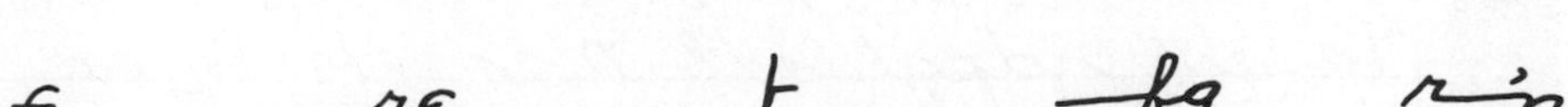

each — *merchandise* — *that-thank* — manufacture — remain

Assignment 3 — **Reading and writing shorthand**. Read each sentence from shorthand until you can read it as rapidly as you can read from print. Write each sentence in shorthand until you can write each one rapidly and accurately.

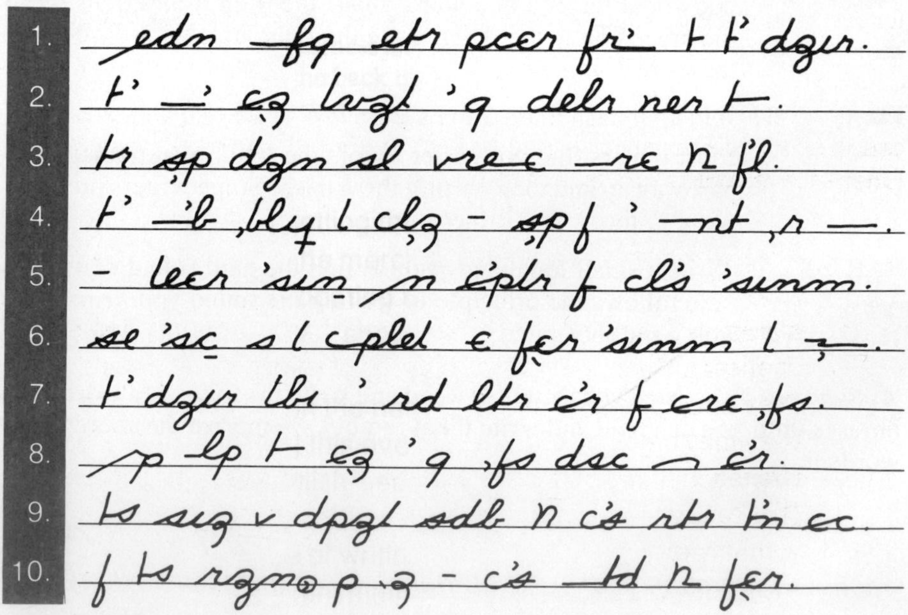

11.
12.
13.
14.

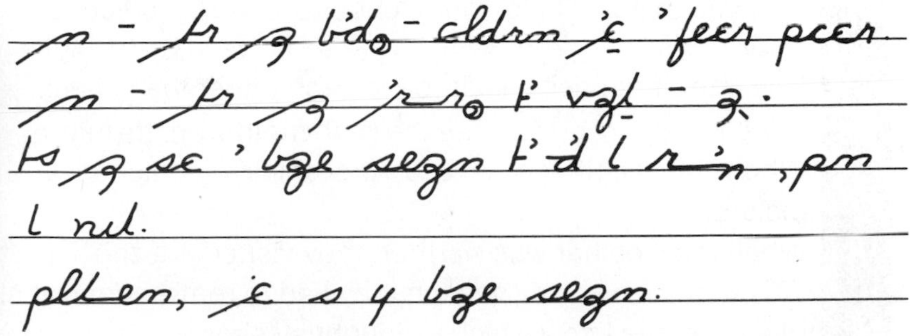

BUILDING SHORTHAND SPEED AND TRANSCRIPTION ACCURACY

Assignment 4 — **Self-testing**. Complete Unit 10 in your *Study Guide* before you proceed with the rest of this chapter.

Assignment 5 — **Taking tape dictation**. To write from dictation the new words and sentences in this chapter, use Cassette 10 Side A from *Theory and Speed-Building Tapes*.

Assignment 6 — **Taking live dictation**. Write from dictation the sentences which are printed at the end of this chapter. Your instructor will dictate each group of 20 words to you at various speeds.

Assignment 7 — **Own-note transcription**. After you have taken the sentences in shorthand, select your best set of notes and transcribe them at your best typing rate. Do not number the sentences.

Assignment 8 — **Supplemental business letters.** If instructed to do so, read and write the additional business letter for this chapter found in "Supplemental Letters for Dictation" at the back of this book.

TRANSCRIPT OF SHORTHAND SENTENCES

1. We do not manufacture either picture frame that they desire.
2. They may choose to visit a good dealer near them. (20)
3. Their shop does not sell very much merchandise in the fall.
4. They may be obliged to close the shop for a month or more. (40)
5. The teacher assigned one chapter for the class assignment.
6. She asked us to complete each future assignment at home. (60)
7. They desire to buy a red leather chair for the church office.

8. Will you please help them choose a good office desk and chair. (80)
9. This size of deposit should be in cash rather than check.
10. For this reason, please use the cash method in the future. (100)
11. When the weather was bad, the children watched a feature picture.
12. When the weather was warmer, they visited the zoo. (120)
13. This was such a busy season they had to remain open at night.
14. Please let me know which is your busy season. (140)

CHAPTER 11

WRITING SOUNDS OF **NG-ING-THING**, **AD-ADD**, AND **TRANS**

Assignment 1 — **Rule discovery**. Follow the three-step plan to learn the new writing principles: (1) Discover the rule for each group of words. (2) Read the shorthand outlines until you can read them rapidly. (3) Cover the shorthand and write each word until you can do so rapidly and accurately.

SOUNDS OF **NG-ING-THING**

earning	giving	bring	coming	evening	building
getting	meeting	among	along	selling	reviewing
thing	planning	bank	blank	think	long	nothing
bringing	something	asking	considering	increasing	
frank	beginning	morning	opening	looking	
following	young	language	English	publishing	

Learning tip: Some words ending in *nk* also have an *ng* sound before the hard *c*. See *bank*, *blank*, and *think* above.

PREFIX **AD-ADD**

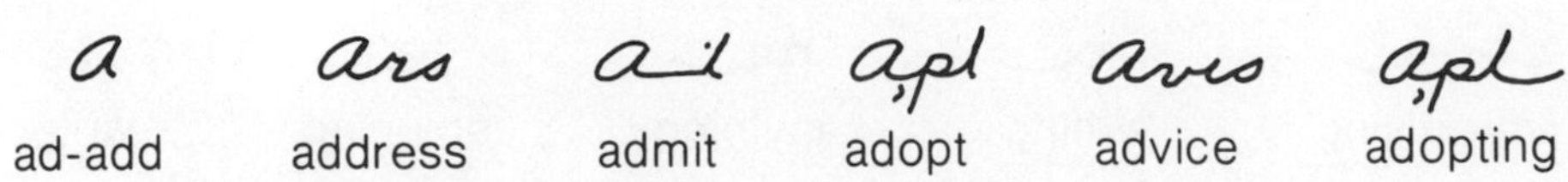

ad-add	address	admit	adopt	advice	adopting

advise added advised adding

PREFIX **TRANS**

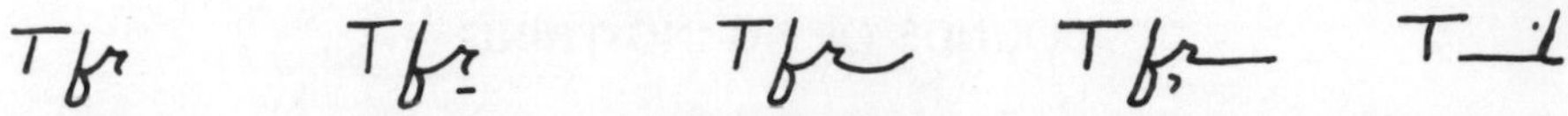

transfer transferred transferring transform transmit

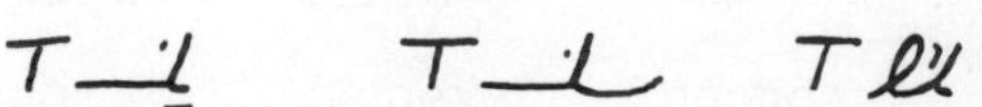

transmitted transmitting translate

WRITING PRINCIPLES

NG-ING-THING Write a long, curved stroke thus  to express the combinations *ng-ing-thing*.

AD-ADD Write a capital  to express the prefix *ad-add*. Use this longhand form of *a* because it can be written quickly and joined easily to other letters.

TRANS Write a capital  to express the prefix *trans*. Any form of capital *T* may be used. The *T* may be joined or disjoined. Example: *transfer*: 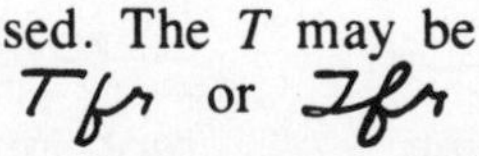 .

Assignment 2 — **New vocabulary**. Read and write the following words and phrases until you can read and write them rapidly. Memorize the abbreviated words.

advertise has business secretary being

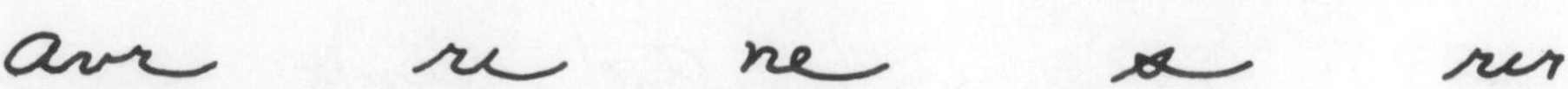

advertising writing anything shipping writer

Assignment 3 — **Reading and writing shorthand**. Read each sentence from shorthand until you can read it as rapidly as you can read from print. Write each sentence in shorthand until you can write each one rapidly and accurately.

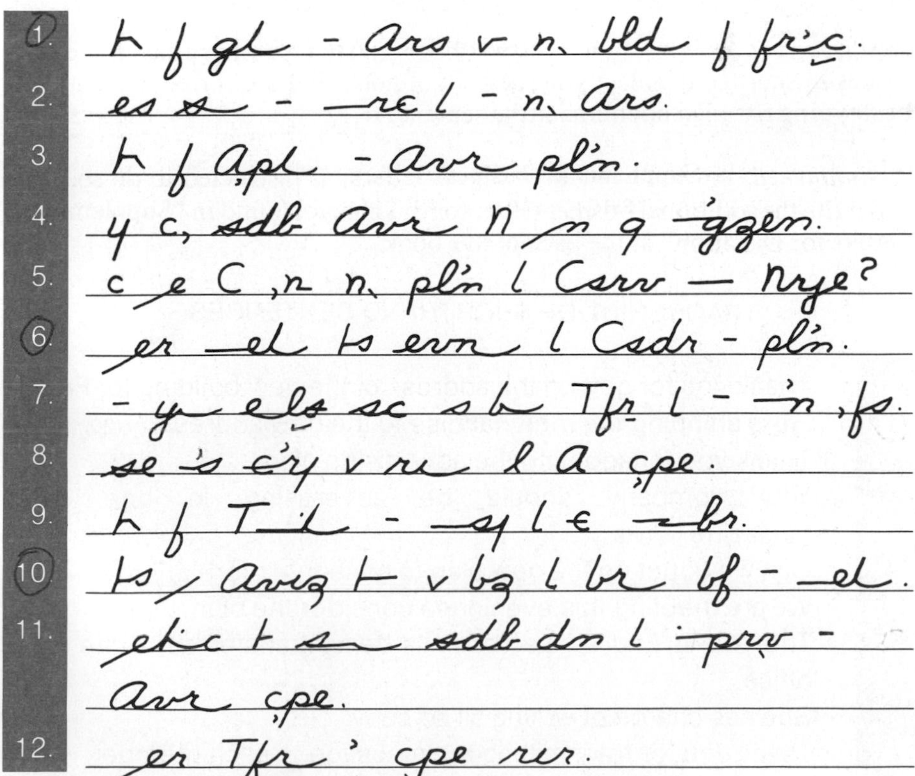

13. 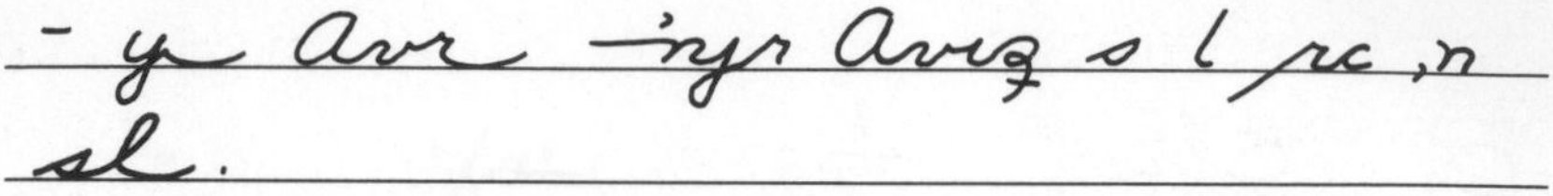

14. 

BUILDING SHORTHAND SPEED AND TRANSCRIPTION ACCURACY

Assignment 4 —**Self-testing**. Complete Unit 11 in your *Study Guide* before you proceed with the rest of this chapter.

Assignment 5 —**Taking tape dictation**. To write from dictation the new words and sentences in this chapter, use Cassette 11 Side A from *Theory and Speed-Building Tapes*.

Assignment 6 —**Taking live dictation**. Write from dictation the sentences which are printed at the end of this chapter. Your instructor will dictate each group of 20 words to you at various speeds.

Assignment 7 —**Own-note transcription**. After you have taken the sentences in shorthand, select your best set of notes and transcribe them at your best typing rate. Do not number the sentences.

Assignment 8 — **Supplemental business letters.** If instructed to do so, read and write the additional business letter for this chapter found in "Supplemental Letters for Dictation" at the back of this book.

TRANSCRIPT OF SHORTHAND SENTENCES

1. Thank you for getting the address of the new building for Frank.
2. He is shipping the merchandise to the new address. (20)
3. Thank you for adopting the advertising plan.
4. Your company should be advertising in one good magazine. (40)
5. Can we count on the new plan to conserve more energy?
6. We are meeting this evening to consider the plan. (60)
7. The young English secretary is being transferred to the main office.
8. She has charge of writing all ad copy. (80)
9. Thank you for transmitting the message to each member.

10. This will advise them of business to bring before the meeting. (100)
11. We think that something should be done to improve the advertising copy.
12. We are transferring a copy writer. (120)
13. The young advertising manager advised us to work on selling.
14. That is a good way to transform the business. (140)

CHAPTER 12

BUSINESS LETTER DICTATION AND TRANSCRIPTION

BUILDING TRANSCRIPTION SKILLS

Assignment 1 — **Punctuating parenthetical words and expressions**. Parenthetical words or expressions are those that can be omitted without changing the meaning of the sentence. Place a comma before and after parenthetical words or expressions. Common parenthetical words and expressions include: *indeed*, *also*, *however*, *therefore*, *perhaps*, *as you know*, *at any rate*, *I believe*, *I think*, *no doubt*, *of course*.

Study the examples below and apply the rule for punctuating parenthetical words and expressions in the letters that follow.

1. My car is, as you know, a terrible gas guzzler.
2. I can reduce my gas consumption, they tell me, if I replace my air filter.
3. I can't do that, I regret to say, because I have a slight financial problem.
4. I am, therefore, forced to wait until pay day.

Assignment 2 — **Punctuating a polite request**. A polite request asks for action rather than an answer. Use a period after a polite request, as in the examples that follow.

1. If you cannot come, will you please telephone me.
2. May I have your new address.
3. Will you please send the books by mail.

Assignment 3 — **Spelling review**. Follow these steps to check your ability to spell correctly the words on page 51.

Step 1. Pronounce each word slowly as you note how each word is spelled.

Step 2. Write the shorthand outline for each word in a column on the left side of your shorthand notebook.

Step 3. Close your textbook and write the transcript of each outline you have written in your notebook.

Step 4. Check your transcript of each word with the spelling in your textbook. Study any words you may have misspelled.

1. approval
2. attach
3. appreciate
4. beginning
5. believe
6. business
7. future
8. machine
9. manufacture
10. merchandise
11. owner
12. planning
13. pleasure
14. receipt
15. receive
16. secretary
17. something
18. summer
19. transfer
20. transferred
21. transferring
22. Wednesday
23. write
24. writing

BUSINESS LETTERS

Assignment 4 — **Letter 1**. Read and write each of the new words and phrases for Letter 1 until you can read and write each one rapidly and accurately. Then read and write the shorthand for Letter 1 to build your writing speed.

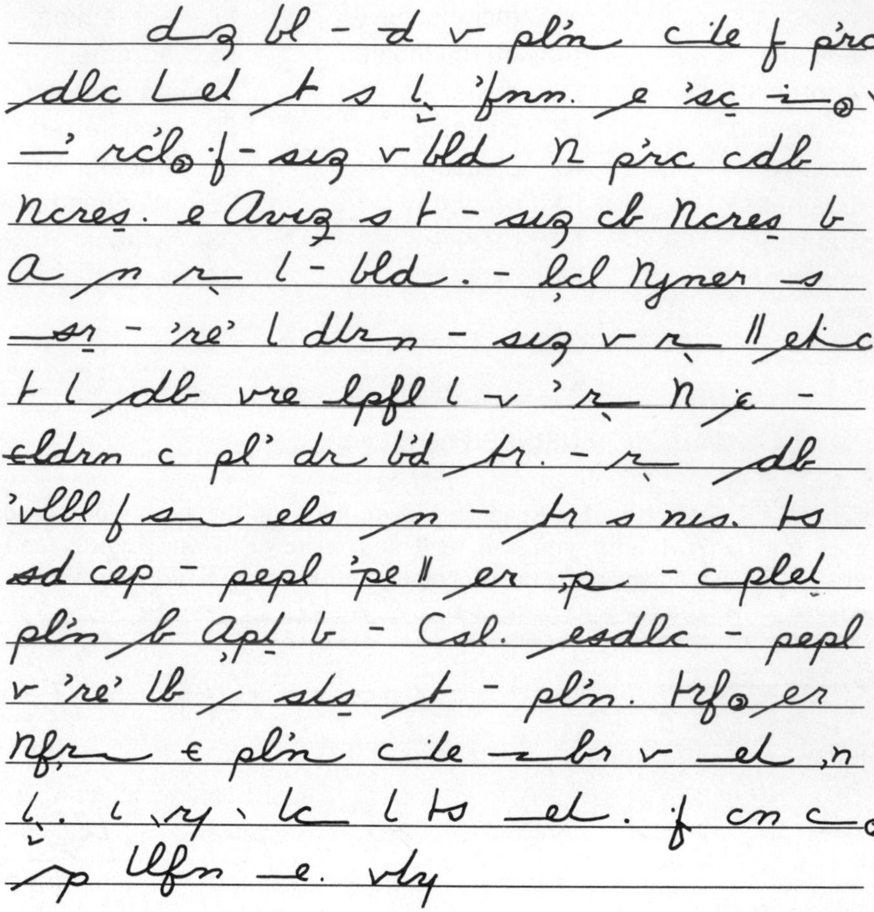

Assignment 5 —**Letter 2**. Read and write each of the new words and phrases for Letter 2 until you can read and write each one rapidly and accurately. Then read and write the shorthand for Letter 2 to build your writing speed.

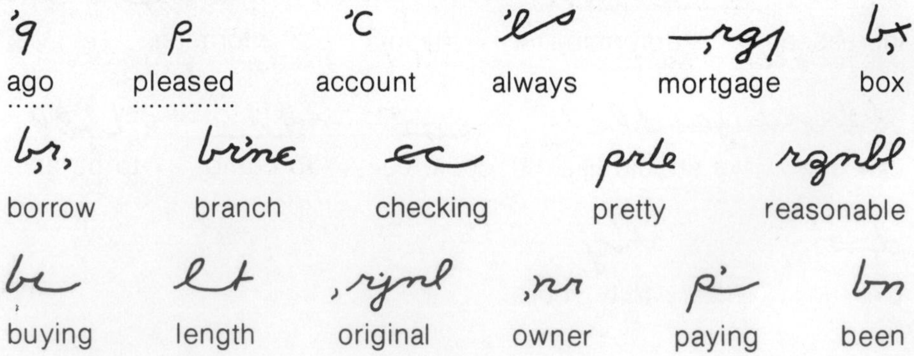

thought safe banking same told we have been

Dear Mr. would have I shall some time at your

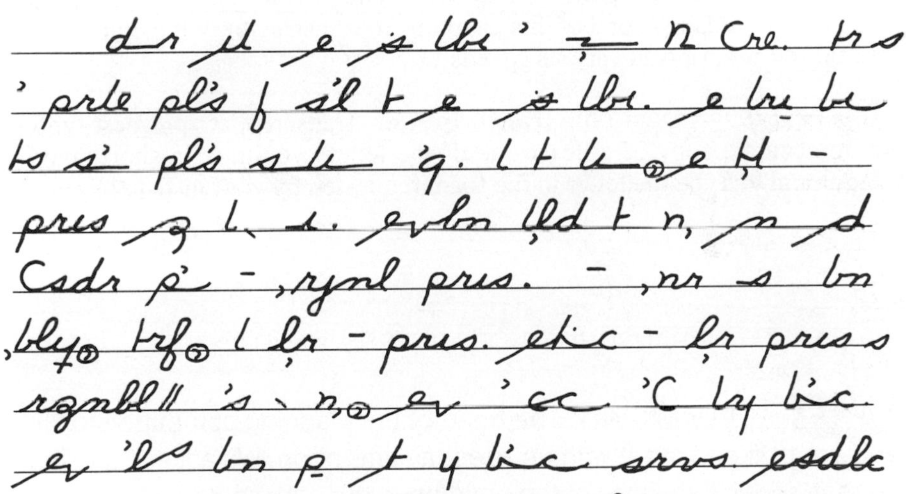

Assignment 6 — **Supplemental business letters.** If instructed to do so, read and write the additional business letter for this chapter found in "Supplemental Letters for Dictation" at the back of this book.

BUILDING SHORTHAND SPEED AND TRANSCRIPTION ACCURACY

Assignment 7 — **Self-testing**. Complete Unit 12 in your *Study Guide* before you proceed with the rest of this chapter.

Assignment 8 — **Taking tape dictation**. To write from dictation the new words and letters in this chapter, use Cassette 12 Side A from *Theory and Speed-Building Tapes*.

Assignment 9 — **Taking live dictation**. Write from dictation the letters which are printed at the end of this chapter. Your instructor will dictate to you from these transcripts at various speeds.

Assignment 10 — **Own-note transcription**. Transcribe at your best typing rate an accurate copy of at least one of the letters you took in shorthand in Assignment 9. Type the letter in the form requested by your instructor.

TRANSCRIPTS OF LETTERS 1 AND 2

Letter 1 Dear Ms. Bell: The head of the planning committee for the park would like to meet with us Tuesday afternoon. We asked (20) him, you may recall, if the size of the building in the park could be increased. He advised us that the size can be (40) increased by adding one room to the building. The local engineer has measured the area to determine (60) the size of the room.

We think that it would be very helpful to have a room in which the children can play during (80) bad weather. The room would be available for something else when the weather is nice. This should keep the people (100) happy.

We are hoping the complete plan will be adopted by the council. We should like the people of the area to (120) be well satisfied with the plan. Therefore, we are informing each planning committee member of the meeting on (140) Tuesday. I urge you to come to this meeting. If you cannot come, will you please telephone me. Very truly yours, (160)

Letter 2 Dear Mr. White: We wish to buy a home in the country. There is a pretty place for sale that we wish to buy. We (20) tried buying this same place some time ago. At that time, we thought the price was too high. We have been told that no one would (40) consider paying the original price. The owner has been obliged, therefore, to lower the price. We think the (60) lower price is reasonable.

As you know, we have a checking account at your bank. We have always been pleased with (80) your banking service. We should like to know if we can count on you to give us a loan. If so, we need to know what (100) rate you would charge on the money we borrow. We also should like to know the length of time we would have to complete (120) payment of the mortgage.

We can meet you at your branch office any afternoon. I shall telephone you soon. Very (140) truly yours, (143)

EXAMINATION 3

Remove and complete Examination 3 at the back of your *Study Guide* before proceeding to Chapter 13 of your textbook.

CHAPTER 13

WRITING **NT-ND**, **AN**, AND **DIS-DES**

Assignment 1 — **Rule discovery**. Follow the three-step plan to learn the new writing principles: (1) Discover the rule for each group of words. (2) Read the shorthand outlines until you can read them rapidly. (3) Cover the shorthand and write each word until you can do so rapidly and accurately.

NT-ND

end event find inventory attend want agent

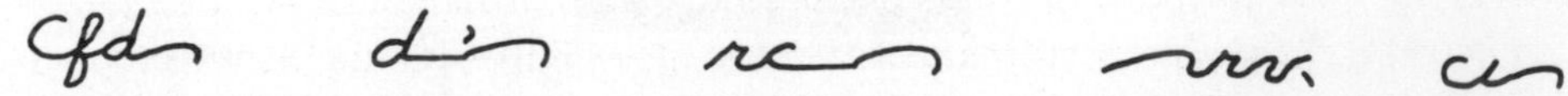

confident demand recommend interview kind

handle different efficient guarantee depend paint

print send-sent printing dependable convenient

Learning tip: The word *interview* is written with the *nt* combination rather than the *in* prefix because the word is pronounced int-er-view.

PREFIX **AN**

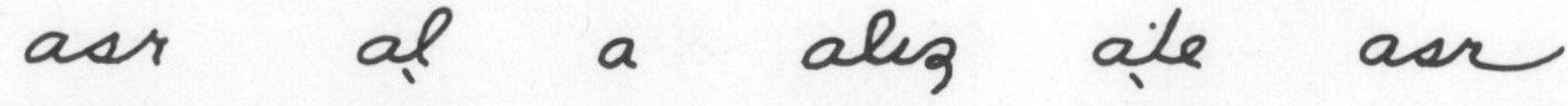

answer annual an analyze annuity answering

PREFIXES **DIS-DES**

discover discuss display discontinue discovered

desperate desolate

WRITING PRINCIPLES

NT-ND Write a curved stroke thus  to express the combinations *nt* or *nd*. Note that this stroke is used for both *nt* as in *event* and for *nd* as in *end*.

AN Write a small longhand *a* to express the prefix *an*.

DIS-DES Write a Capital D thus  to express the prefixes *dis* and *des*. Some writers prefer to write the capital D thus . Either is correct.

Assignment 2 — **New vocabulary**. Read and write the following words and phrases until you can read and write them rapidly. Memorize the abbreviated words.

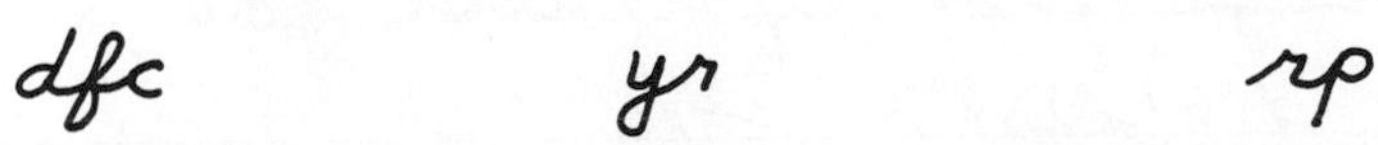

difficult-difficulty year represent-representative

gentlemen September Thursday memorandum

memo accountant discount sometime somebody

several Miss case sure mailed worker

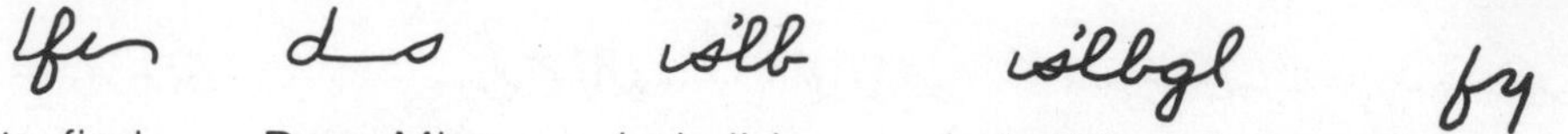

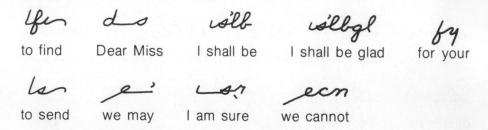

to find | Dear Miss | I shall be | I shall be glad | for your

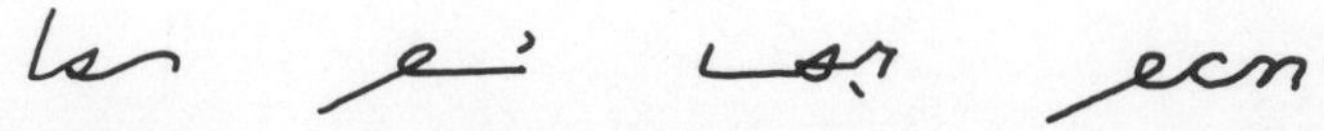

to send | we may | I am sure | we cannot

Assignment 3 — **Reading and writing shorthand**. Read each sentence from shorthand until you can read it as rapidly as you can read from print. Write each sentence in shorthand until you can write each one rapidly and accurately.

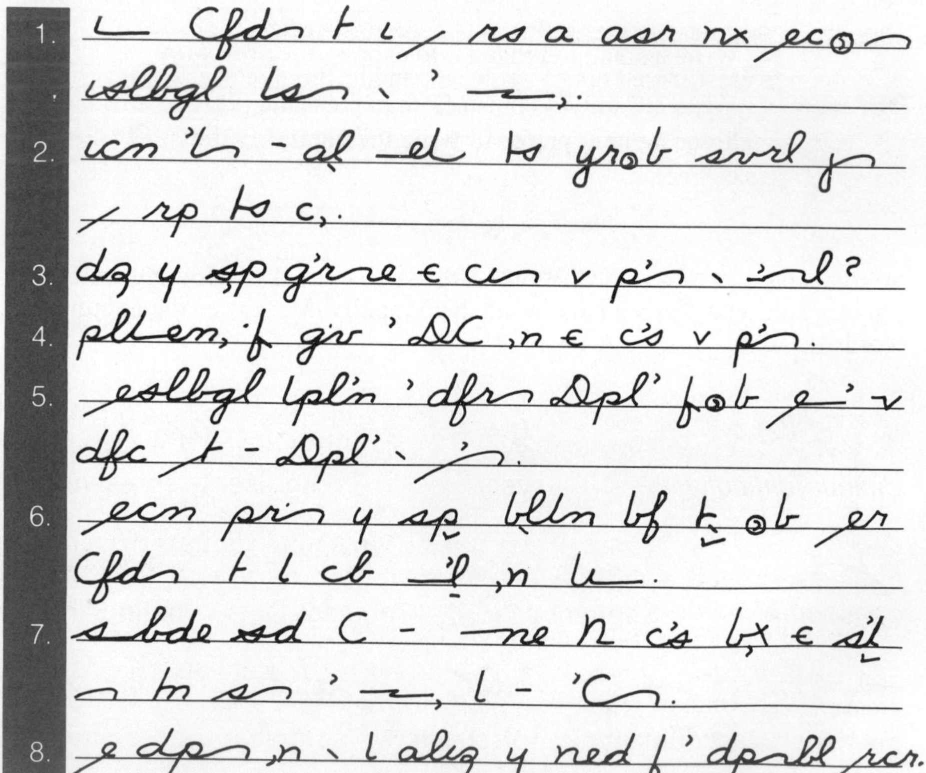

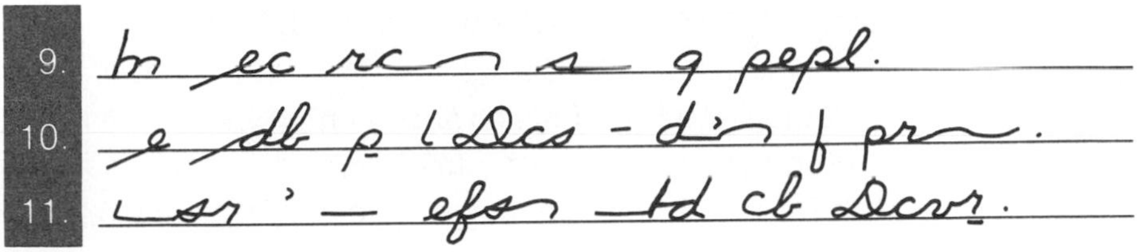

BUILDING TRANSCRIPTION SKILLS

Assignment 4 — **Punctuating compound sentences**. The shorthand sentences in Assignment 3 include *compound sentences*. Study the punctuation rule and examples that follow, and apply the rule when transcribing the sentences.

A compound sentence is two sentences joined together. The two sentences are usually joined by a connecting word (conjunction). Common connecting words are: *and*, *but*, *for*, *either*, *or*, *nor*, and *neither*. Place a comma before the connecting word in a compound sentence.

1. John overestimated his gas mileage, and he ran out of gas.
2. He will come to the meeting, but he may arrive late.
3. I will mail you a ticket to the game, or you may pick up your ticket at the box office.

BUILDING SHORTHAND SPEED AND TRANSCRIPTION ACCURACY

Assignment 5 — **Self-testing**. Complete Unit 13 in your *Study Guide* before you proceed with the rest of this chapter.

Assignment 6 — **Taking tape dictation**. To write from dictation the new words and sentences in this chapter, use Cassette 13 Side A from *Theory and Speed-Building Tapes*.

Assignment 7 — **Taking live dictation**. Write from dictation the sentences which are printed at the end of this chapter. Your instructor will dictate each group of 20 words to you at various speeds.

Assignment 8 — **Own-note transcription**. After you have taken the sentences in shorthand, select your best set of notes and transcribe them at your best typing rate. Do not number the sentences.

Assignment 9 — **Supplemental business letters.** If instructed to do so, read and write the additional business letter for this chapter found in "Supplemental Letters for Dictation" at the back of this book.

TRANSCRIPT OF SHORTHAND SENTENCES

1. I am confident that I will receive an answer next week, and I shall be glad to send you a memorandum. (20)
2. I cannot attend the annual meeting this year, but several gentlemen will represent this company. (40)
3. Does your shop guarantee each kind of paint you handle?
4. Please let me know if you give a discount on each case of paint. (60)
5. We shall be glad to plan a different display for you, but we may have difficulty with the display you want. (80)
6. We cannot print your September bulletin before Thursday, but we are confident that it can be mailed on time. (100)
7. Somebody should count the money in the cash box each Saturday and then send a memo to the accountant. (120)
8. We depend on you to analyze your need for a dependable worker.
9. Then we can recommend some good people. (140)
10. We would be pleased to discuss the demand for printing.
11. I am sure a more efficient method can be discovered. (160)

CHAPTER 14

WRITING **QU**, **INCL-ENCLOSE**, AND **LY**

Assignment 1 — **Rule discovery**. Follow the three-step plan to learn the new writing principles: (1) Discover the rule for each group of words. (2) Read the shorthand outlines until you can read them rapidly. (3) Cover the shorthand and write each word until you can do so rapidly and accurately.

QU

quote quality quite quoted acquainted equip

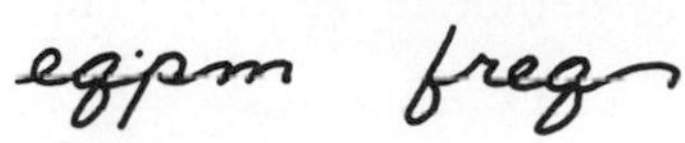

equipment frequent

INCL-ENCLOSE

include included including incline inclined

inclusive enclose enclosure enclosing enclosed

LY

easily quickly clearly daily surely monthly

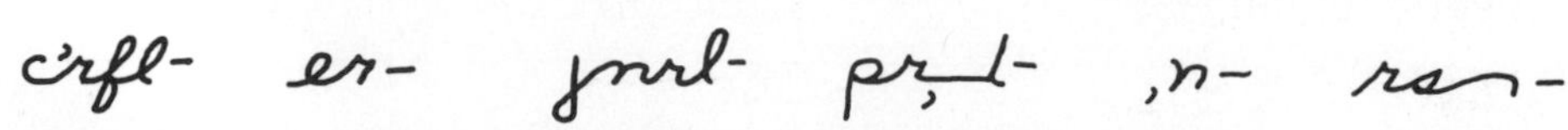

carefully early generally promptly only recently

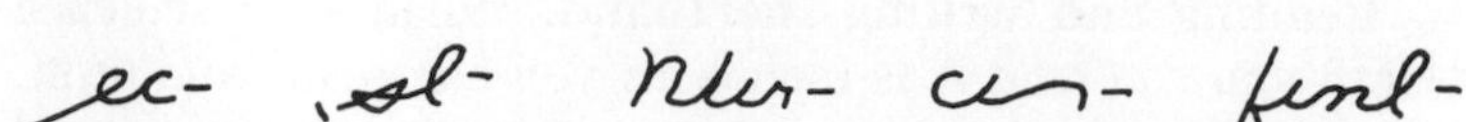

weekly usually entirely kindly finally

WRITING PRINCIPLES

QU Write only *q* for the combination *qu*.

INCL ENCLOSE Write a capital longhand *I* thus *I* to express the combination *incl* and the following vowel and the word *enclose*. The capital *I* must be written so it cannot be confused with the longhand *l*. The form shown above is recommended.

LY Write a short, disjoined dash close to the word to which it belongs to express the ending *ly*. Write words in full that end in *l* and then add the *ly* dash, as in *carefully* c'rfl- and *fully* fl-.

Assignment 2 — **New vocabulary**. Read and write the following words and phrases until you can read and write them rapidly. Memorize the abbreviated words.

q'n	q	rq	dpl	g	
quantity	question	require	department	going	
gr-	yr-	rq	rqm	gl-	fr
greatly	yearly	required	requirement	gladly	form
nrlm	-prv	tx	lsn	rsn	fr=
enrollment	improved	tax	lesson	recent	formed
nel	lasr	-erfr	ny		
any time-anytime	to answer	hear from	in your		
plle					
please let me					

Assignment 3 — **Reading and writing shorthand**. Read each sentence from shorthand until you can read it as rapidly as you can read from print. Write each sentence in shorthand until you can write each one rapidly and accurately.

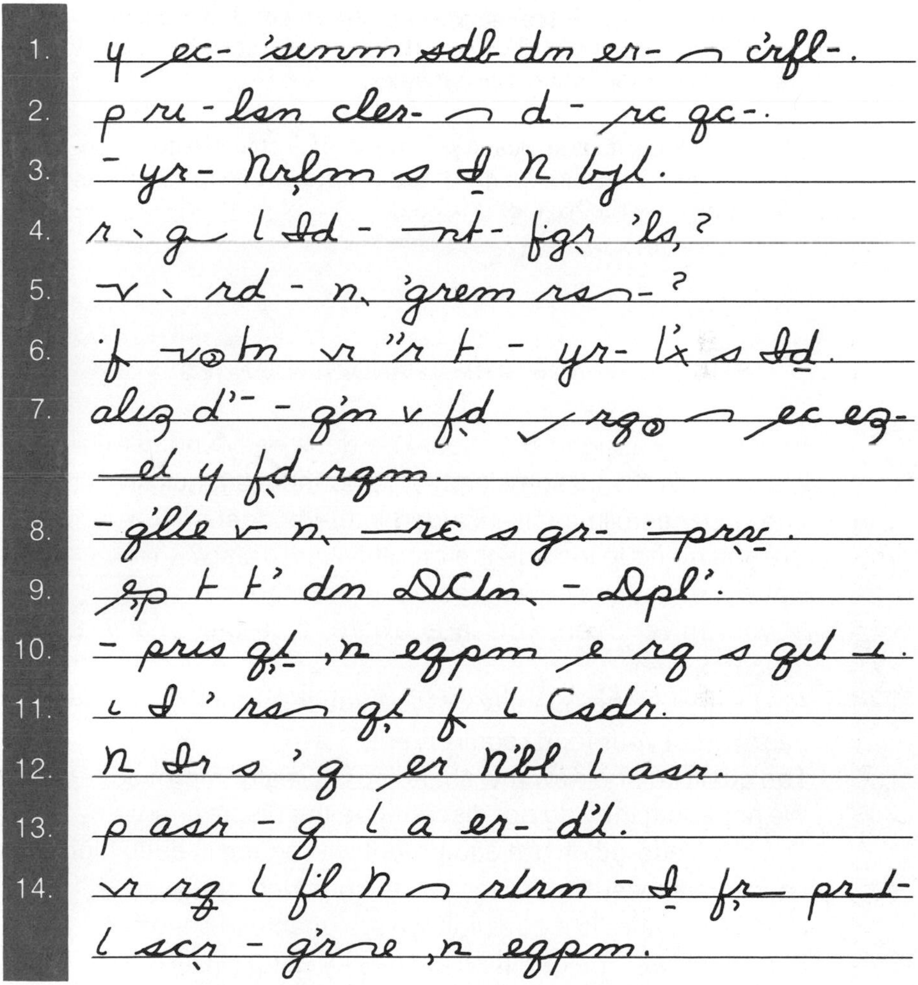

BUILDING SHORTHAND SPEED AND TRANSCRIPTION ACCURACY

Assignment 4 — **Self-testing**. Complete Unit 14 in your *Study Guide* before you proceed with the rest of this chapter.

Assignment 5 — **Taking tape dictation**. To write from dictation the new words and sentences in this chapter, use Cassette 14 Side A from *Theory and Speed-Building Tapes*.

Assignment 6 — **Taking live dictation**. Write from dictation the sentences which are printed at the end of this chapter. Your instructor will dictate each group of 20 words to you at various speeds.

Assignment 7 — **Own-note transcription**. After you have taken the sentences in shorthand, select your best set of notes and transcribe them at your best typing rate. Do not number the sentences.

Assignment 8 — **Supplemental business letters.** If instructed to do so, read and write the additional business letter for this chapter found in "Supplemental Letters for Dictation" at the back of this book.

TRANSCRIPT OF SHORTHAND SENTENCES

1. Your weekly assignment should be done early and carefully.
2. Please write the lesson clearly and do the work quickly. (20)
3. The yearly enrollment is included in the budget.
4. Are you going to include the monthly figure also? (40)
5. Have you read the new agreement recently?
6. If you have, then you are aware that the yearly tax is included. (60)
7. Analyze daily the quantity of food you will require, and we can easily meet your food requirement. (80)
8. The quality of the new merchandise is greatly improved.
9. We hope that they do not discontinue the display. (100)
10. The price quoted on the equipment we require is quite high.
11. I enclose a recent quote for you to consider. (120)
12. In the enclosure is a question we are unable to answer.
13. Please answer the question at an early date. (140)
14. You are required to fill in and return the enclosed form promptly to secure the guarantee on the equipment. (160)

CHAPTER 15

ADDING S TO ROOT WORDS AND WRITING EVER-EVERY

Assignment 1 – **Rule discovery**. Follow the three-step plan to learn the new writing principles: (1) Discover the rule for each group of words. (2) Read the shorthand outlines until you can read them rapidly. (3) Cover the shorthand and write each word until you can do so rapidly and accurately.

ADDING S TO ROOT WORDS

advises answers banks bills checks

thinks copies damages figures days says

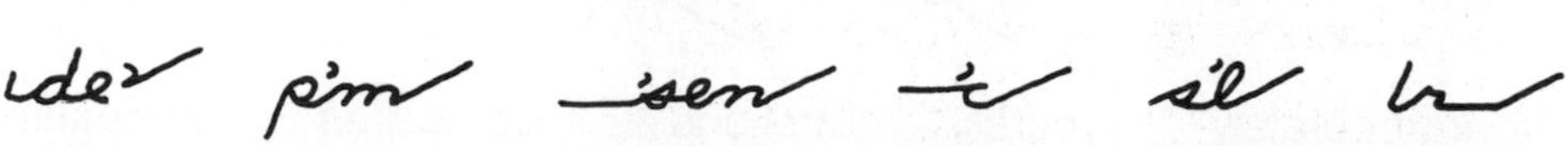

ideas payments machines makes sales terms

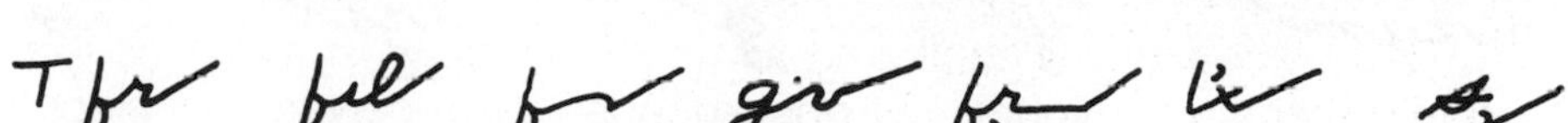

transfers files funds gives forms taxes shows

assures

PREFIX OR SUFFIX EVER-EVERY

everybody everyone ever-every whenever everything

WRITING PRINCIPLES

ADDING S Write an upward, slanted, straight stroke joined to the last letter or symbol of a word to add *s* to a root word. This same stroke is used to add *s* to a word to form the possessive. (See punctuation of possessives in Chapter 16.) Note how the *s* symbol is joined to words that end in a vowel symbol. Some writers prefer to *double* the symbol to indicate *s* with such words. Examples: *days* d˘ or d" ; *shows* ... or ... .

EVER-EVERY Write a disjoined capital *V* thus V for the words *ever* and *every* and the prefixes and suffixes *ever-every*. Make the first stroke of the *V* with a straight slanted line so it will not look like a *t*.

Assignment 2 — **New vocabulary**. Read and write the following words and phrases until you can read and write them rapidly. Memorize the abbreviated words.

Assignment 3 — **Reading and writing shorthand**. Read each sentence from shorthand until you can read it as rapidly as you can read from print. Write each sentence in shorthand until you can write each one rapidly and accurately.

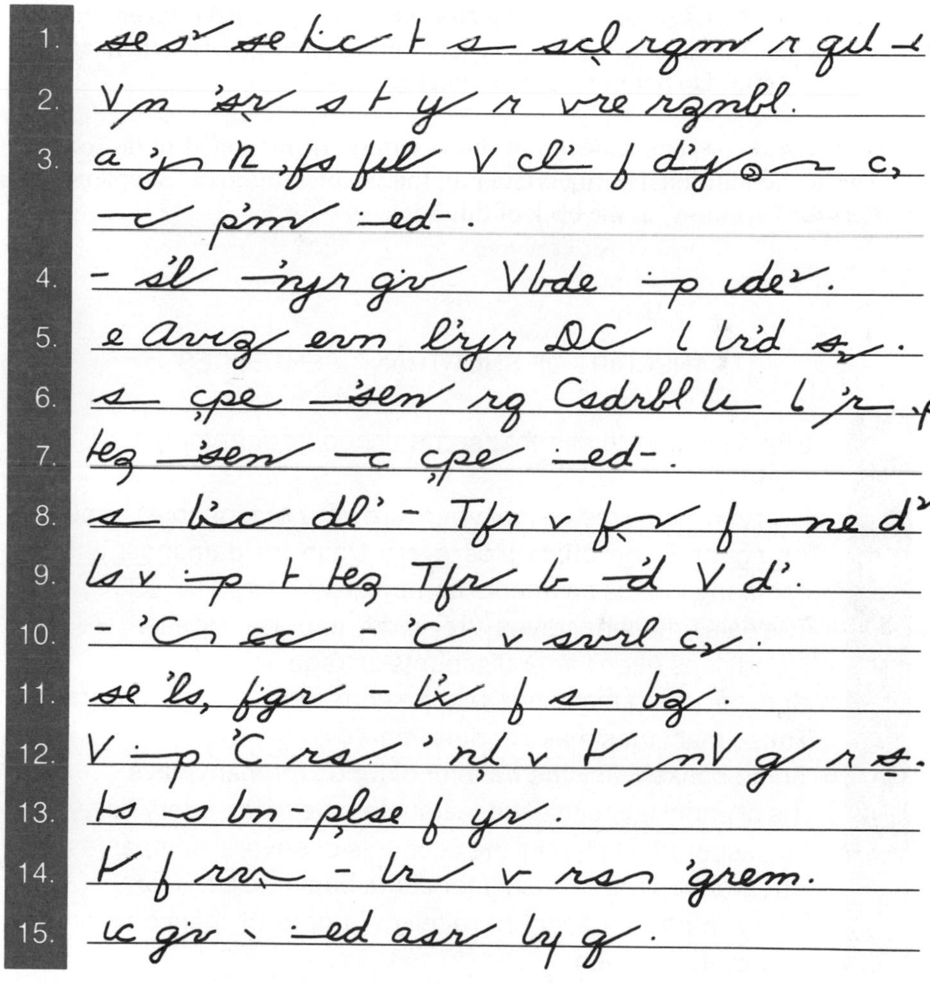

BUILDING SHORTHAND SPEED AND TRANSCRIPTION ACCURACY

Assignment 4 — **Self-testing**. Complete Unit 15 in your *Study Guide* before you proceed with the rest of this chapter.

Assignment 5 — **Taking tape dictation**. To write from dictation the new words and sentences in this chapter, use Cassette 15 Side A from *Theory and Speed-Building Tapes*.

Assignment 6 — **Taking live dictation**. Write from dictation the sentences which are printed at the end of this chapter. Your instructor will dictate each group of 20 words to you at various speeds.

Assignment 7 — **Own-note transcription**. After you have taken the sentences in shorthand, select your best set of notes and transcribe them at your best typing rate. Do not number the sentences.

Assignment 8 — **Supplemental business letters.** If instructed to do so, read and write the additional business letter for this chapter found in "Supplemental Letters for Dictation" at the back of this book.

TRANSCRIPT OF SHORTHAND SENTENCES

1. She says she thinks that some school requirements are quite high.
2. Everyone assures us that yours are very reasonable. (20)
3. An agent in the office files every claim for damages, and the company makes payments immediately. (40)
4. The sales manager gives everybody important ideas.
5. He advises even larger discounts at trade shows. (60)
6. Some copying machines require considerable time to warm up.
7. These machines make copies immediately. (80)
8. Some banks delay the transfer of funds for many days.
9. It is of importance that these transfers be made every day. (100)
10. The accountant checks the accounts of several companies.
11. She also figures the taxes for some businesses. (120)
12. Every important account receives a note of thanks whenever goods are shipped.
13. This has been the policy for years. (140)
14. Thanks for reviewing the terms of the recent agreement.
15. I can give you immediate answers to your questions. (160)

CHAPTER 16

BUSINESS LETTER DICTATION AND TRANSCRIPTION

BUILDING TRANSCRIPTION SKILLS

Assignment 1 — **Forming the singular possessive**. In the letters that follow are some words that require the possessive form. Study the rule and the examples and apply the rule when you transcribe.

To form the possessive of a singular word, add an *apostrophe* and an *s* to the word. In the examples, note that each possessive indicates "belonging to" or "of."

1. The boy's coat was torn. (coat belonging to the boy)
2. The company's balance sheet is printed. (the balance sheet belonging to the company)
3. The society is planning next year's meeting. (meeting of next year)
4. The manager's representative will meet you. (representative of the manager)
5. The customer's request came to the department head. (request of the customer).

Assignment 2 — **Spelling review**. Follow the steps outlined in Chapter 12 to check your ability to spell the following words correctly:

1. account	8. copies	15. immediately
2. available	9. different	16. mortgage
3. always	10. difficulty	17. original
4. annual	11. final	18. receiving
5. answer	12. finally	19. recommend
6. carefully	13. generally	20. several
7. convenient	14. guarantee	21. Tuesday
		22. usually

BUSINESS LETTERS

Assignment 3 — **Letter 1**. Read and write each of the new words and phrases for Letter 1 until you can read and write each one rapidly and accurately. Then read and write the shorthand for Letter 1 to build your writing speed.

dissatisfied inside doing advertisements receiving

adequate shopping charges lighting reaching

areas growing appear pictures desirable rapidly

serves renting center discussed buildings

services shown friend indicated modern design

talked retail appears rates touch kinds rent

Yours very truly

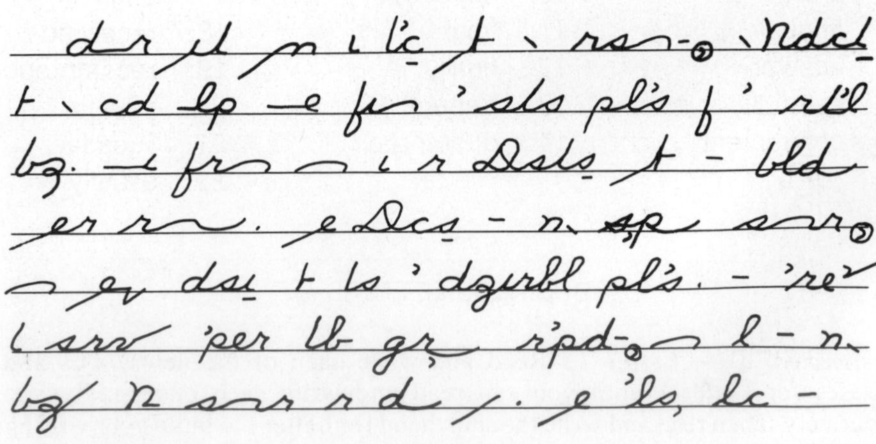

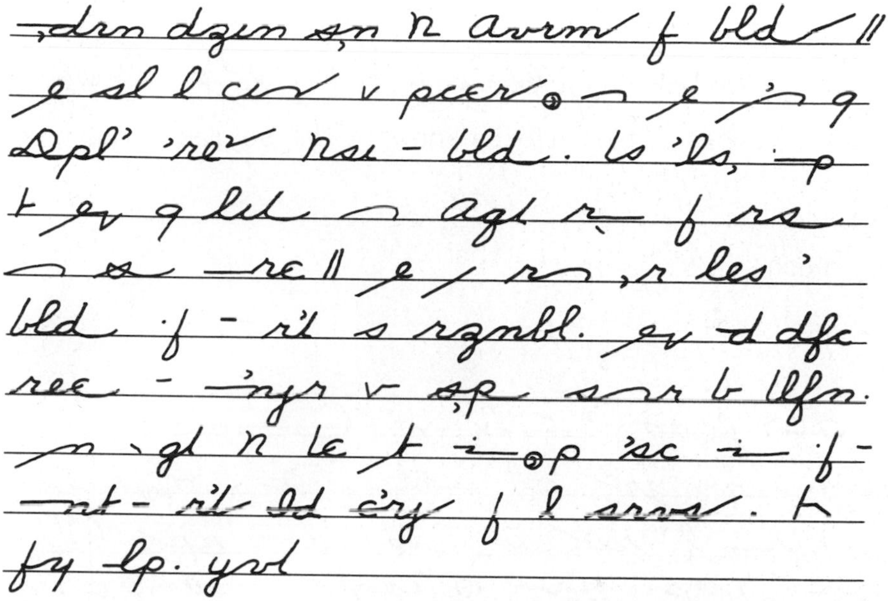

Assignment 4 — Letter 2. Read and write each of the new words and phrases for Letter 2 until you can read and write each one rapidly and accurately. Then read and write the shorthand for Letter 2 to build your writing speed.

November	representatives	accounting	attended	both
cooperate	determining	double	meetings	held
hotels	Jackson	leading	society	second
managers	manager's	major	single	needs	year's

rs	prss	pllsn,	bgl	vn
rooms	prices	please let us know	will be glad	have not

vrec
very much

dr jcsn, cle v C ssile s
pln nx yr al el. 's . n,olry
c, fr l 're v Cre sn rp l
tez el. nx yr el b ld
er - scn ec v nvon ep t l b
/ 'l ll - cle ned y lp n dlrn
- nbr v rs t - led, Tl c
g'rsef el. e 'ls, ned - prss
v bt sl n dbl rs. sp 'sc -
nyr v jr, Tl lgv . tez fgr.
usr t' bgl l cprl ll pllsn, - nbr
v rs t r 'vlbl ssns psbl. t
vrec fy lp. yvl

Assignment 5 **—Supplemental business letters**. If instructed to do so, read and write the additional business letter for this chapter found in "Supplemental Letters for Dictation" at the back of this book.

BUILDING SHORTHAND SPEED AND TRANSCRIPTION ACCURACY

Assignment 6 — **Self-testing**. Complete Unit 16 in your *Study Guide* before you proceed with the rest of this chapter.

Assignment 7 — **Taking tape dictation**. To write from dictation the new words and letters in this chapter, use Cassette 16 Side A from *Theory and Speed-Building Tapes*.

Assignment 8 — **Taking live dictation**. Write from dictation the letters which are printed at the end of this chapter. Your instructor will dictate to you from these transcripts at various speeds.

Assignment 9 — **Own-note transcription**. Transcribe at your best typing rate an accurate copy of at least one of the letters you took in shorthand in Assignment 8. Type the letter in the form requested by your instructor.

TRANSCRIPTS OF LETTERS 1 AND 2

Letter 1 Dear Mr. White: When I talked with you recently, you indicated that you could help me find a satisfactory (20) place for a retail business. My friend and I are dissatisfied with the building we are renting. We discussed (40) the new shopping center, and we have decided that it is a desirable place. The areas it serves appear (60) to be growing rapidly, and all the new businesses in the center are doing well. We also like the (80) modern design shown in the advertisements for the buildings.

We sell all kinds of pictures, and we want good display (100) areas inside the building. It is also important that we have good lighting and adequate room for (120) receiving and shipping merchandise.

We will rent or lease a building if the rate is reasonable. We have had (140) difficulty reaching the manager of the shopping center by telephone. When you get in touch with him, please ask (160) him if the monthly rates include charges for all services. Thank you for your help. Yours very truly, (178)

Letter 2 Dear Mr. Jackson: A committee of the accounting society is planning next year's annual meeting. As (20) you know, large companies from all areas of the country send representatives to these meetings. Next year's meeting (40) will be held here the second week of November, and we hope that it will be well attended.

The committee (60) needs your help in determining the number of rooms that the leading hotels can guarantee for the meeting. We (80) also need the prices of both single and double rooms. Will you please ask the managers of the major hotels (100) to give you these figures. I am sure they will be glad to cooperate.

Please let us know the number of rooms that (120) are available as soon as possible. Thanks very much for your help. Yours very truly, (136)

REVIEWING THE WRITING PRINCIPLES

All the writing principles, abbreviated words, and standard abbreviations you have learned in Chapters 9 through 16 are reviewed on Tape 18 Side A of the *Theory and Speed-Building Tapes*. Take dictation from this tape before completing Examination 4.

EXAMINATION 4

Remove and complete Examination 4 at the back of your *Study Guide* before proceeding to Chapter 17 of your textbook.

CHAPTER 17

WRITING **ST** AND **SITY-CITY**

Assignment 1 — **Rule discovery**. Follow the three-step plan to learn the new writing principles: (1) Discover the rule for each group of words. (2) Read the shorthand outlines until you can read them rapidly. (3) Cover the shorthand and write each word until you can do so rapidly and accurately.

ST

SITY-CITY

capacity publicity university city simplicity

WRITING PRINCIPLES

ST Write a capital *S* thus *S* to express the *st* combination. The use of the capital *S* for the combination *st* helps when reading shorthand notes because one knows immediately that there is no vowel between the *s* and the *t*. When one sees *st*, a vowel must come between the *s* and the *t*.

SITY CITY Write a disjoined capital *S* thus *S* to express the combinations *sity-city* and the preceding vowel. Write the disjoined capital *S* close to the word to which it belongs.

Assignment 2 — **New vocabulary**. Read and write the following words and phrases until you can read and write them rapidly. Memorize the abbreviated words.

administer because suggest acknowledge estimate

its it's estimated suggests greatest

manufacturing computer computing market limited

airline travel attends data apply small benefit

easy showed computers we must as well as

at this time

Learning tip: The outline for the contraction *it's* (meaning *it is*) should be written with an apostrophe inserted as shown on page 76. The apostrophe is a reminder to insert the apostrophe when transcribing. See Chapter 31 for more help with contractions.

Assignment 3 — **Reading and writing shorthand**. Read each sentence from shorthand until you can read it as rapidly as you can read from print. Write each sentence in shorthand until you can write each one rapidly and accurately.

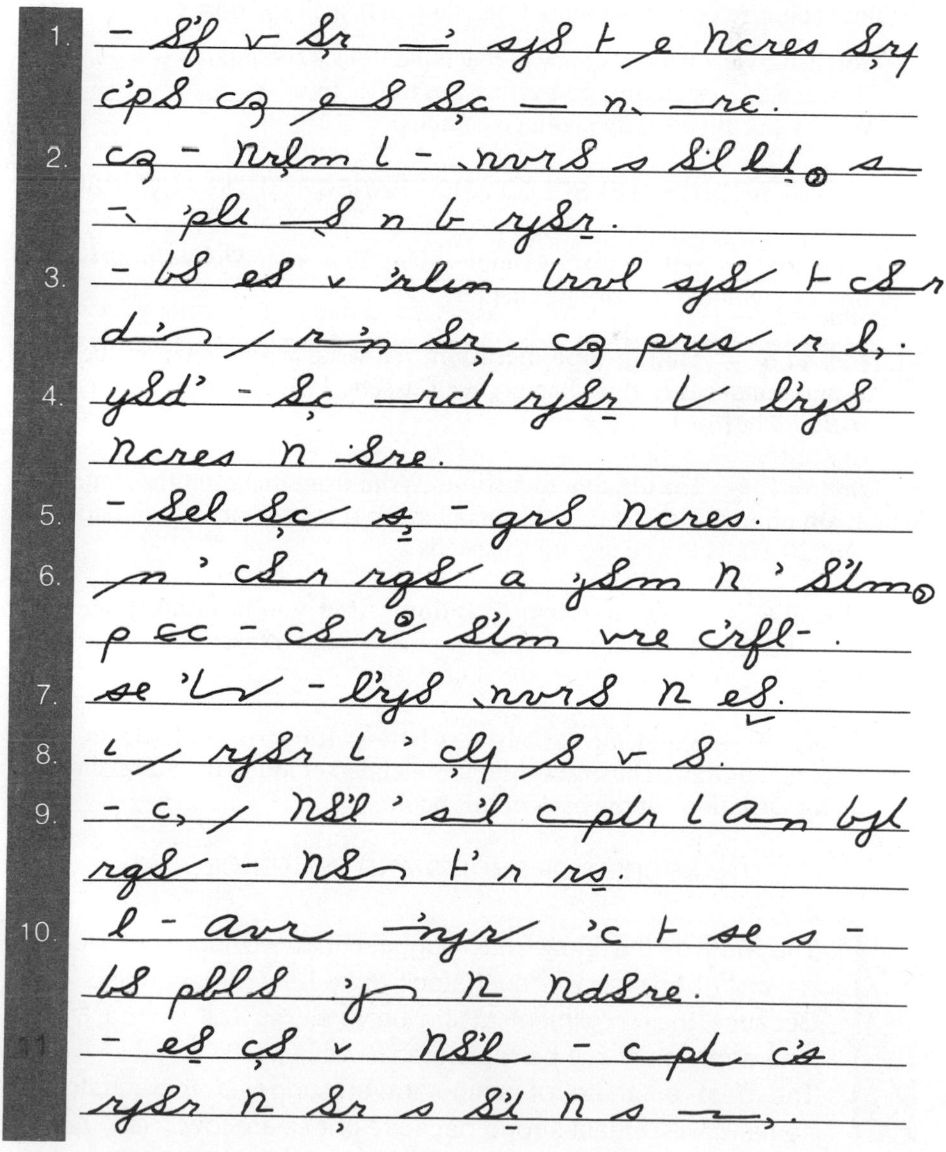

BUILDING TRANSCRIPTION SKILLS

Assignment 4 — **Capitalizing geographical sections of a country**. Capitalize compass points when they name specific geographic regions. Apply the rule when transcribing.

1. She lives in the East.
2. Our geology class will visit the desert in the Southwest.
3. The Rocky Mountains are in the West.

Do not capitalize compass points when they indicate direction.

1. You drive west from Calgary to reach the Rocky Mountains.
2. To reach the restaurant, go north at the traffic light.
3. We live northwest of the college campus.

BUILDING SHORTHAND SPEED AND TRANSCRIPTION ACCURACY

Assignment 5 — **Self-testing**. Complete Unit 17 in your *Study Guide* before you proceed with the rest of this chapter.

Assignment 6 — **Taking tape dictation**. To write from dictation the new words and sentences in this chapter, use Cassette 1 Side B from *Theory and Speed-Building Tapes*.

Assignment 7 — **Taking live dictation**. Write from dictation the sentences which are printed at the end of this chapter. Your instructor will dictate each group of 20 words to you at various speeds.

Assignment 8 — **Own-note transcription**. After you have taken the sentences in shorthand, select your best set of notes and transcribe them at your best typing rate. Do not number the sentences.

Assignment 9 — **Supplemental business letters.** If instructed to do so, read and write the additional business letter for this chapter found in "Supplemental Letters for Dictation" at the back of this book.

TRANSCRIPT OF SHORTHAND SENTENCES

1. The staff of the store may suggest that we increase storage capacity because we must stock more new merchandise. (20)
2. Because the enrollment at the university is still limited, some who apply must not be registered. (40)
3. The best estimate of airline travel suggests that customer demand will remain strong because prices are low. (60)

4. Yesterday the stock market registered its largest increase in history.
5. The steel stocks showed the greatest increase. (80)
6. When a customer requests an adjustment in a statement, please check the customer's statement very carefully. (100)
7. She attends the largest university in the East.
8. I will register at a college west of the city. (120)
9. The company will install a small computer to administer budget requests the instant they are received. (140)
10. All the advertising managers acknowledge that she is the best publicity agent in the industry. (160)
11. The estimated cost of installing the computing cash register in the store is stated in his memo. (180)

CHAPTER 18

WRITING SOUNDS OF **OU-OW**, **OUT**, AND **SELF**

Assignment 1 – **Rule discovery**. Follow the three-step plan to learn the new writing principles: (1) Discover the rule for each group of words. (2) Read the shorthand outlines until you can read them rapidly. (3) Cover the shorthand and write each word until you can do so rapidly and accurately.

SOUND OF **OU-OW**

brown doubt allowed aloud amount found

house south ground now power how down

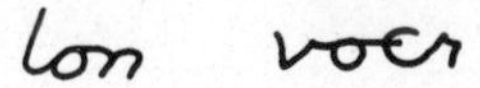

town voucher

PREFIX OR SUFFIX **OUT**

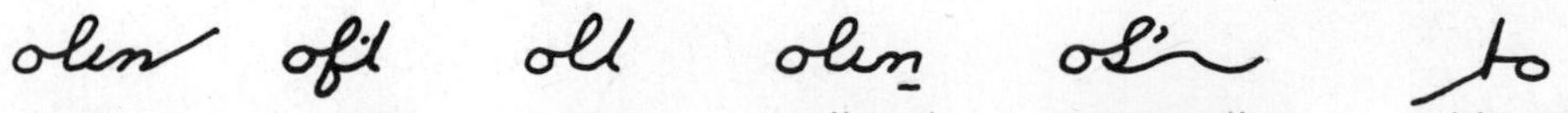

outlines outfit outlet outlined outstanding without

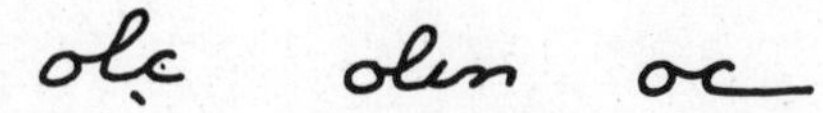

outlook outline outcome

PREFIX OR SUFFIX **SELF**

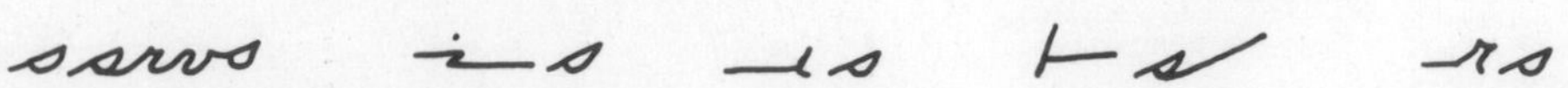

self-service himself myself themselves herself

sArs	sDpln
self-addressed	self-discipline

WRITING PRINCIPLES

OU-OW Write a small longhand *o* to express *ou-ow*. Write the longhand *o* in a clockwise direction thus o so that you can form the *o* quickly.

OUT Write a small longhand *o* to express the prefix or suffix *out*.

SELF Write a small disjoined longhand *s* thus s to express the prefix or suffix *self*. The suffix *selves* is expressed by adding the *s*-added stroke to the suffix *self*, as shown in the word *themselves*.

Assignment 2 — **New vocabulary**. Read and write the following words and phrases until you can read and write them rapidly. Memorize the abbreviated words.

'bo	f8	o	8	'g	sn
about	first	our-out-hour	street	August	Sunday
osi	ys	sj8	s	cllg	
outside	yourself	suggested	sending	catalogs	
'gn	cps	rtrn	mtrel	rl	l8
again	campus	returned	materials	rating	test
f-	rsrc	rvz	ters	r	lv
family	research	revised	teachers	wrong	live
Sde	scjl	Csll	rvz	jnrs	
study	schedule	consult	revise	generous	

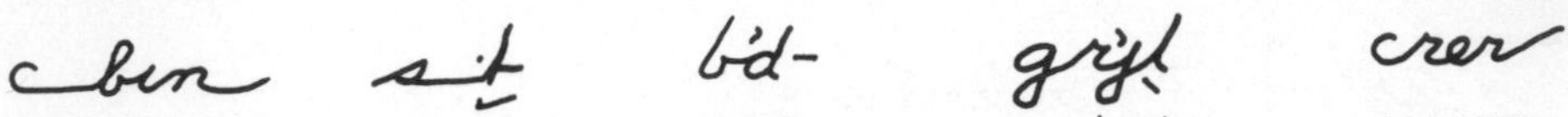

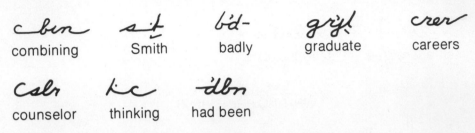

combining Smith badly graduate careers

counselor thinking had been

Assignment 3 — **Reading and writing shorthand**. Read each sentence from shorthand until you can read it as rapidly as you can read from print. Write each sentence in shorthand until you can write each one rapidly and accurately.

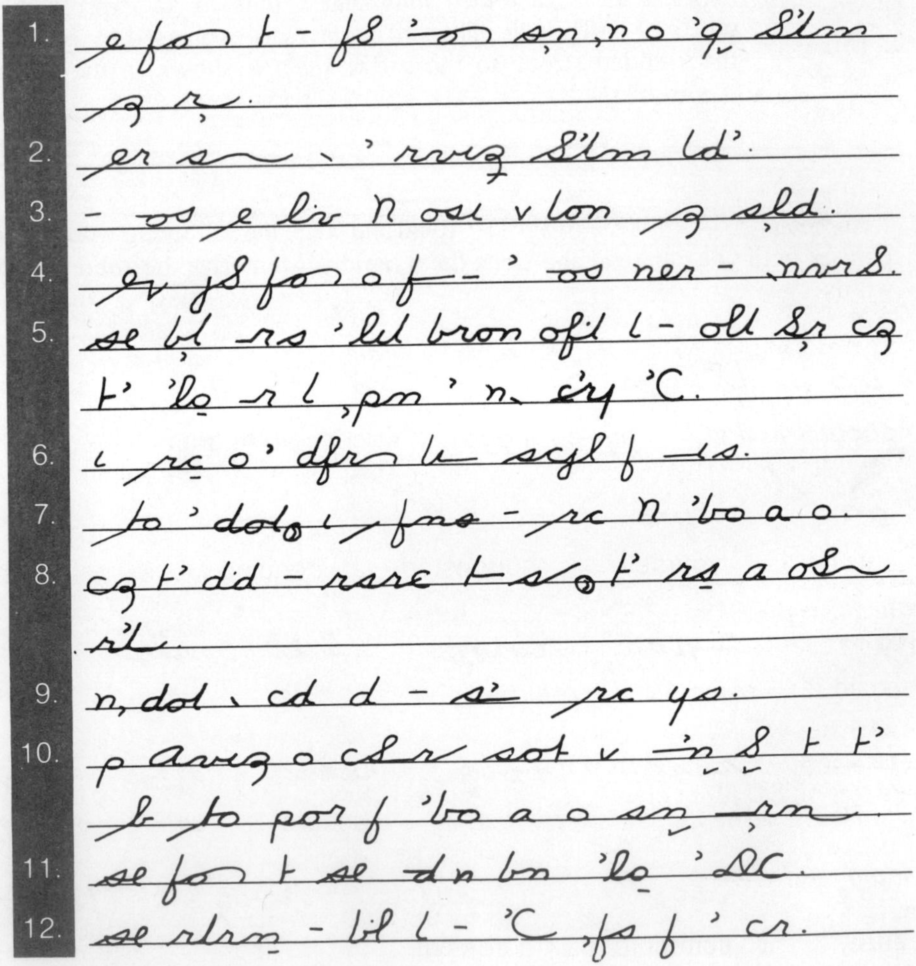

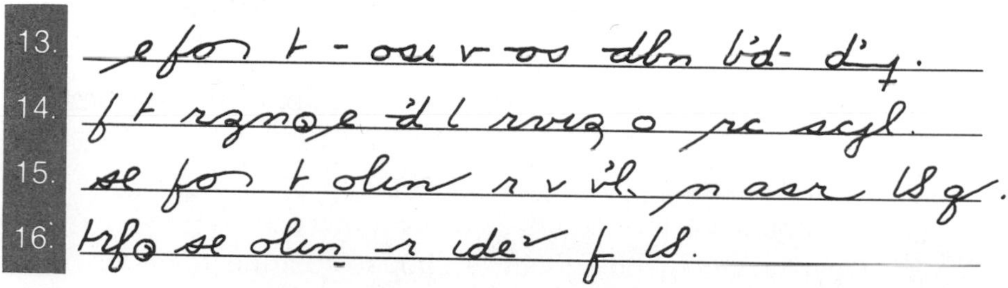

BUILDING TRANSCRIPTION SKILLS

Assignment 4 — **Capitalizing names of states, towns, streets, avenues, boulevards, and routes**. Because these are proper nouns, they are capitalized. Study the examples below and remember to capitalize such proper nouns when transcribing.

1. We live two blocks south of Main Street.
2. Many large companies have offices on Park Avenue.
3. Sunset Boulevard runs through Hollywood, California.
4. To go from Portland to Seattle, you go north on Route 5.

BUILDING SHORTHAND SPEED AND TRANSCRIPTION ACCURACY

Assignment 5 — **Self-testing**. Complete Unit 18 in your *Study Guide* before you proceed with the rest of this chapter.

Assignment 6 — **Taking tape dictation**. To write from dictation the new words and sentences in this chapter, use Cassette 2 Side B from *Theory and Speed-Building Tapes*.

Assignment 7 — **Taking live dictation**. Write from dictation the sentences which are printed at the end of this chapter. Your instructor will dictate each group of 20 words to you at various speeds.

Assignment 8 — **Own-note transcription**. After you have taken the sentences in shorthand, select your best set of notes and transcribe them at your best typing rate. Do not number the sentences.

Assignment 9 — **Supplemental business letters.** If instructed to do so, read and write the additional business letter for this chapter found in "Supplemental Letters for Dictation" at the back of this book.

TRANSCRIPT OF SHORTHAND SENTENCES

1. We found that the first amount shown on our August statement was wrong.
2. We are sending you a revised statement today. (20)
3. The house we live in outside of town was sold.
4. We have just found our family a house near the university. (40)
5. She bought herself a light brown outfit at the outlet store because they allowed her to open a new charge account. (60)
6. I worked out a different time schedule for myself.
7. Without a doubt, I will finish the work in about an hour. (80)
8. Because they did the research themselves, they received an outstanding rating.
9. No doubt you could do the same work yourself. (100)
10. Please advise our customers south of Main Street that they will be without power for about an hour Sunday morning. (120)
11. She found that she had not been allowed a discount.
12. She returned the bill to the accounting office for a credit. (140)
13. We found that the outside of the house had been badly damaged.
14. For that reason, we had to revise our work schedule. (160)
15. She found that outlines are of value when answering test questions.
16. Therefore, she outlined her ideas for the test. (180)

CHAPTER 19

WRITING THE SOUND OF **SHUN**

Assignment 1 — **Rule discovery**. Follow the three-step plan to learn the new writing principles: (1) Discover the rule for each group of words. (2) Read the shorthand outlines until you can read them rapidly. (3) Cover the shorthand and write each word until you can do so rapidly and accurately.

SOUND OF **SHUN**

WRITING PRINCIPLES

SHUN Write a short, vertical, downward stroke under the last letter or symbol of a word to express the *shun* sound and the preceding vowel. Note how additional endings are added to the *shun* symbol.

Assignment 2 — **New vocabulary**. Read and write the following words and phrases until you can read and write them rapidly. Memorize the abbreviated words.

Assignment 3 — **Reading and writing shorthand**. Read each sentence from shorthand until you can read it as rapidly as you can read from print. Write each sentence in shorthand until you can write each one rapidly and accurately.

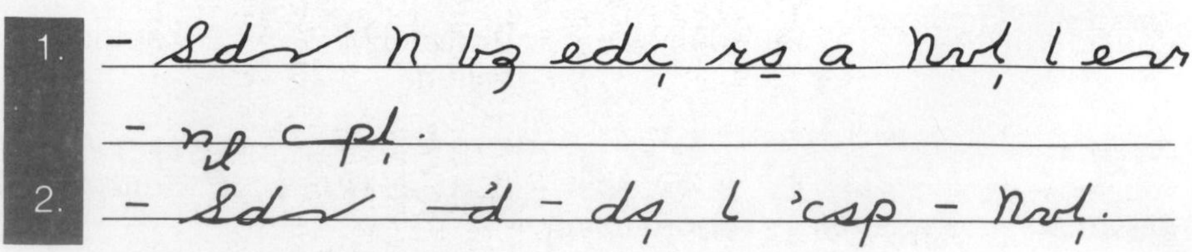

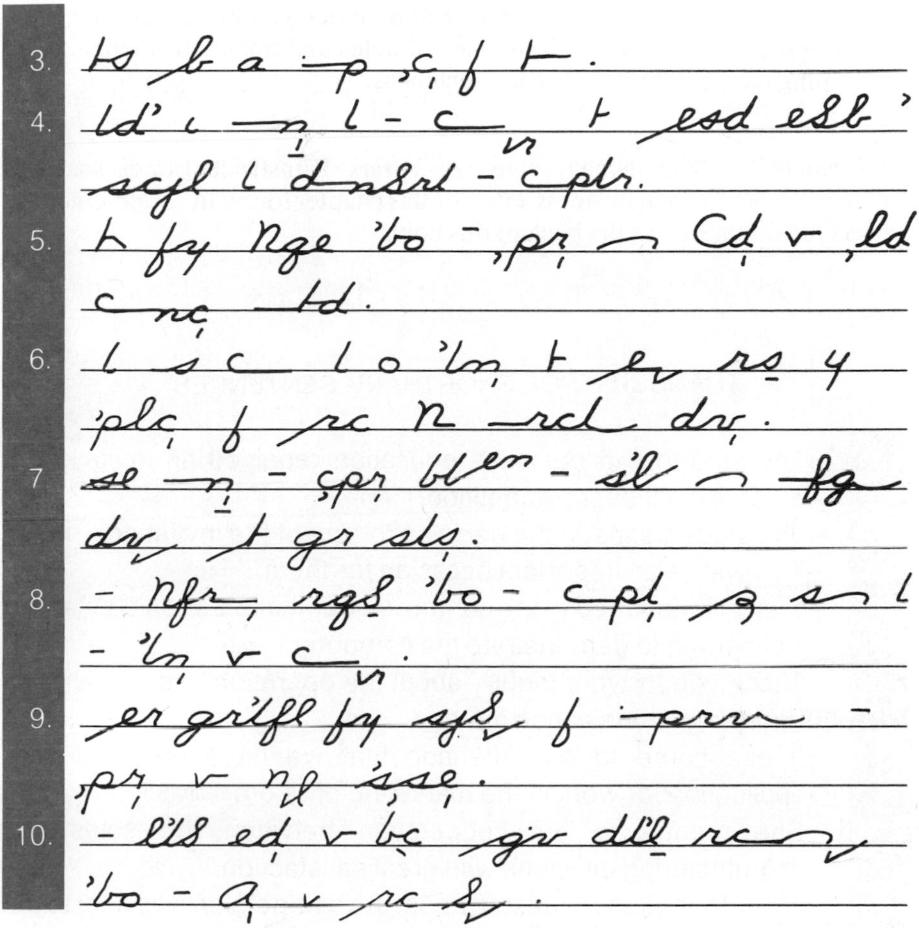

BUILDING SHORTHAND SPEED AND TRANSCRIPTION ACCURACY

Assignment 4 — **Self-testing**. Complete Unit 19 in your *Study Guide* before you proceed with the rest of this chapter.

Assignment 5 — **Taking tape dictation**. To write from dictation the new words and sentences in this chapter, use Cassette 3 Side B from *Theory and Speed-Building Tapes*.

Assignment 6 — **Taking live dictation**. Write from dictation the sentences which are printed at the end of this chapter. Your instructor will dictate each group of 20 words to you at various speeds.

Assignment 7 — **Own-note transcription**. After you have taken the sentences in shorthand, select your best set of notes and transcribe them at your best typing rate. Do not number the sentences.

Assignment 8 — **Supplemental business letters.** If instructed to do so, read and write the additional business letter for this chapter found in "Supplemental Letters for Dictation" at the back of this book.

TRANSCRIPT OF SHORTHAND SENTENCES

1. The students in business education received an invitation to enter the national competition. (20)
2. The students made the decision to accept the invitation.
3. This will be an important occasion for them. (40)
4. Today I mentioned to the commissioner that we should establish a schedule to demonstrate the computer. (60)
5. Thank you for your inquiry about the operation and condition of the old communication method. (80)
6. It has come to our attention that we have received your application for work in the marketing division. (100)
7. She mentioned the cooperation between the sales and manufacturing divisions with great satisfaction. (120)
8. The information requested about the competition was sent to the attention of the commissioner. (140)
9. We are grateful for your suggestions for improving the operation of the national association. (160)
10. The latest edition of the book will give detailed recommendations about the addition of work stations. (180)

CHAPTER 20

BUSINESS LETTER DICTATION AND TRANSCRIPTION

BUILDING TRANSCRIPTION SKILLS

Assignment 1 — **Capitalization**. Names of businesses, organizations, associations, governmental agencies, schools, and colleges are proper nouns. They should be capitalized when transcribing. Study the examples that follow and remember to capitalize such proper nouns when transcribing.

1. I have a savings account at the Dollar Savings Bank.
2. Our football team at Northern High School is known as the Tigers.
3. The Dominion Insurance Company has its home office in our town.
4. We attended the convention of the Future Business Leaders last summer.
5. We belong to the North American Association of Insurance Agencies.

Assignment 2 – **Spelling review**. Follow the steps outlined in Chapter 12 to check your ability to spell the following words correctly:

1. acknowledge
2. again
3. association
4. attention
5. appear
6. benefit
7. between
8. condition
9. cooperation
10. discussion
11. division
12. double
13. doubt
14. estimate
15. grateful
16. history
17. install
18. occasion
19. request
20. shop
21. shopping
22. suggest

BUSINESS LETTERS

Assignment 3 — **Letter 1**. Read and write each of the new words and phrases until you can read and write each one rapidly and accurately. Then read and write the shorthand for Letter 1 to build your writing speed.

administration ....

organized ....

suggestion ....

hours-ours ....

classes	maintain	committees	visits	members
methods	helps	conditions	superior	various
teaching	introduction	courses	inviting	similar
world	skills	valuable	bond	advisory
matters	off	sometimes	times	used
vocational	black	to serve	to get	at this

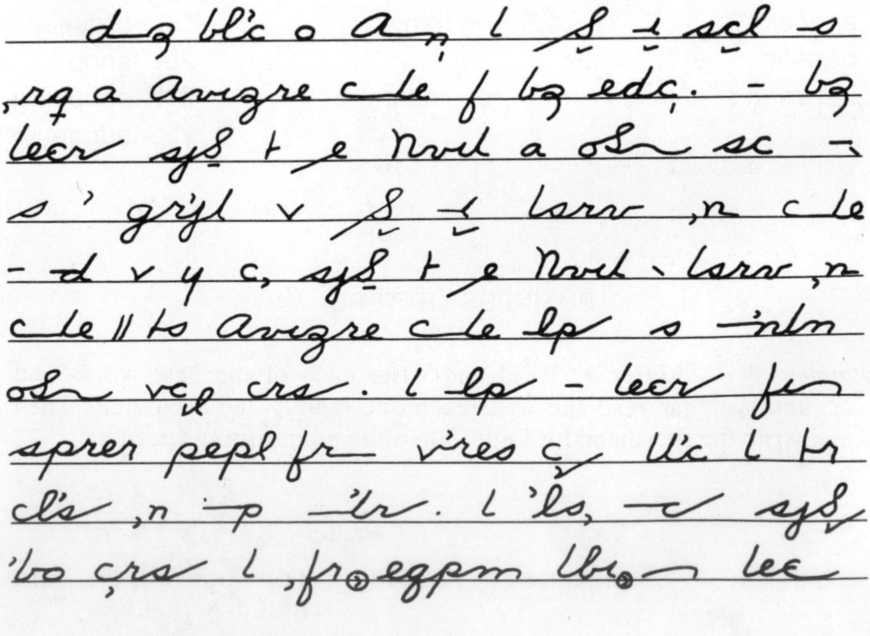

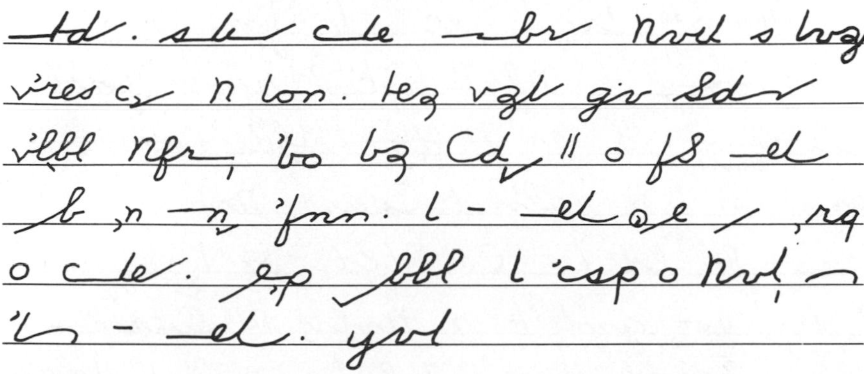

Assignment 4 — **Letter 2**. Read and write each of the new words and phrases for Letter 2 until you can read and write each one rapidly and accurately. Then read and write the shorthand for Letter 2 to build your writing speed.

December	represented	states	associations		
undoubtedly	someone	entire	conservation	phone	
met	use (n)	federal	hearings	hearing	reduction
recommendations	involved	revising	session	sessions	
plans	might	least	officials	winter	officers
users	series	to this	this is	let us know	at least
there are					

Learning tip:: The (n) after the word *use* means the word is a noun.

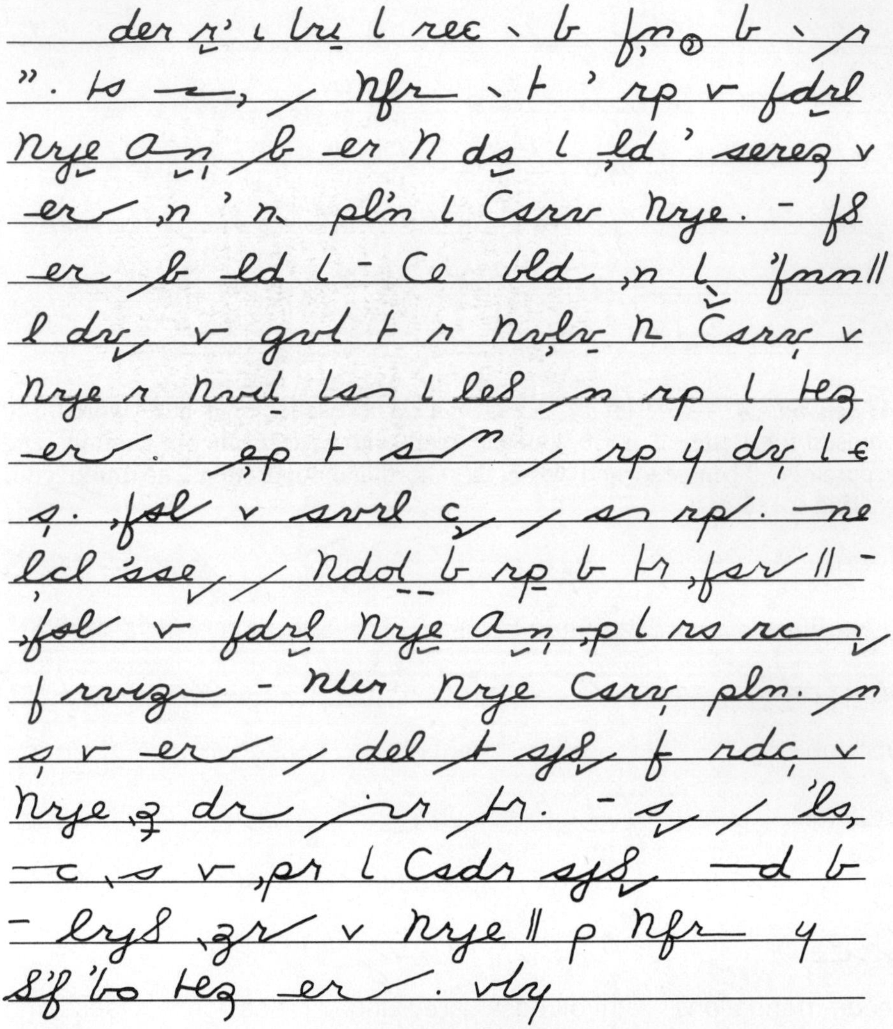

Assignment 5 — **Supplemental business letters.** If instructed to do so, read and write the additional business letter for this chapter found in "Supplemental Letters for Dictation" at the back of this book.

BUILDING SHORTHAND SPEED AND TRANSCRIPTION ACCURACY

Assignment 6 — **Self-testing**. Complete Unit 20 in your *Study Guide* before you proceed with the rest of this chapter.

Assignment 7 — **Taking tape dictation**. To write from dictation the new words and letters in this chapter, use Cassette 4 Side B from *Theory and Speed-Building Tapes*.

Assignment 8 — **Taking live dictation**. Write from dictation the letters which are printed at the end of this chapter. Your instructor will dictate to you from these transcripts at various speeds.

Assignment 9 — **Own-note transcription**. Transcribe at your best typing rate an accurate copy of at least one of the letters you took in shorthand in Assignment 8. Type the letter in the form requested by your instructor.

TRANSCRIPTS OF LETTERS 1 AND 2

Letter 1 Dear Ms. Black: Our administration at West High School has organized an advisory committee for business (20) education. The business teachers suggested that we invite an outstanding secretary who is a (40) graduate of West High to serve on the committee. The head of your company suggested that we invite you to (60) serve on the committee.

This advisory committee helps us maintain outstanding vocational courses. It (80) helps the teachers find superior people from various companies to talk to their classes on important matters. (100) It also makes suggestions about courses to offer, equipment to buy, and teaching methods. Sometimes (120) committee members invite us to visit various companies in town. These visits give students valuable (140) information about business conditions.

Our first meeting will be on Monday afternoon. At the meeting, we (160) will organize our committees. We hope you will be able to accept our invitation and attend the meeting. (180) Yours very truly, (184)

Letter 2 Dear Ray: I tried to reach you by phone, but you were away. This memo will inform you that a representative (20) of the Federal Energy Administration will be here in December to hold a series of hearings (40) on a new plan to conserve energy. The first hearing will be held at the county building on Tuesday afternoon. (60)

All divisions of the government that are involved in the conservation of energy are invited (80) to send at least one representative to these hearings. We hope that someone will represent your division (100) at each session. Officials of several companies will send representatives. Many local associations (120) will undoubtedly be represented by their officers.

The officials of the Federal Energy (140) Administration hope to receive recommendations for revising the entire energy conservation (160) plan. One session of the hearings will deal with suggestions for the reduction of energy used during winter (180) weather. The sessions will also make use of the opportunity to consider suggestions made by the largest (200) users of energy.

Please inform your staff about these hearings. Very truly yours, (215)

EXAMINATION 5

Remove and complete Examination 5 at the back of your *Study Guide* before proceeding to Chapter 21 of your textbook.

CHAPTER 21

WRITING **SP**, **CT**, AND **INSTR**

Assignment 1 — **Rule discovery.** Follow the three-step plan to learn the new writing principles: (1) Discover the rule for each group of words. (2) Read the shorthand outlines until you can read them rapidly. (3) Cover the shorthand and write each word until you can do so rapidly and accurately.

SP

ssl	essl-	sr	s's	sl-d	sc
special	especially	spring	space	splendid	spoke
ssfc (check)	,sll	sec	ssfc	ssf	
specifications	hospital	speak	specific	specify	

CT

sbjc	crc	clc	drc	Dlrc	'c
subject	correct	collect	direct	district	act
C8rc	nsc	efcv	drcr	drc (underlined)	
construct	inspect	effective	director	directed	
'cv	fc/	ddc	nsc/	drc/	
active	facts	deduct	inspects	directs	

INSTR

nc	nc (check)	nc (underlined)	ncr	nm
instruct	instructions	instructed	instructor	instrument

WRITING PRINCIPLES

SP Write a small printed *s* thus s to express the *sp* combination when no vowel occurs between the *s* and *p*.

CT Omit *t* in the combination *ct* when *ct* ends a word because the *t* is lightly sounded. The *t* is also omitted when *ct* is followed by a common word ending such as *ed*, *ly*, *ing*, *ive*, etc.

INSTR Write a disjoined capital *N* thus n to express the combination *instr* and the following vowel. Write the disjoined capital *N* close to the word to which it belongs.

Assignment 2 — **New Vocabulary**. Read and write the following words and phrases until you can read and write them rapidly. Memorize the abbreviated words.

Assignment 3 — **Reading and writing shorthand**. Read each sentence from shorthand until you can read it as rapidly as you can read from print. Write each sentence in shorthand until you can write each one rapidly and accurately.

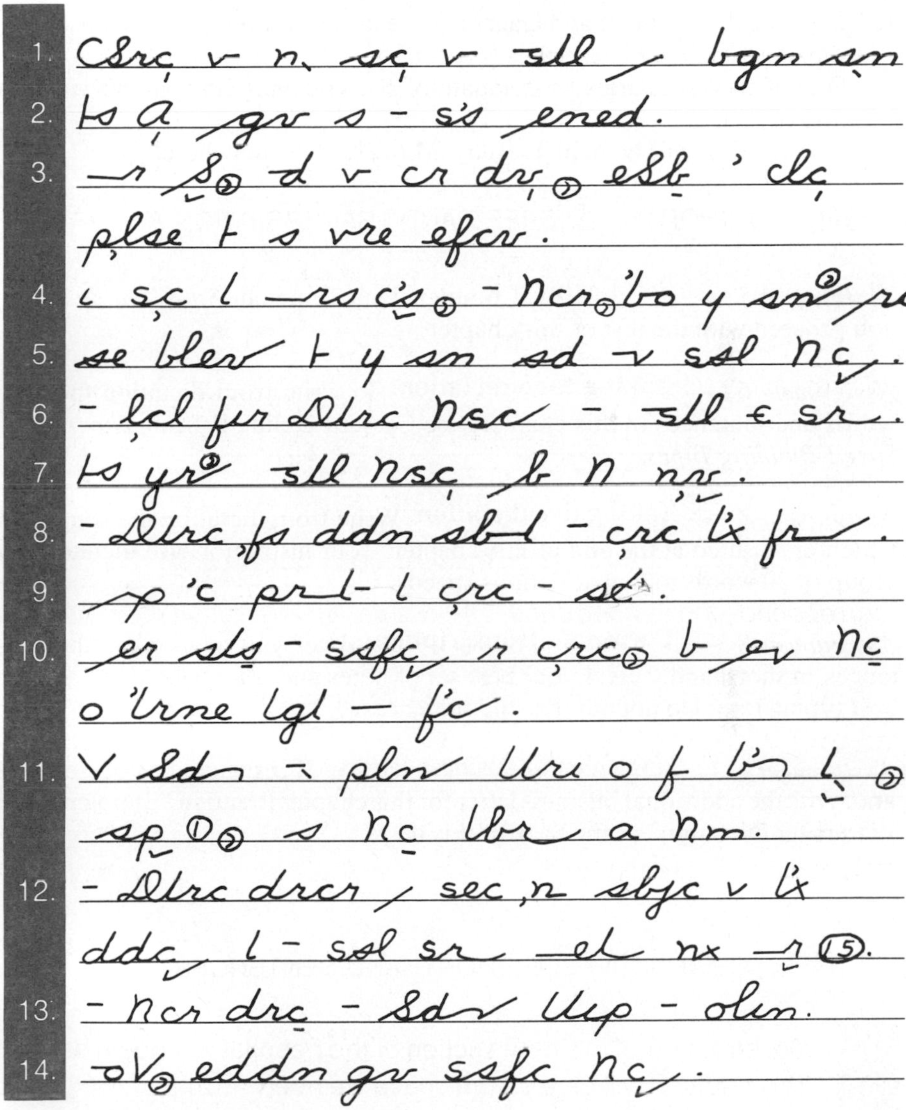

Learning tip: Note that the numbers in sentences 11 and 12 are circled in the shorthand notes above. When writing numbers in shorthand, circle them so that you can transcribe them easily.

BUILDING TRANSCRIPTION SKILLS

Assignment 4 — **Punctuating appositives**. Words and phrases that describe or explain a preceding word or expression are called *appositives*. *Place a comma before and after appositives.*

1. Mr. Jones, our shorthand teacher, gave us an easy test. (The phrase, *our shorthand teacher*, describes Mr. Jones.)
2. One of the secretaries, a graduate of our college, can type 80 words a minute.
3. The meeting will be held Tuesday, May 21, at the new hotel.

BUILDING SHORTHAND SPEED AND TRANSCRIPTION ACCURACY

Assignment 5 — **Self-testing**. Complete Unit 21 in your *Study Guide* before you proceed with the rest of this chapter.

Assignment 6 — **Taking tape dictation**. To write from dictation the new words and sentences in this chapter, use Cassette 5 Side B from *Theory and Speed-Building Tapes*.

Assignment 7 — **Taking live dictation**. Write from dictation the sentences which are printed at the end of this chapter. Your instructor will dictate each group of 20 words to you at various speeds.

Assignment 8 — **Own-note transcription**. After you have taken the sentences in shorthand, select your best set of notes and transcribe them at your best typing rate. Do not number the sentences.

Assignment 9 — **Supplemental business letters.** If instructed to do so, read and write the additional business letter for this chapter found in "Supplemental Letters for Dictation" at the back of this book.

TRANSCRIPT OF SHORTHAND SENTENCES

1. Construction of the new section of the hospital will begin soon.
2. This addition will give us the space we need. (20)
3. Mr. West, head of the credit division, established a collection policy that is very effective. (40)
4. I spoke to Mrs. Case, the instructor, about your son's work.
5. She believes that your son should have special instructions. (60)
6. The local fire district inspects the hospital each spring.
7. This year's hospital inspection will be in November. (80)
8. The district office did not submit the correct tax forms.
9. Will you please act promptly to correct the situation. (100)

10. We are satisfied the specifications are correct, but we have instructed our attorney to get more facts. (120)
11. Every student who plans to try out for the band Tuesday, September 1, is instructed to bring an instrument. (140)
12. The district director will speak on the subject of tax deductions at the special spring meeting next March 15. (160)
13. The instructor directed the students to type the outline.
14. However, he did not give specific instructions. (180)

CHAPTER 22

WRITING **RT-RD** AND **RITY**

Assignment 1 — **Rule discovery**. Follow the three-step plan to learn the new writing principles: (1) Discover the rule for each group of words. (2) Read the shorthand outlines until you can read them rapidly. (3) Cover the shorthand and write each word until you can do so rapidly and accurately.

RT-RD

record report according records board third

transportation standard article ordinary cards

heard-herd hard effort part reports support

card start quarter started quarterly guards

RITY

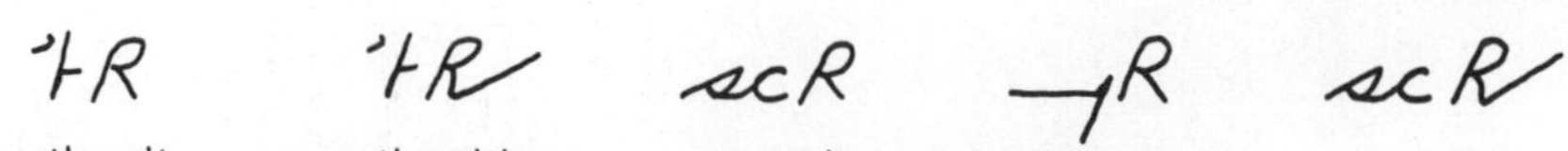

authority authorities security majority securities

WRITING PRINCIPLES

RT-RD Write a capital *R* thus *R* to express *rt-rd* when no vowel occurs between the letters. When writing the capital *R*, begin the letter on the line and write upward thus ↗*R* .

RITY Write a disjoined capital *R* to express the combination *rity* and the preceding vowel. Write the disjoined capital *R* close to the word to which it belongs.

Assignment 2 — **New vocabulary**. Read and write the following words and phrases until you can read and write them rapidly. Memorize the abbreviated words.

sR	certificate
R	order
pRc	particular
Db	distribute
jn	January
,rg	organizations-organizes
pRc-	particularly
R	orders
qn	quantities
,dl	model
,css	anxious
ned	needed
sntl	central
rcgnz	recognize
sfs	sufficient
cld	cold
Nvlp	envelopes
s	spend-spent
rtn	written
dvlp	develop
sRn-	certainly
drcr	directors
S	cities
S'	city's
Nts	in this
NRl	in order to
nb	will not be
evd	we have had

Assignment 3 — **Reading and writing shorthand**. Read each sentence from shorthand until you can read it as rapidly as you can read from print. Write each sentence in shorthand until you can write each one rapidly and accurately.

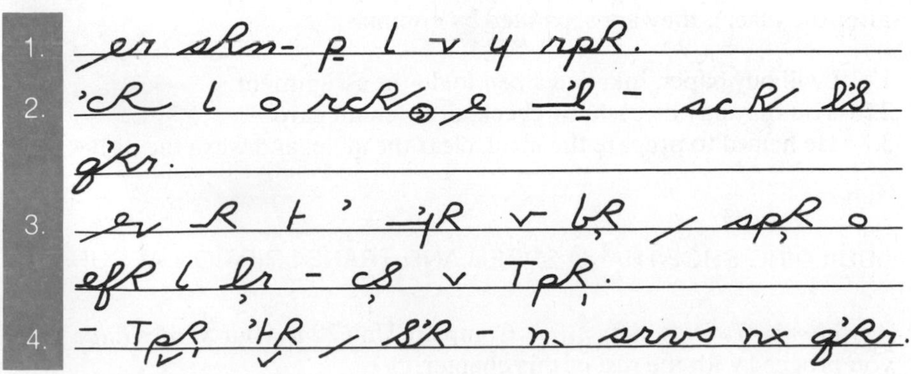

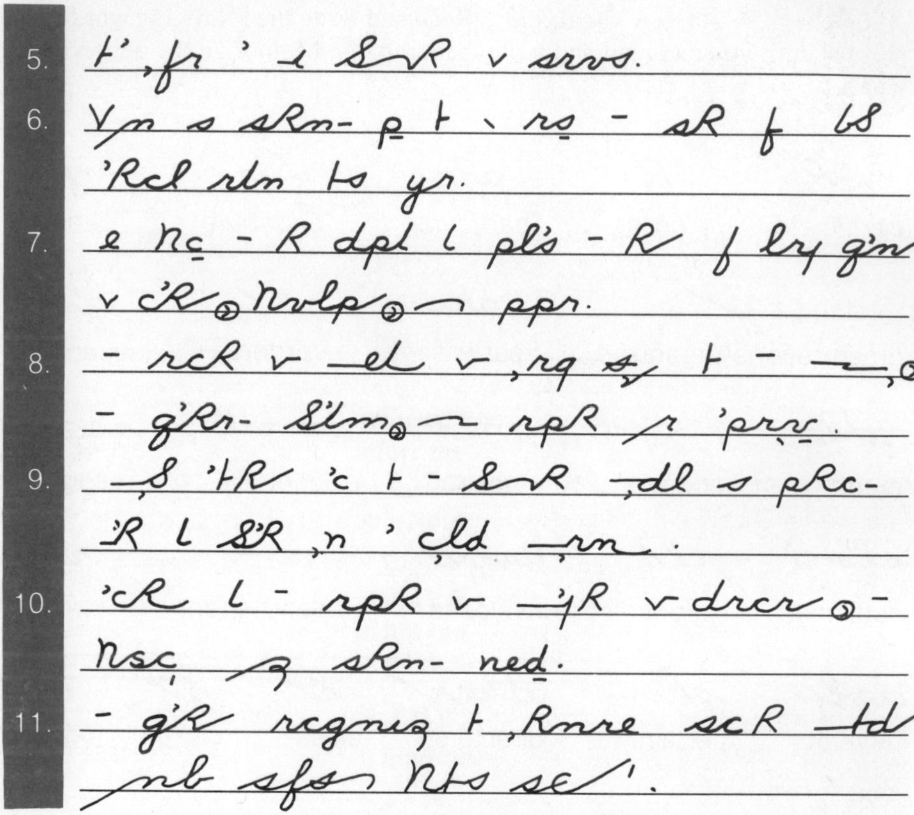

BUILDING TRANSCRIPTION SKILLS

Assignment 4 — **Punctuating a series**. Study the following rule and examples. Apply this rule when transcribing.

When two or more words, phrases, or clauses appear in a series (one after the other), they are separated by commas.

1. I will buy paper, ink, and a pen to do the assignment.
2. You may pay by cash, by check, or by credit card.
3. He helped to prepare the meal, clear the table, and wash the dishes.

BUILDING SHORTHAND SPEED AND TRANSCRIPTION ACCURACY

Assignment 5 — **Self-testing**. Complete Unit 22 in your *Study Guide* before you proceed with the rest of this chapter.

Assignment 6 — **Taking tape dictation**. To write from dictation the new words and sentences in this chapter, use Cassette 6 Side B from *Theory and Speed-Building Tapes*.

Assignment 7 — **Taking live dictation**. Write from dictation the sentences which are printed at the end of this chapter. Your instructor will dictate each group of 20 words to you at various speeds.

Assignment 8 — **Own-note transcription**. After you have taken the sentences in shorthand, select your best set of notes and transcribe them at your best typing rate. Do not number the sentences.

Assignment 9 — **Supplemental business letters.** If instructed to do so, read and write the additional business letter for this chapter found in "Supplemental Letters for Dictation" at the back of this book.

TRANSCRIPT OF SHORTHAND SENTENCES

1. We are certainly pleased to have your report.
2. According to our records, we mailed the securities last quarter. (20)
3. We have heard that a majority of the board will support our effort to lower the cost of transportation. (40)
4. The Transportation Authority will start the new service next quarter.
5. They offer a high standard of service. (60)
6. Everyone is certainly pleased that you received the certificate for the best article written this year. (80)
7. He instructed the order department to place the orders for large quantities of cards, envelopes, and paper. (100)
8. The record of the meeting of the organization shows that the memo, the quarterly statement, and the report were approved. (120)
9. Most authorities acknowledge that the standard model is particularly hard to start on a cold morning. (140)
10. According to the report of the majority of the directors, the inspection was certainly needed. (160)
11. The guards recognize that ordinary security methods will not be sufficient in this situation. (180)

CHAPTER 23

WRITING SOUNDS OF **OI-OY**, **NCE-NSE**, AND **POST** AND **POSITION**

Assignment 1 — **Rule discovery.** Follow the three-step plan to learn the new writing principles: (1) Discover the rule for each group of words. (2) Read the shorthand outlines until you can read them rapidly. (3) Cover the shorthand and write each word until you can do so rapidly and accurately.

SOUND OF **OI-OY**

bi	bi'	il	eplie	'pinm
boys	boy's	oil	employees	appointment
eplim	cis	eplir	Neplim	pi
employment	choice	employer	unemployment	point
'vid	bilr	ril		
avoid	boiler	royal		

NCE-NSE

'cRn	b'ln	r-ln	sn	rsnbl
accordance	balance	remittance	since	responsible
'jne	Nsrn	Cfrn	aonm	
agency	insurance	conference	announcement	
sin	avn	dfrn	aon	cn
science	advances	differences	announced	chances
Cvenen	nnsn			
convenience	nonsense			

POST AND **POSITION**

post-position disposition postponed postage posted

WRITING PRINCIPLES

OI-OY Write a dotted *i* to express the sound *oi-oy.*

NCE-NSE Write a small, disjoined *n* to express the combinations *nce-nse* and the preceding vowel. Write the disjoined *n* close to the word to which it belongs.

POST-POSITION Write a capital *P* to express the prefix and suffix *post* and *position*. Start the first stroke of *P* on the line and write upward.

Assignment 2 — **New vocabulary**. Read and write the following words and phrases until you can read and write them rapidly. Memorize the abbreviated words.

sincere-sincerely remember purchase order invoice

October regard February regarding post office

correction cases remaining efforts warns

answered deducted securing charged decrease

despite known error making gas claims suit

ladies mistake has been

Assignment 3 — **Reading and writing shorthand**. Read each sentence from shorthand until you can read it as rapidly as you can read from print. Write each sentence in shorthand until you can write each one rapidly and accurately.

1. - eplir asr o g re eplim.
2. o En v scr ' cis fb 'per q.
3. - b'ln v Nsrn bl -sbn pd.
4. tss N 'cRn t o 'grem l o Cfrn.
5. v gvl 'yne s rsnbl f — c ' sn efR l dcres Neplim.
6. e sn blev o eplie / 'csp s rc l - fb Cfrn.
7. dsul rs avn N sin ev n, cis b l Cln, o efR l Csrv g's il.
8. - drcr v P,fs aont se -s rs a 'pirm l a -p P.
9. l - al Cfrn a 'lrne Dcs - dfrn N DP v c's.
10. sn rs y rs rqS o eplim 'yne Ppn - aonm v n P.
11. c r t c I - rln f b'ln ,r Nv fr - Nsrn c,.

BUILDING SHORTHAND SPEED AND TRANSCRIPTION ACCURACY

Assignment 4 — **Self-testing**. Complete Unit 23 in your *Study Guide* before you proceed with the rest of this chapter.

Assignment 5 — **Taking tape dictation**. To write from dictation the new words and sentences in this chapter, use Cassette 7 Side B from *Theory and Speed-Building Tapes*.

Assignment 6 — **Taking live dictation**. Write from dictation the sentences which are printed at the end of this chapter. Your instructor will dictate each group of 20 words to you at various speeds.

Assignment 7 — **Own-note transcription**. After you have taken the sentences in shorthand, select your best set of notes and transcribe them at your best typing rate. Do not number the sentences.

Assignment 8 — **Supplemental business letters.** If instructed to do so, read and write the additional business letter for this chapter found in "Supplemental Letters for Dictation" at the back of this book.

TRANSCRIPT OF SHORTHAND SENTENCES

1. The employer answered our questions regarding employment.
2. Our chances of securing a choice job appear good. (20)
3. The balance of the insurance bill has been paid.
4. This is in accordance with our agreement at our conference. (40)
5. Every government agency is responsible for making a sincere effort to decrease unemployment. (60)
6. He sincerely believes our employees will accept his recommendations at the February conference. (80)
7. Despite recent advances in science, we have no choice but to continue our efforts to conserve gas and oil. (100)
8. The director of the post office announced that she has received an appointment to an important position. (120)
9. At the annual conference, an attorney discussed the differences in the disposition of the cases. (140)
10. Since receiving your recent request, our employment agency postponed the announcement of the new position. (160)
11. I remember that I enclosed the remittance for the balance on the invoice from the insurance company. (180)

CHAPTER 24

BUSINESS LETTER DICTATION AND TRANSCRIPTION

BUILDING TRANSCRIPTION SKILLS

Assignment 1 — **Hyphenating words**. In the letters that follow are some words that require a hyphen. Study the rule and the examples and apply the rule when you transcribe.

Two or more words that are used as a single descriptive word should be hyphenated when they come before the word they describe.

1. Fred will take a full-time job. (Note that *full-time* describes the kind of job Fred will take.)
2. I can take a part-time job, but I cannot work full time. (In this case, *full time* does not have a hyphen because the words do not come before a noun they describe.)
3. She is a well-known actress, but the leading man is not well known.
4. The dance will be our main fund-raising event this year.

Assignment 2 — **Setting up business letters**. Names and addresses are given for each of the remaining letters in this text. Unless your instructor tells you otherwise, you should transcribe the business letters in this and the remaining chapters in business-letter form.

Examine the example of a business letter in *block style* on page 203 of your text. This style is used in many offices. Use this style when transcribing the letters in this text unless your instructor asks you to use a different letter style.

For each letter, your instructor will give you the name of the person signing the letter.

Names and addresses are seldom dictated in offices. The secretary gets this information from previous correspondence. Therefore, names and addresses are not included in the word count of the letters. Your instructor will start timing the dictation with the salutation.

Assignment 3 — **Spelling review.** Follow the steps outlined in Chapter 12 to check your ability to spell the following words correctly:

1. according	9. federal	17. quantity
2. achievement	10. hospital	18. quantities
3. assistance	11. insurance	19. remittance
4. balance	12. least	20. special
5. classes	13. maintain	21. specific
6. collection	14. model	22. valuable
7. conference	15. organization	23. various
8. February	16. particularly	24. written

BUSINESS LETTERS

Assignment 4 — **Letter 1.** Read and write each of the new words and phrases until you can read and write each one rapidly and accurately. Then read and write the shorthand for Letter 1 to build your writing speed.

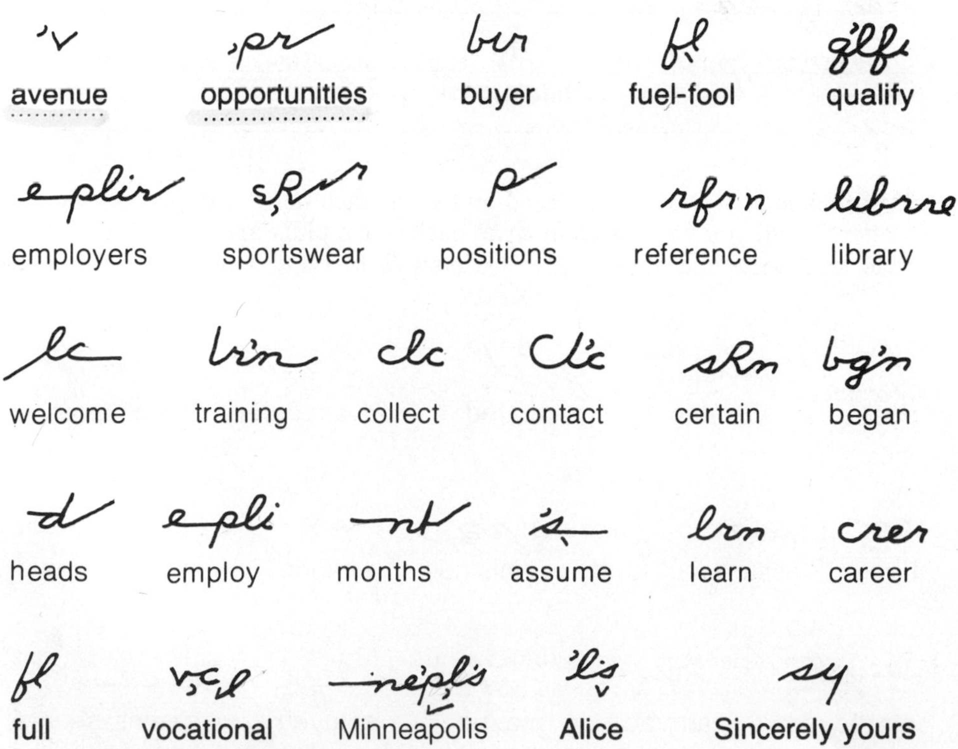

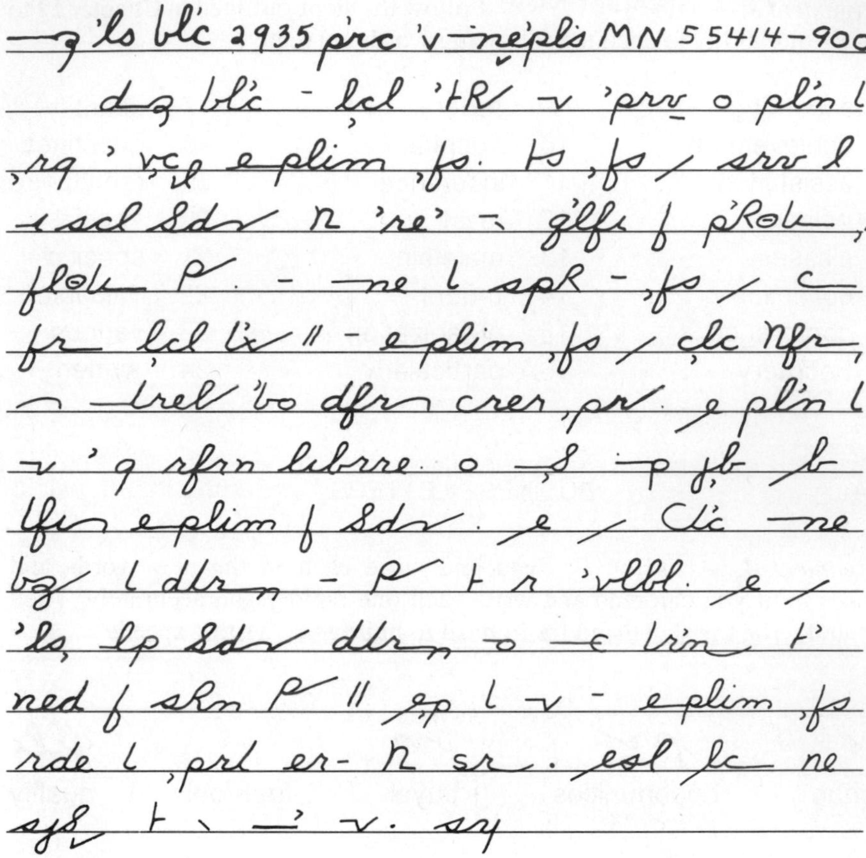

Assignment 5 – **Letter 2**. Read and write each new word and phrase for Letter 2 until you can read and write each one rapidly and accurately. Then read and write the shorthand for Letter 2 to build your writing speed.

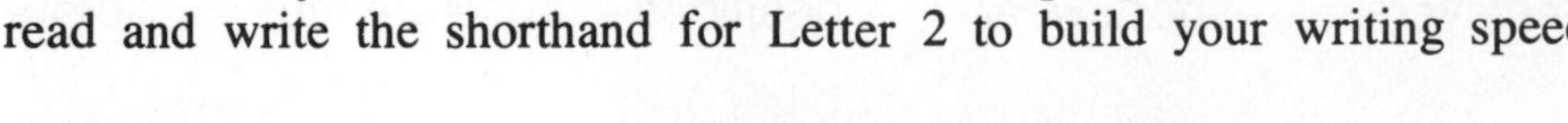

posts applying graduated advancement assurance

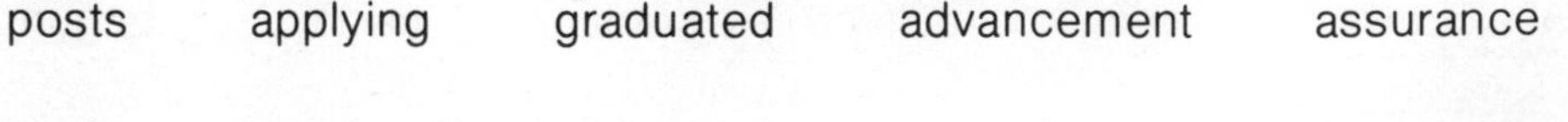

Eve assure fund raising chance often rapid

employed arrived maybe enjoyed seems-seams

alumni offers Martin wise Lansing to do so

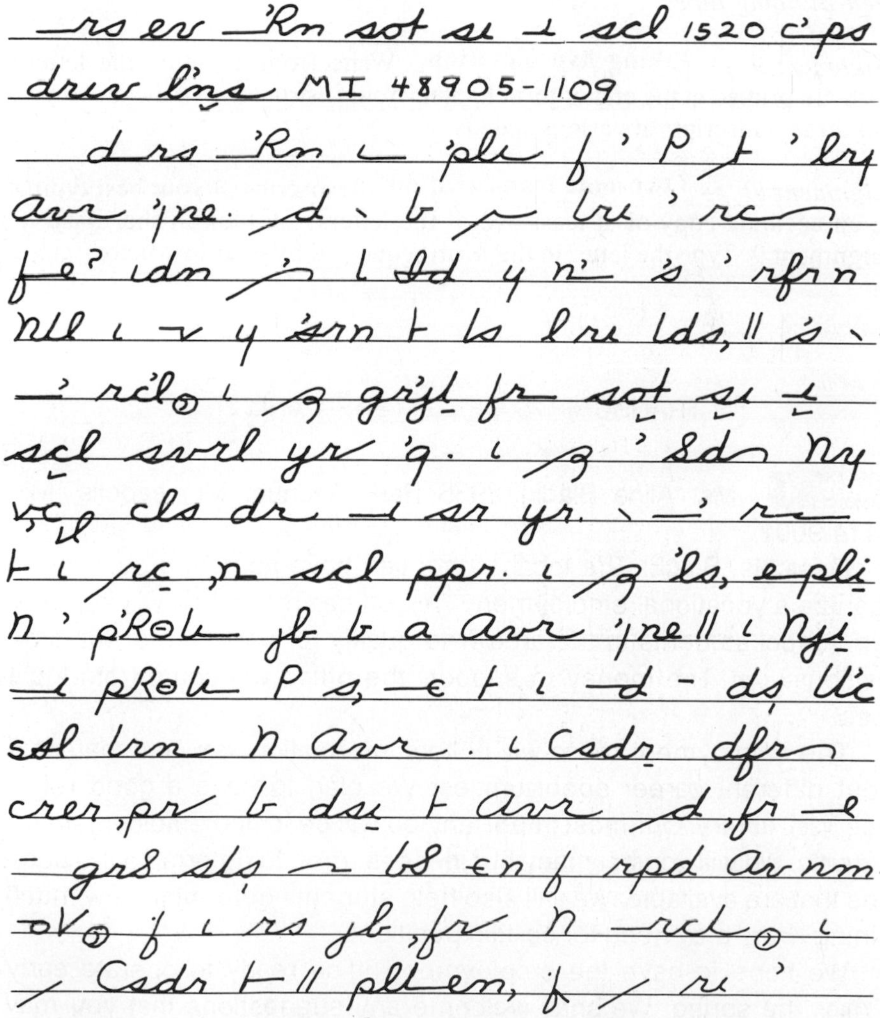

Assignment 6 — **Supplemental business letters.** If instructed to do so, read and write the additional business letter for this chapter found in "Supplemental Letters for Dictation" at the back of this book.

BUILDING SHORTHAND SPEED AND TRANSCRIPTION ACCURACY

Assignment 7 — **Self-testing**. Complete Unit 24 in your *Study Guide* before you proceed with the rest of this chapter.

Assignment 8 — **Taking tape dictation**. To write from dictation the new words and letters in this chapter, use Cassette 8 Side B from *Theory and Speed-Building Tapes*.

Assignment 9 — **Taking live dictation**. Write from dictation the letters which are printed at the end of this chapter. Your instructor will dictate to you from these transcripts at various speeds.

Assignment 10 — **Own-note transcription**. Transcribe at your best typing rate an accurate copy of at least one of the letters you took in shorthand in Assignment 9. Type the letter in the form requested by your instructor.

TRANSCRIPTS OF LETTERS 1 AND 2

Letter 1 Ms. Alice Black, 2935 Park Avenue, Minneapolis, MN 55414-9001

Dear Ms. Black: The local authorities have approved our plan to organize a vocational employment (20) office. This office will serve all high school students in the area who qualify for part-time or full-time positions. (40) The money to support the office will come from local taxes.

The employment office will collect information (60) and materials about different career opportunities. We plan to have a good reference (80) library. Our most important job will be to find employment for students. We will contact many businesses (100) to determine the positions that are available. We will also help students determine how much training (120) they need for certain positions.

We hope to have the employment office ready to operate early in (140) the spring. We shall welcome any suggestions that you may have. Sincerely yours, (154)

Letter 2 Mrs. Eve Martin, South Side High School, 1520 Campus Drive, Lansing, MI 48905-1109

Dear Mrs. Martin: I am applying for a position with a large advertising agency. Would you be (20) willing to write a recommendation for me? I do not want to include your name as a reference until (40) I have your assurance that it is all right to do so.

As you may recall, I was graduated from South Side (60) High School several years ago. I was a student in your vocational class during my senior year. You may (80) remember that I worked on the school paper. I was also employed in a part-time job by an advertising (100) agency.

I enjoyed my part-time position so much that I made the decision to take special training in (120) advertising. I considered different career opportunities but decided that advertising would (140) offer me the greatest satisfaction and the best chance for rapid advancement. However, if I receive job (160) offers in marketing, I will consider them.

Please let me know if you will write a recommendation for me. (180) I shall appreciate your help. Sincerely yours, (189)

REVIEWING THE WRITING PRINCIPLES

All the writing principles, abbreviated words, and standard abbreviations you have learned in Chapters 17 through 24 are reviewed on Tape 17 Side B of the *Theory and Speed-Building Tapes*. Take dictation from this tape before completing Examination 6.

EXAMINATION 6

Remove and complete Examination 6 at the back of your *Study Guide* before proceeding to Chapter 25 of your textbook.

CHAPTER 25

WRITING **FOR-FORE-FER-FUR**, **BILITY**, AND **LETTER-LITER**

Assignment 1 — **Rule discovery.** Follow the three-step plan to learn the new writing principles: (1) Discover the rule for each group of words. (2) Read the shorthand outlines until you can read them rapidly. (3) Cover the shorthand and write each word until you can do so rapidly and accurately.

PREFIXES **FOR-FORE-FER-FUR**

furnace furnish further formerly formal former

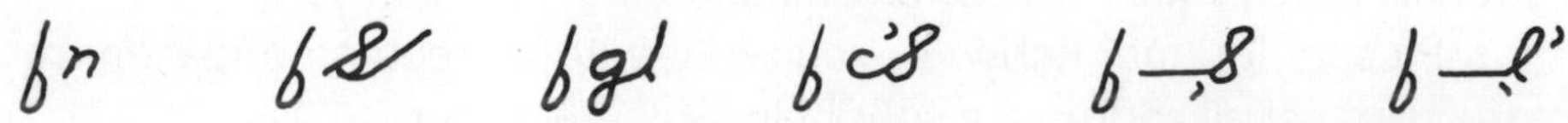

foreign forests forget forecast foremost formula

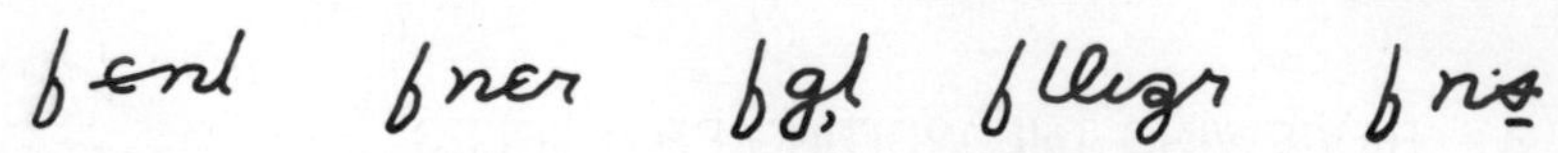

fortunate furniture forgot fertilizer furnished

BILITY

ability eligibility liability possibility flexibility

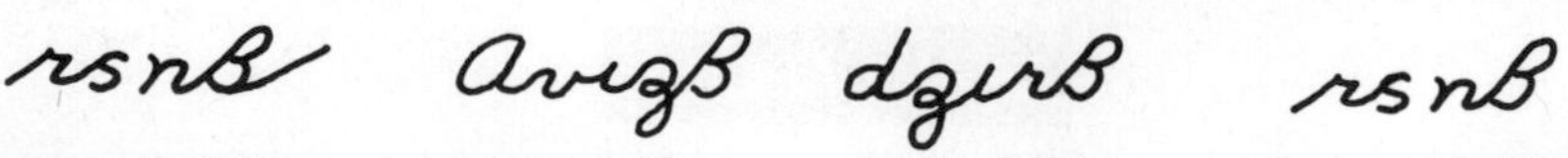

responsibilities advisability desirability responsibility

LETTER-LITER

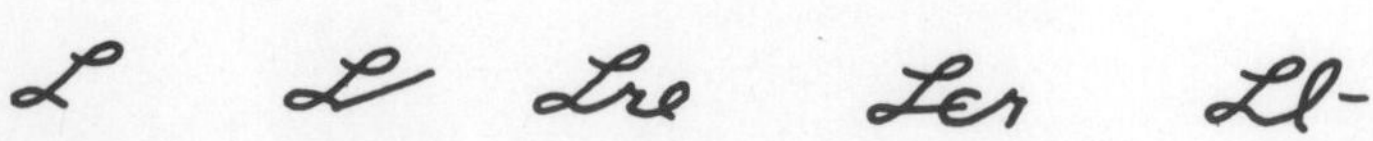

letter letters literary literature literally

WRITING PRINCIPLES

FOR-FORE FER-FUR — Write a disjoined *f* for the prefixes *for-fore-fer-fur*. The disjoined *f* is used *only* when it represents a syllable. Note the following example: *form* *formal* . The *f* is joined in the word *form* because the *for* is not a syllable.

BILITY — Write a capital *B* to express the combination *bility* and the preceding vowel. When writing the capital *B*, begin on the line and write upward thus .

LETTER-LITER — Write a capital *L* thus to express the combinations *letter-liter*. Do not write a printed *L* for the combinations *letter* and *liter* because the printed *L* could be taken for the shorthand *t-m*.

Assignment 2 — **New vocabulary**. Read and write the following words and phrases until you can read and write them rapidly.

furthermore, shipments, conserving, difference

quotation, American, requesting, typing, turn

warranty, western, applicants, sports, Gonzales

helped, wants, wrote, north, Alfredo, publication

countries, Atlanta, to call, there is

Assignment 3 — **Reading and writing shorthand**. Read each sentence from shorthand until you can read it as rapidly as you can read from print. Write each sentence in shorthand until you can write each one rapidly and accurately.

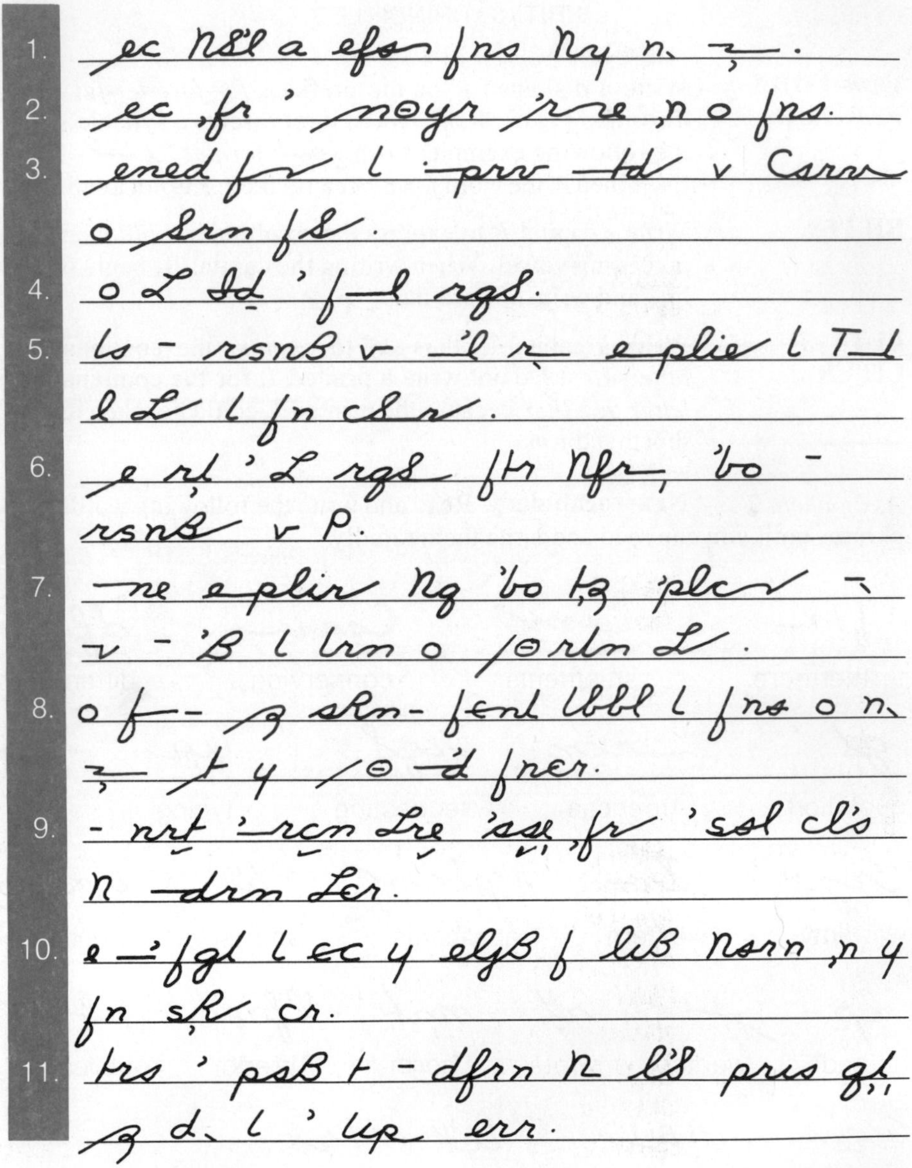

BUILDING SHORTHAND SPEED AND TRANSCRIPTION ACCURACY

Assignment 4 — **Self-testing**. Complete Unit 25 in your *Study Guide* before you proceed with the rest of this chapter.

Assignment 5 — **Taking tape dictation**. To write from dictation the new words and sentences in this chapter, use Cassette 9 Side B from *Theory and Speed-Building Tapes*.

Assignment 6 — **Taking live dictation.** Write from dictation the sentences which are printed at the end of this chapter. Your instructor will dictate each group of 20 words to you at various speeds.

Assignment 7 — **Own-note transcription.** After you have taken the sentences in shorthand, select your best set of notes and transcribe them at your best typing rate. Do not number the sentences.

Assignment 8 — **Supplemental business letters.** If instructed to do so, read and write the additional business letter for this chapter found in "Supplemental Letters for Dictation" at the back of this book.

TRANSCRIPT OF SHORTHAND SENTENCES

1. We can install an efficient furnace in your new home.
2. We can offer a one-year warranty on our furnace. (20)
3. We need funds to improve methods of conserving our western forests.
4. Our letter included a formal request. (40)
5. It is the responsibility of the mail room employees to transmit all letters to foreign customers. (60)
6. We wrote a letter requesting further information about the responsibilities of the position. (80)
7. Many employers inquire about those applicants who have the ability to turn out well-written letters. (100)
8. Our family was certainly fortunate to be able to furnish our new home with your well-made furniture. (120)
9. The North American Literary Association offers a special class in modern literature. (140)
10. He may forget to check your eligibility for liability insurance on your foreign sports car. (160)
11. There is a possibility that the difference in the last price quotation was due to a typing error. (180)

CHAPTER 26

WRITING **PRE-PRI-PRO-PER-PUR**

Assignment 1 – **Rule discovery**. Follow the three-step plan to learn the new writing principles: (1) Discover the rule for each group of words. (2) Read the shorthand outlines until you can read them rapidly. (3) Cover the shorthand and write each word until you can do so rapidly and accurately.

PRE-PRI-PRO-PER-PUR

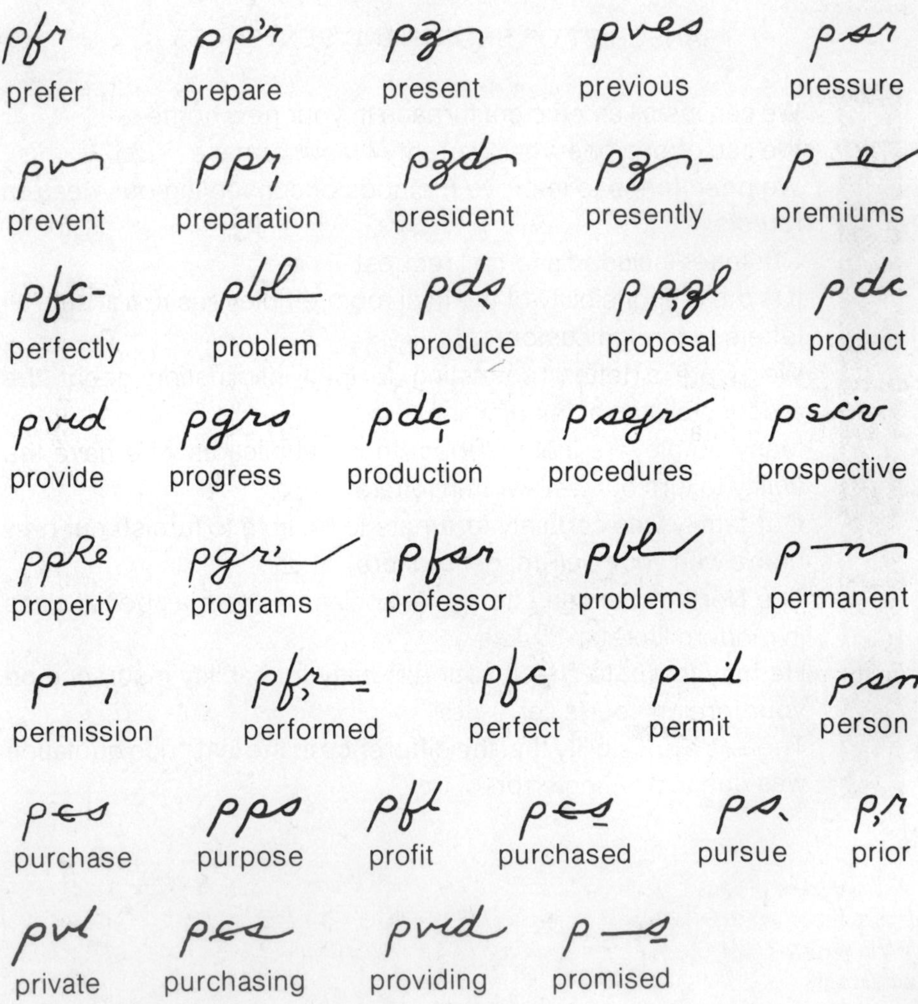

WRITING PRINCIPLES

PRE-PRI-PRO-PER-PUR Write a small disjoined *p* to express the combinations *pre-pri-pro-per-pur* when they begin a word containing more than one syllable. Write the disjoined *p* close to the remainder of the word. Note the following examples:

press preside prove provide price priority

Assignment 2 — **New vocabulary**. Read and write the following words and phrases until you can read and write them rapidly.

appreciated manufacturer attendance supervisor

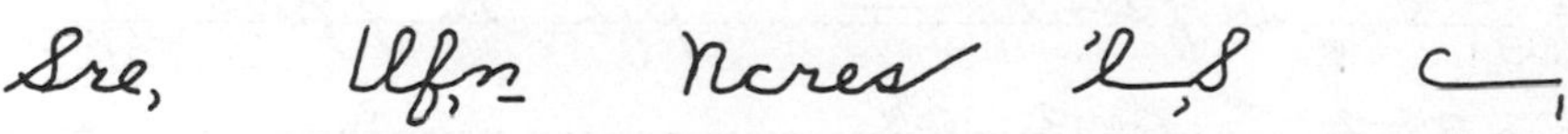

stereo telephoned increases almost commission

against Rita appointed demonstrated additional

studying continued trouble complaint refused

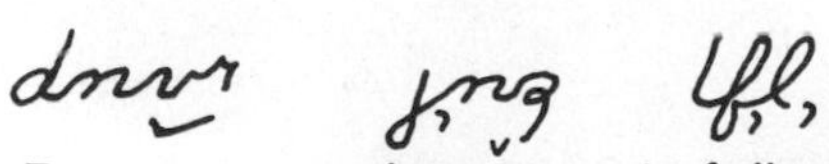

Denver Jones to follow

Assignment 3 — **Reading and writing shorthand**. Read each sentence from shorthand until you can read it as rapidly as you can read from print. Write each sentence in shorthand until you can write each one rapidly and accurately.

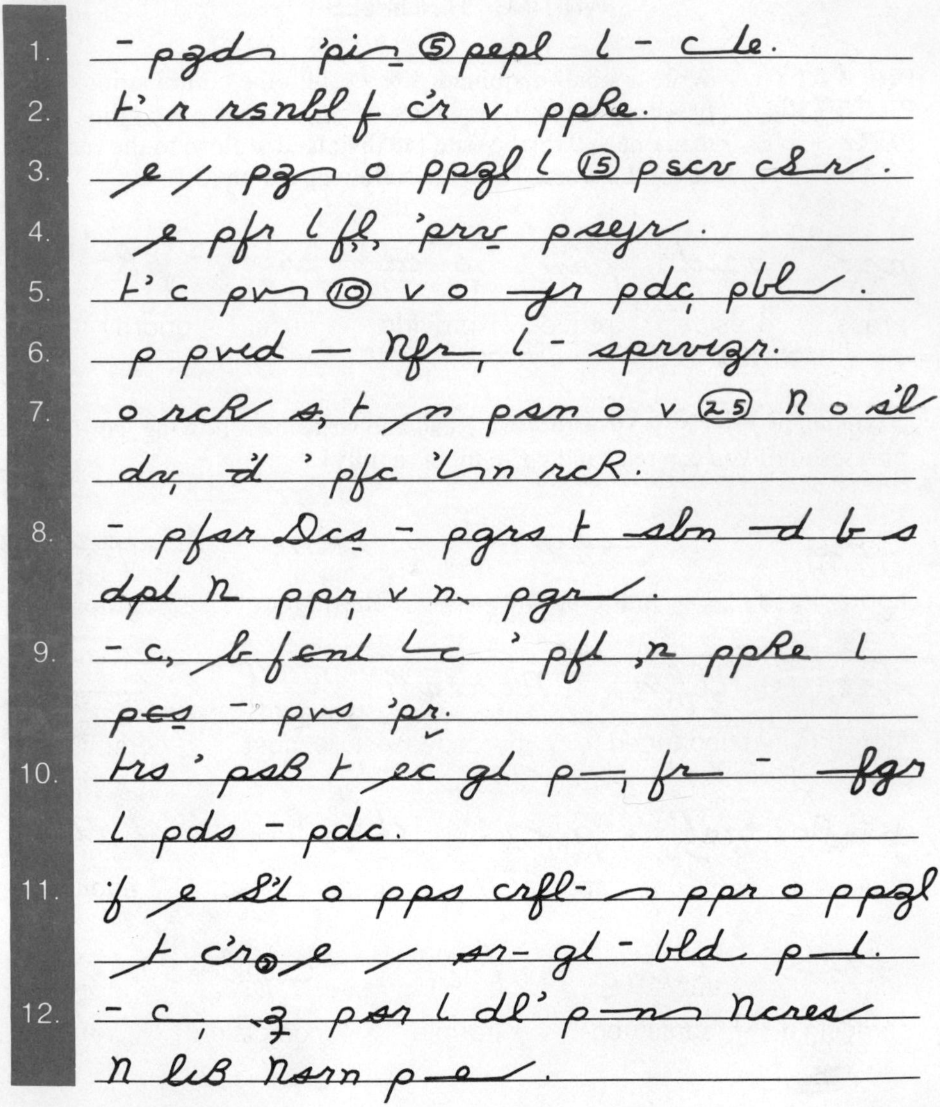

BUILDING TRANSCRIPTION SKILLS

Assignment 4 — **Transcribing numbers**.

1. Spell out numbers that begin a sentence.
   - Thirty-five students from our class will attend the game.
2. Spell out isolated numbers from one to ten.
   - I went to the library two times today.
   - There are five books and three magazines in my bag.

3. Use figures for other numbers (numbers of 11 and over, amounts of money, dates, percentages, and figures to denote time).
   - All 35 students in our class will attend the game.
   - Tomorrow's assignment begins on page 64.
   - Each ticket sells for $2.50, and we paid $45 to rent the bus.
   - We will return on November 5 at 2 p.m.
   - Our sales have increased 25 percent this year.
4. Use the same style to express related numbers above and below 10. (If any of the numbers are above 10, place all numbers in figures).
   - There are 5 books and 14 magazines in my bag.

BUILDING SHORTHAND SPEED AND TRANSCRIPTION ACCURACY

Assignment 5 — **Self-testing**. Complete Unit 26 in your *Study Guide* before you proceed with the rest of this chapter.

Assignment 6 — **Taking tape dictation**. To write from dictation the new words and sentences in this chapter, use Cassette 10 Side B from *Theory and Speed-Building Tapes*.

Assignment 7 — **Taking live dictation**. Write from dictation the sentences which are printed at the end of this chapter. Your instructor will dictate each group of 20 words to you at various speeds.

Assignment 8 — **Own-note transcription**. After you have taken the sentences in shorthand, select your best set of notes and transcribe them at your best typing rate. Do not number the sentences.

Assignment 9 — **Supplemental business letters**. If instructed to do so, read and write the additional business letter for this chapter found in "Supplemental Letters for Dictation" at the back of this book.

TRANSCRIPT OF SHORTHAND SENTENCES

1. The president appointed five people to the committee.
2. They are responsible for the care of property. (20)
3. We will present our proposal to 15 prospective customers.
4. We prefer to follow approved procedures. (40)
5. They can prevent ten of our major production problems.
6. Please provide more information to the supervisor. (60)
7. Our records show that 1 person out of 25 in our sales division had a perfect attendance record. (80)

8. The professor discussed the progress that has been made by his department in the preparation of new programs. (100)
9. The company will be fortunate to make a profit on the property it purchased the previous April. (120)
10. There is a possibility that we can get permission from the manufacturer to produce the product. (140)
11. If we state our purpose carefully and prepare our proposal with care, we will surely get the building permit. (160)
12. The commission used pressure to delay permanent increases in liability insurance premiums. (180)

CHAPTER 27

WRITING **AX-EX-OX** AND **NGE**

Assignment 1 — **Rule discovery**. Follow the three-step plan to learn the new writing principles: (1) Discover the rule for each group of words. (2) Read the shorthand outlines until you can read them rapidly. (3) Cover the shorthand and write each word until you can do so rapidly and accurately.

PREFIXES **AX-EX-OX**

expense except expect examples examine exact

expected excellent export explain extend-extent

expects extension experience exceptionally

explained expensive extending examination

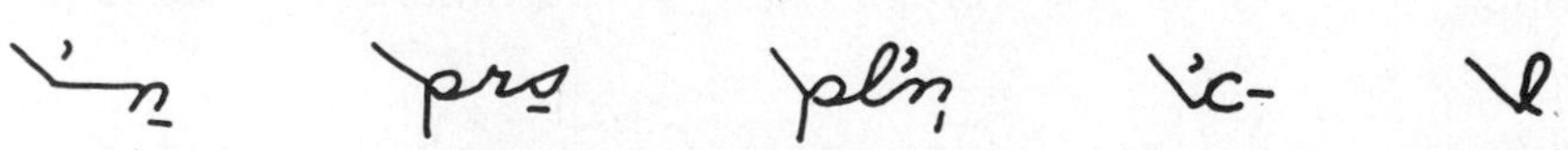

examined expressed explanation exactly axle-excel

oxygen express

NGE

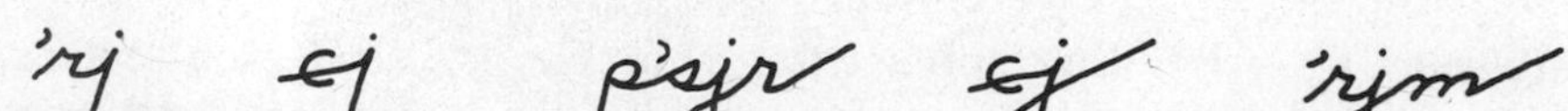

arrange change passengers changes arrangements

WRITING PRINCIPLES

AX-EX-OX Write a long, straight slanted, downward stroke to express the prefixes *ax*, *ex*, and *ox*. Be sure to slant the stroke so you will not confuse it with the letter *t*.

NGE Write a dotted *j* to express the combination *nge*.

Assignment 2 — **New vocabulary**. Read and write the following words and phrases until you can read and write them rapidly. Memorize the abbreviated words.

Assignment 3 — **Reading and writing shorthand**. Read each sentence from shorthand until you can read it as rapidly as you can read from print. Write each sentence in shorthand until you can write each one rapidly and accurately.

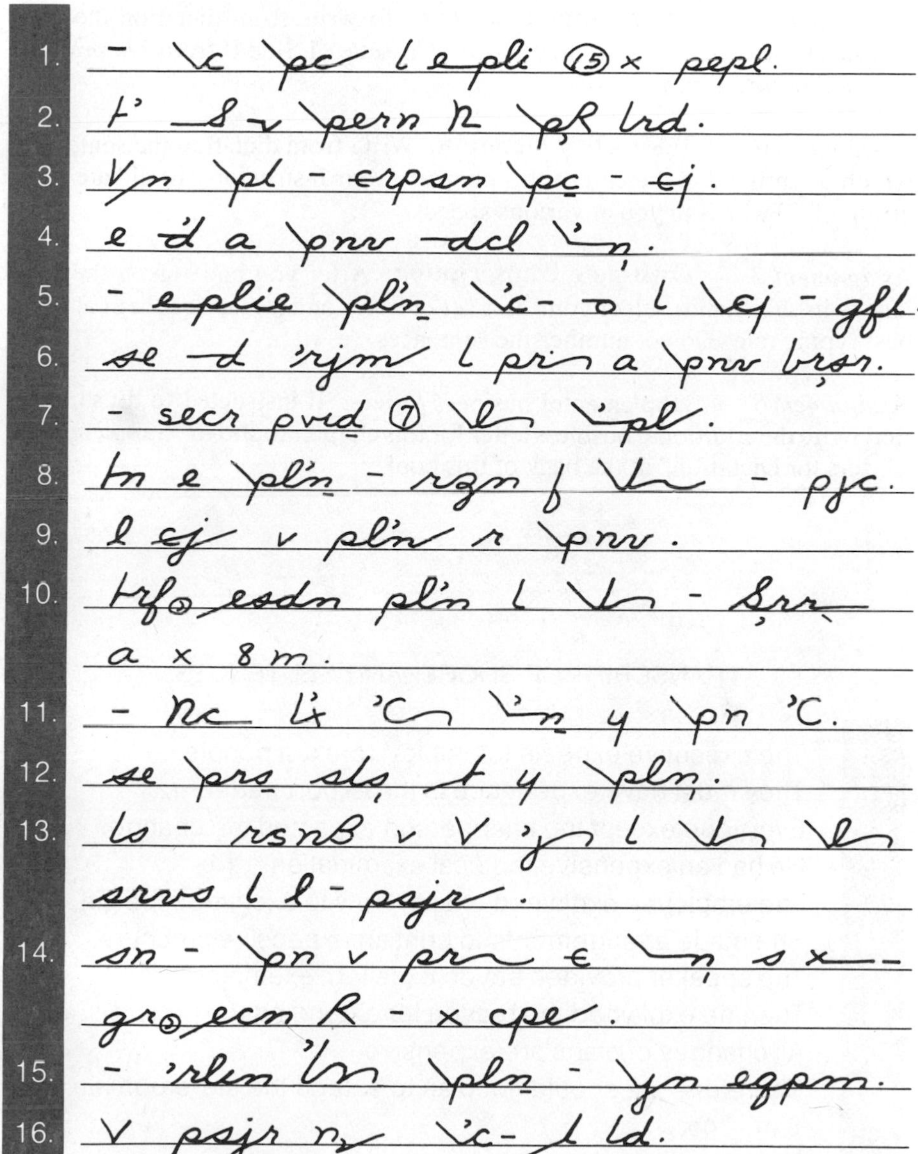

BUILDING SHORTHAND SPEED AND TRANSCRIPTION ACCURACY

Assignment 4 — **Self-testing**. Complete Unit 27 in your *Study Guide* before you proceed with the rest of this chapter.

Assignment 5 — **Taking tape dictation**. To write from dictation the new words and sentences in this chapter, use Cassette 11 Side B from *Theory and Speed-Building Tapes*.

Assignment 6 — **Taking live dictation**. Write from dictation the sentences which are printed at the end of this chapter. Your instructor will dictate each group of 20 words to you at various speeds.

Assignment 7 — **Own-note transcription**. After you have taken the sentences in shorthand, select your best set of notes and transcribe them at your best typing rate. Do not number the sentences.

Assignment 8 — **Supplemental business letters.** If instructed to do so, read and write the additional business letter for this chapter found in "Supplemental Letters for Dictation" at the back of this book.

TRANSCRIPT OF SHORTHAND SENTENCES

1. The executive expects to employ 15 extra people.
2. They must have experience in the export trade. (20)
3. Everyone except the chairperson expected the change.
4. He had an expensive medical examination. (40)
5. The employee explained exactly how to exchange the gift.
6. She made arrangements to print an expensive brochure. (60)
7. The speaker provided seven excellent examples.
8. Then he explained the reason for extending the project. (80)
9. All changes of plans are expensive.
10. Therefore, we should not plan to extend the storeroom an extra 8 m. (100)
11. The income tax accountant examined your expense account.
12. She expressed satisfaction with your explanation. (120)
13. It is the responsibility of every agent to extend excellent service to all the passengers. (140)
14. Since the expense of printing each examination is extremely great, we cannot order the extra copies. (160)
15. The airline attendant explained the oxygen equipment.
16. Every passenger knows exactly what do do. (180)

CHAPTER 28

BUSINESS LETTER DICTATION AND TRANSCRIPTION

BUILDING TRANSCRIPTION SKILLS

Assignment 1 — **Spelling review**. Follow the steps outlined in Chapter 12 to check your ability to spell the following words correctly:

1. attendance
2. almost
3. buyer
4. career
5. employee
6. errors
7. excellent
8. exceptionally
9. expense
10. experience
11. extremely
12. foreign
13. library
14. literature
15. permit
16. permitted
17. president
18. previous
19. quotation
20. reference
21. responsibilities
22. responsible
23. supervisor
24. type
25. typing
26. welcome

BUSINESS LETTERS

Assignment 2 — **Letter 1**. Read and write each of the new words and phrases until you can read and write each one rapidly and accurately. Then read and write the shorthand for Letter 1 to build your writing speed. Memorize the standard abbreviation.

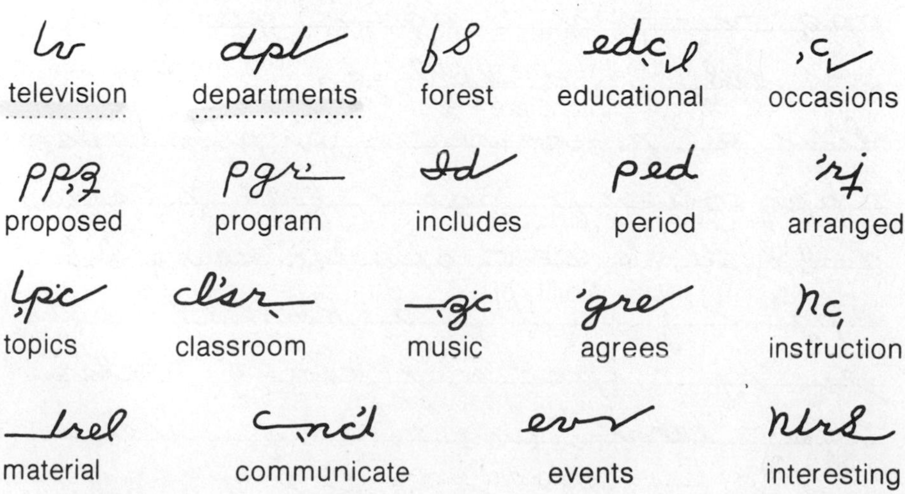

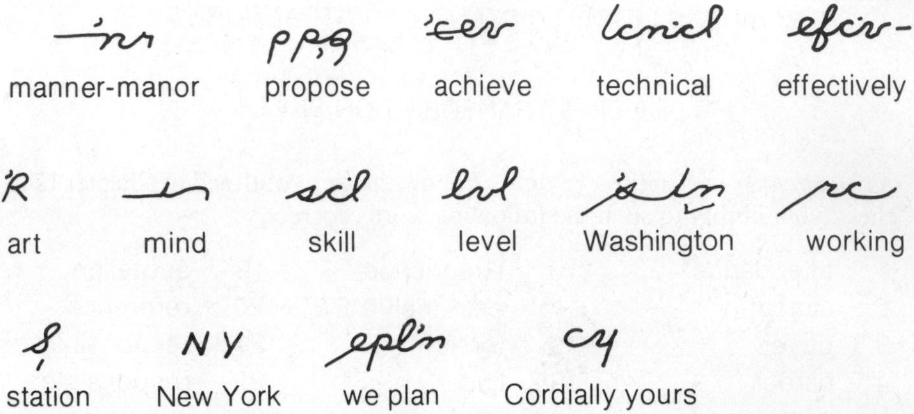
manner-manor
propose
achieve
technical
effectively
art
mind
skill
level
Washington
working
station
New York
we plan
Cordially yours

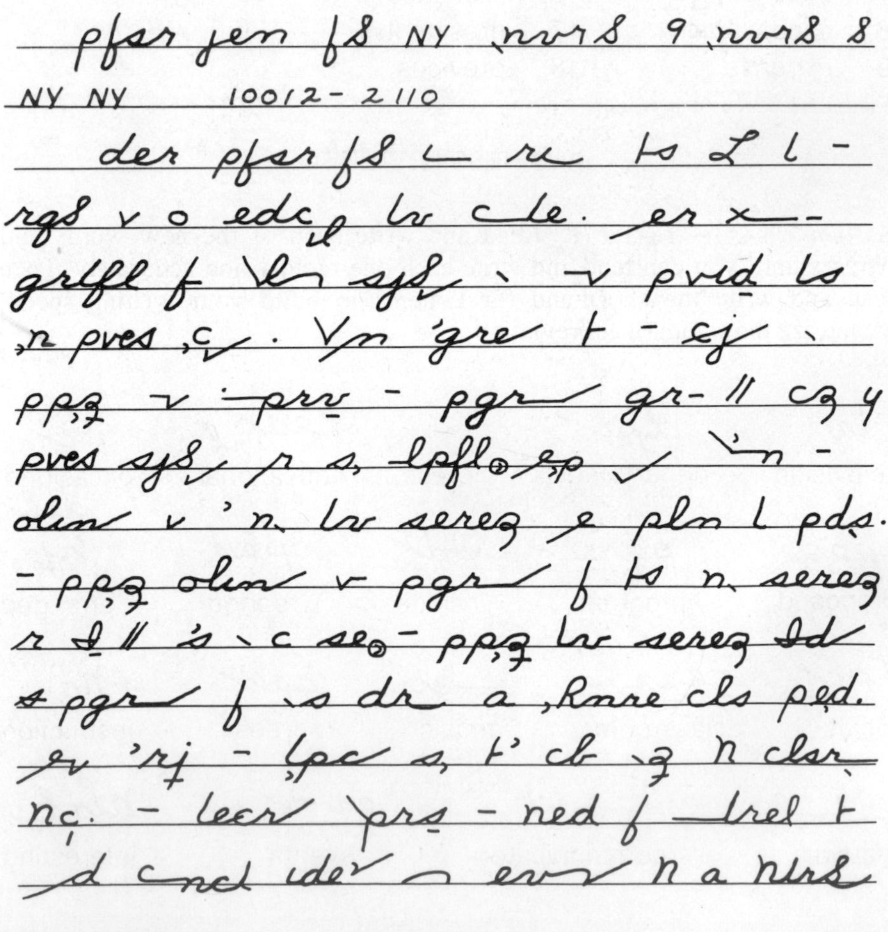

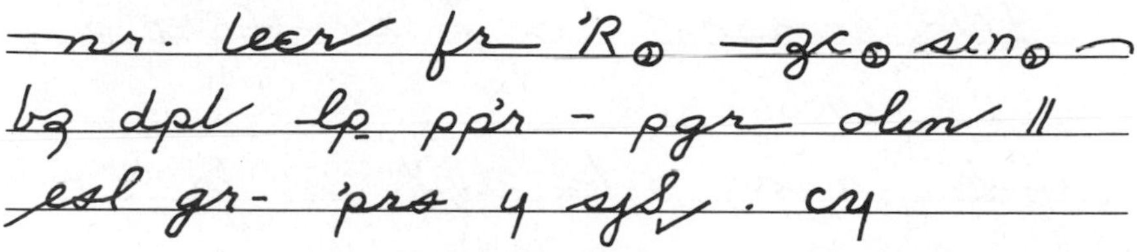

Assignment 3 — **Letter 2**. Read and write each new word and phrase for Letter 2 until you can read and write each one rapidly and accurately. Then read and write the shorthand for Letter 2 to build your writing speed.

copyright	writers	distribution	economics	textbook	
published	consumer	produced	title	workbook	
basic	unfortunately	Chicago	actual	workbooks	
textbooks	mimeograph	photocopies	favorable	reply	
informative	text	magazines	protection	deals	
Rosa.	printed	schools	books	Boston	editor
law-lay	producer	we may not be able	Yours sincerely		

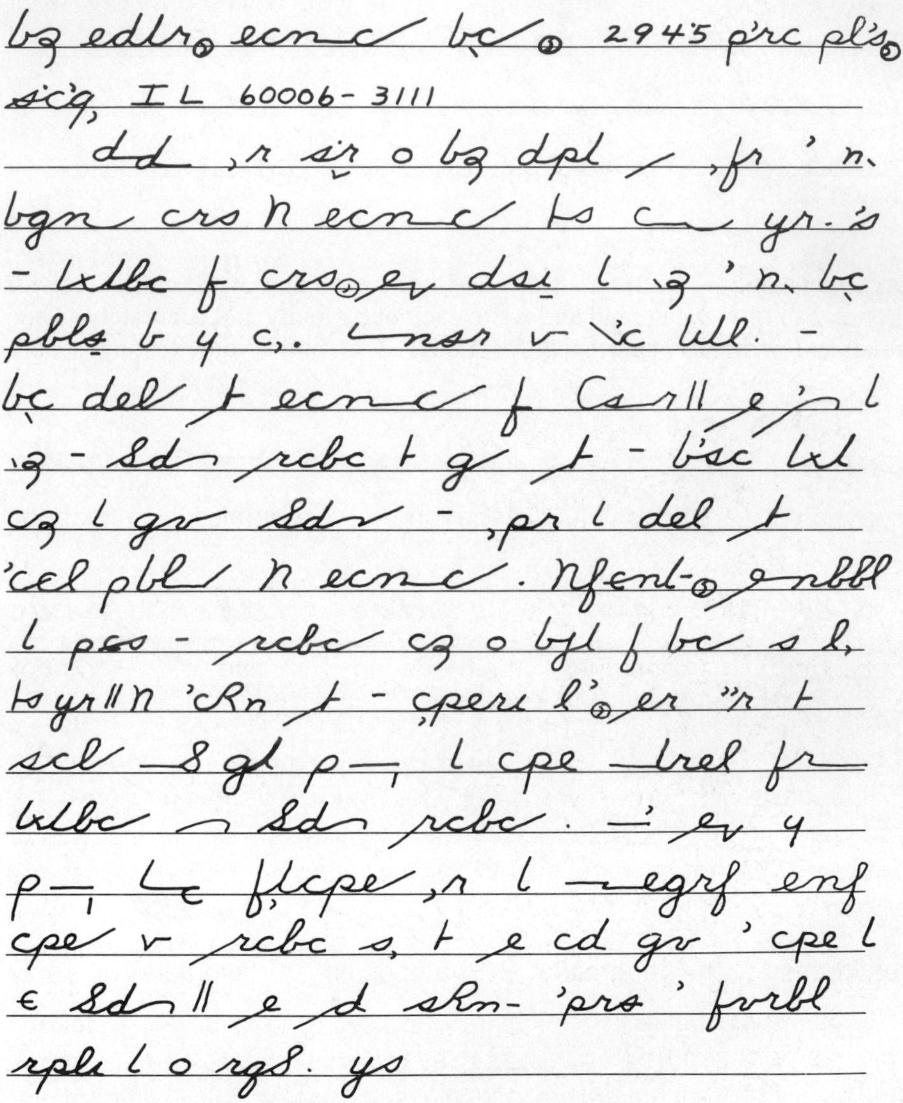

Assignment 4 — **Supplemental business letters.** If instructed to do so, read and write the additional business letter for this chapter found in "Supplemental Letters for Dictation" at the back of this book.

BUILDING SHORTHAND SPEED AND TRANSCRIPTION ACCURACY

Assignment 5 — **Self-testing**. Complete Unit 28 in your *Study Guide* before you proceed with the rest of this chapter.

Assignment 6 — **Taking tape dictation.** To write from dictation the new words and letters in this chapter, use Cassette 12 Side B from *Theory and Speed-Building Tapes*.

Assignment 7 — **Taking live dictation.** Write from dictation the letters printed at the end of this chapter. Your instructor will dictate to you from these transcripts at various speeds.

Assignment 8 — **Own-note transcription.** Transcribe at your best typing rate an accurate copy of at least one of the letters you took in shorthand in Assignment 7. Type the letter in the form requested by your instructor.

TRANSCRIPTS OF LETTERS 1 AND 2

Letter 1 Professor Jean Forest, New York University, 9 University Street, New York, NY 10012-2110

Dear Professor Forest: I am writing this letter at the request of our educational television (20) committee. We are extremely grateful for the excellent suggestions you have provided to us on previous (40) occasions. Everyone agrees that the changes you proposed have improved the programs greatly.

Because your (60) previous suggestions were so helpful, we hope you will examine the outlines of a new television series (80) we plan to produce. The proposed outlines of the programs for this new series are enclosed.

As you can see, the proposed (100) television series includes short programs for use during an ordinary class period. We have arranged (120) the topics so they can be used in classroom instruction. The teachers expressed the need for material that would (140) communicate ideas and events in an interesting manner. Teachers from art, music, science, and (160) business departments helped prepare the program outlines.

We shall greatly appreciate your suggestions. Cordially yours, (180)

Letter 2 Business Editor, Economics Books, 2945 Park Place, Chicago, IL 60006-3111

Dear Madam or Sir: Our business department will offer a new beginning course in economics this coming (20) year. As the textbook for the course, we have decided to use a new book published by your company. I am not (40) sure of the exact title. The book deals with economics for the consumer.

We want to use the student workbook (60) that goes with the basic text because it gives students the opportunity to deal with actual problems in (80) economics. Unfortunately, we may not be able to purchase the workbooks because our budget for books (100) is low this year.

In accordance with the copyright law, we are aware that schools must get permission to copy (120) material from textbooks and student workbooks. May we have your permission to make photocopies or to (140) mimeograph enough copies of the workbook so that we could give a copy to each student.

We would certainly (160) appreciate a favorable reply to our request. Yours sincerely, (174)

EXAMINATION 7

Remove and complete Examination 7 at the back of your *Study Guide* before proceeding to Chapter 29 of your textbook.

11-19-90

CHAPTER 29

WRITING **SYS-SESS-SUS-SIS-CESS-CIS**, **ULATE**, AND **SCRIBE-SCRIPT**

Assignment 1 — **Rule discovery**. Follow the three-step plan to learn the new writing principles: (1) Discover the rule for each group of words. (2) Read the shorthand outlines until you can read them rapidly. (3) Cover the shorthand and write each word until you can do so rapidly and accurately.

SYS-SESS-SUS-SIS-CESS-CIS

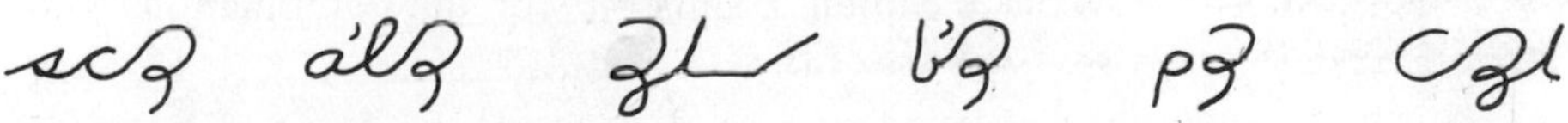

success analysis systems basis process consist

processing systematic successful necessity

assistance assist excess access insist possess

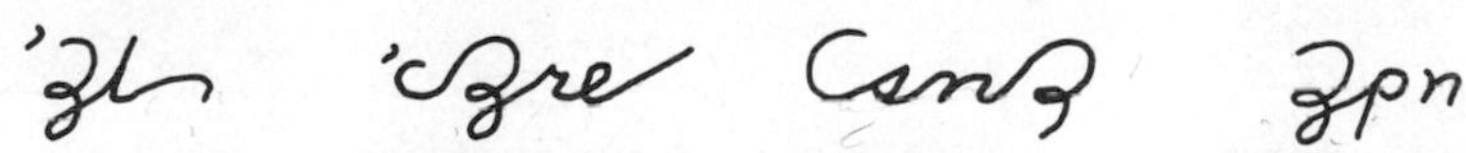

assistant accessories consensus suspense

ULATE

regulation congratulated formulated stimulate

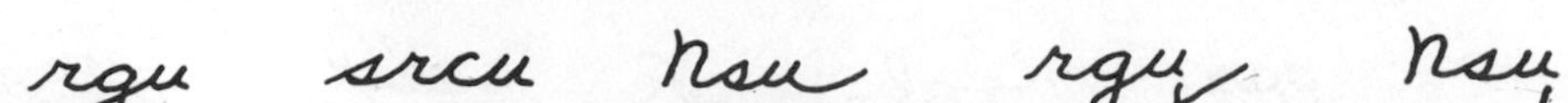

regulate circulate insulating regulations insulation

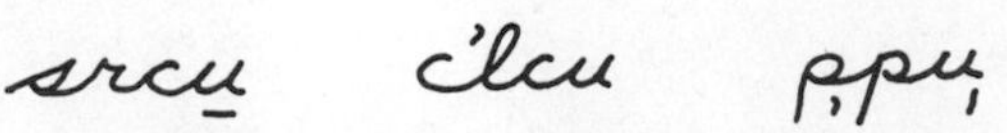

circulated calculate population

SCRIBE-SCRIPT

sbS subscribe · dS description · sbS subscription · TS transcription

dS describes · nS inscribe · pS prescribe · pS prescription

WRITING PRINCIPLES

SYS-SESS-SUS-SIS-CESS-CIS	Write a capital *Z* thus ʒ for the combinations *sys-sess-sus-sis-cess-cis*.
ULATE	Write a small longhand *u* to express the combination *ulate*.
SCRIBE-SCRIPT	Write a printed capital *S* to express the combinations *scribe-script*. The *S* may be joined or disjoined.

Assignment 2 — **New vocabulary**. Read and write the following words and phrases until you can read and write them rapidly. Memorize the abbreviated words.

necessary · debit · junior · administrative · railroad

Roger · booklet · promoted · filing · corporation · profits

public · relations · saving · depends · errors · regional

word · proper · example · expert · Seattle · products

allowing

Assignment 3 — **Reading and writing shorthand**. Read each sentence from shorthand until you can read it as rapidly as you can read from print. Write each sentence in shorthand until you can write each one rapidly and accurately.

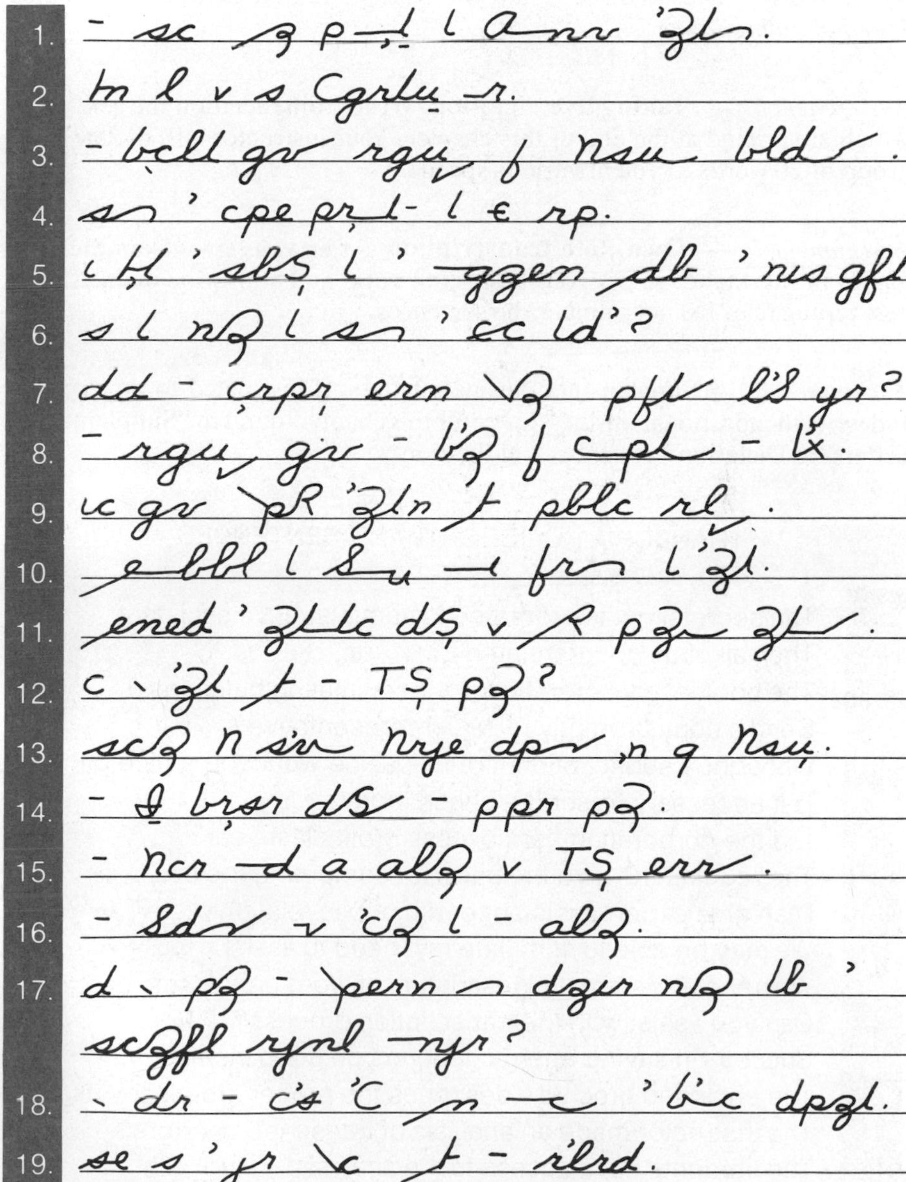

BUILDING SHORTHAND SPEED AND TRANSCRIPTION ACCURACY

Assignment 4 — **Self-testing**. Complete Unit 29 in your *Study Guide* before you proceed with the rest of this chapter.

Assignment 5 — **Taking tape dictation**. To write from dictation the new words and sentences in this chapter, use Cassette 13 Side B from *Theory and Speed-Building Tapes*.

Assignment 6 — **Taking live dictation**. Write from dictation the sentences which are printed at the end of this chapter. Your instructor will dictate each group of 20 words to you at various speeds.

Assignment 7 — **Own-note transcription**. After you have taken the sentences in shorthand, select your best set of notes and transcribe them at your best typing rate. Do not number the sentences.

Assignment 8 — **Supplemental business letters.** If instructed to do so, read and write the additional business letter for this chapter found in "Supplemental Letters for Dictation" at the back of this book.

TRANSCRIPT OF SHORTHAND SENTENCES

1. The secretary was promoted to administrative assistant.
2. Then all of us congratulated her. (20)
3. The booklet gives regulations for insulating buildings.
4. Send a copy promptly to each representative. (40)
5. I thought a subscription to a magazine would be a nice gift.
6. Is it necessary to send a check today? (60)
7. Did the corporation earn excess profits last year?
8. The regulations give the basis for computing the tax. (80)
9. I can give expert assistance with public relations.
10. We may be able to stimulate my friend to assist. (100)
11. We need a systematic description of word processing systems.
12. Can you assist with the transcription process? (120)
13. Success in saving energy depends on good insulation.
14. The enclosed brochure describes the proper process. (140)
15. The instructor made an analysis of transcription errors.
16. The students have access to the analysis. (160)

17. Do you possess the experience and desire necessary to be a successful regional manager? (180)
18. You debit the cash account when making a bank deposit.
19. She is a junior executive with the railroad. (200)

CHAPTER 30

WRITING **CONTR**, **OVER-OTHER**, AND **UNDER**

Assignment 1 — **Rule discovery**. Follow the three-step plan to learn the new writing principles: (1) Discover the rule for each group of words. (2) Read the shorthand outlines until you can read them rapidly. (3) Cover the shorthand and write each word until you can do so rapidly and accurately.

CONTR

contract	contribute	control	contracts	contributions
contributed	controls	contribution	contrast	controller

OVER-OTHER

over-other	another	overseas	otherwise	overcharged
overdue	overlook	overcharge	overlooked	overloaded
overtime	oversight	overnight	overcome	others

UNDER

under	understand	understanding	understood

ul'c	-sus8'	-sus8'—
undertake	misunderstand	misunderstanding
-sus8d	ugro—	
misunderstood	underground	

WRITING PRINCIPLES

CONTR Write a small longhand *k* to express the combination *contr* and the following vowel. Avoid writing extra strokes when writing the longhand *k*.

OVER-OTHER Write a joined or disjoined capital *O* to express *over* and *other*.

UNDER Write a small longhand *u* to express the combination *under*.

Assignment 2 — **New vocabulary**. Read and write the following words and phrases until you can read and write them rapidly. Memorize the abbreviated words.

pr'c	$	spl	'cspbl	c/
practical	dollar	superintendent	acceptable	company's
pp—	,pr/	Csq—-	pp'r	rf—
perhaps	operations	consequently	prepared	refund
ddc	psnl	d'l's	evn	
deduct	personal-personnel	Dallas	we have not	
zn				
was not				

Assignment 3 **Reading and writing shorthand.** Read each sentence from shorthand until you can read it as rapidly as you can read from print. Write each sentence in shorthand until you can write each one rapidly and accurately.

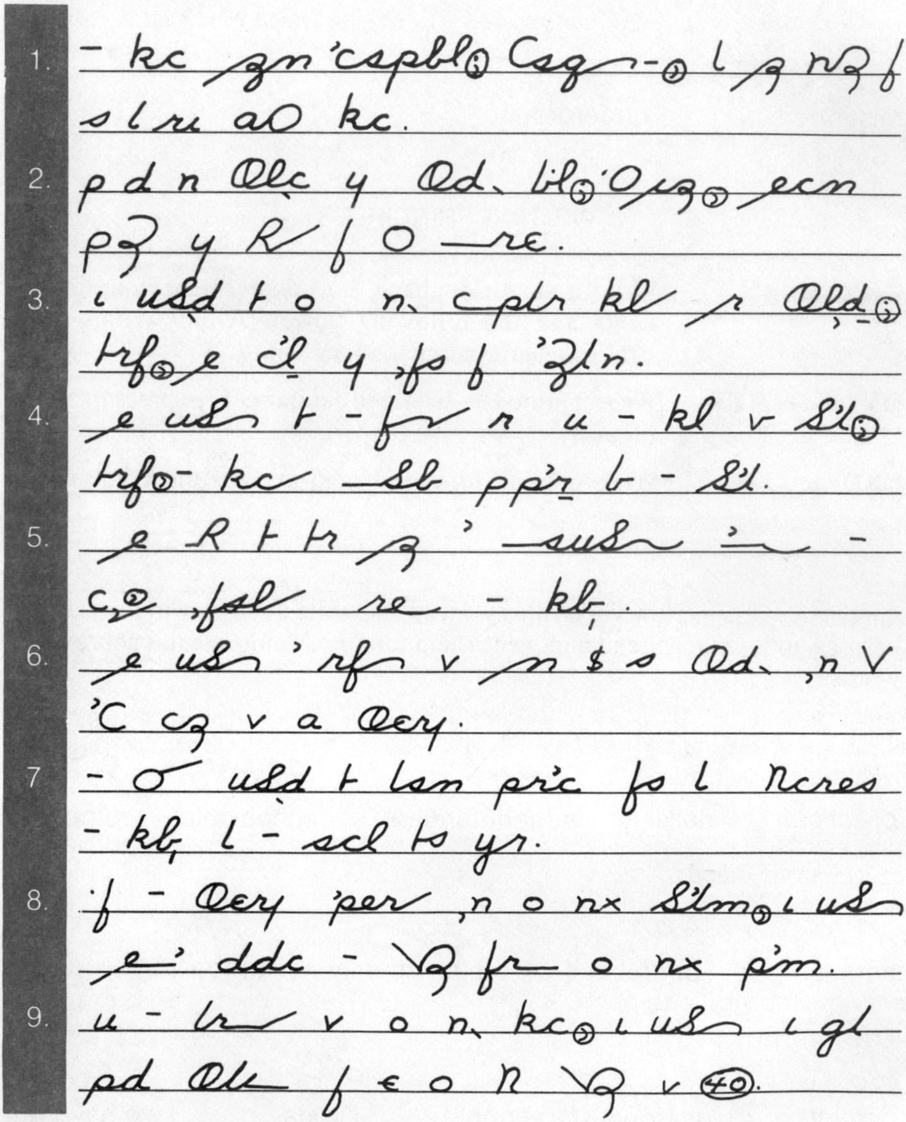

BUILDING TRANSCRIPTION SKILLS

Assignment 4 — **Punctuating sentences joined by a transitional word.** Place a semicolon before and a comma after a transitional word or phrase that joins two sentences. Common transitional words and phrases include: *therefore*, *however*, *accordingly*, *consequently*, *in fact*, *as a result*. Study the examples that follow and apply this rule when transcribing.

1. Our sales are up; therefore, we have hired several new sales clerks. (Note that the transitional word, *therefore*, joins the two sentences.)
2. We have not received your check; consequently, we cannot ship the merchandise to you.
3. We can ship the present model; however, you should know that next year's model will be available in one month.
4. We are in first place in our baseball league; in fact, our team is having its best year yet.

BUILDING SHORTHAND SPEED AND TRANSCRIPTION ACCURACY

Assignment 5 — **Self-testing**. Complete Unit 30 in your *Study Guide* before you proceed with the rest of this chapter.

Assignment 6 — **Taking tape dictation**. To write from dictation the new words and sentences in this chapter, use Cassette 14 Side B from *Theory and Speed-Building Tapes*.

Assignment 7 — **Taking live dictation**. Write from dictation the sentences which are printed at the end of this chapter. Your instructor will dictate each group of 20 words to you at various speeds.

Assignment 8 — **Own-note transcription**. After you have taken the sentences in shorthand, select your best set of notes and transcribe them at your best typing rate. Do not number the sentences.

Assignment 9 — **Supplemental business letters.** If instructed to do so, read and write the additional business letter for this chapter found in "Supplemental Letters for Dictation" at the back of this book.

TRANSCRIPT OF SHORTHAND SENTENCES

1. The contract was not acceptable; consequently, it was necessary for us to write another contract. (20)
2. Please do not overlook your overdue bill; otherwise, we cannot process your orders for other merchandise. (40)

3. I understood that our new computer controls were overloaded; therefore, we called your office for assistance. (60)
4. We understand that the funds are under the control of the state; therefore, the contracts must be prepared by the state. (80)
5. We heard that there was a misunderstanding among the company's officials regarding the contribution. (100)
6. We understand a refund of one dollar is overdue on every account because of an overcharge. (120)
7. The others understood that it is not practical for us to increase the contribution to the school this year. (140)
8. If the overcharge appears on our next statement, I understand we may deduct the excess from our next payment. (160)
9. Under the terms of our new contract, I understand I get paid overtime for each hour in excess of 40. (180)

CHAPTER 31

WRITING **ELECTR**, **OLOGY**, AND **ITIS-ICITIS**

Assignment 1 — **Rule discovery**. Follow the three-step plan to learn the new writing principles: (1) Discover the rule for each group of words. (2) Read the shorthand outlines until you can read them rapidly. (3) Cover the shorthand and write each word until you can do so rapidly and accurately.

ELECTR

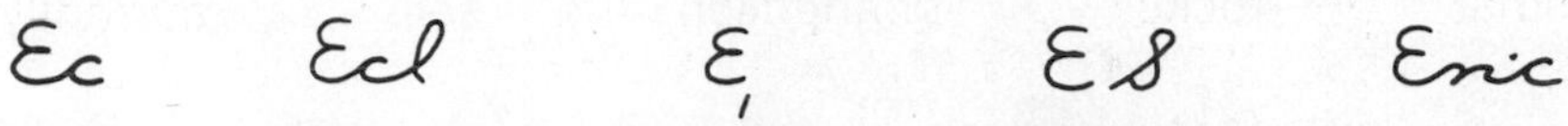

electric electrical electrician electricity electronic

OLOGY

biology geology psychology psychological sociology

ITIS-ICITIS

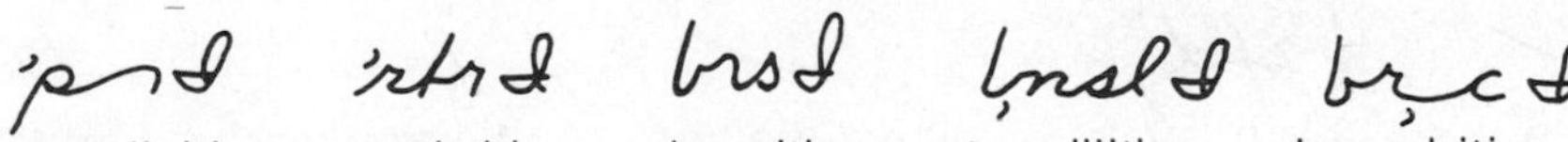

appendicitis arthritis bursitis tonsillitis bronchitis

WRITING PRINCIPLES

ELECTR Write a capital *E* thus to express the combination *electr* and the following vowel.

OLOGY Write a small disjoined to express the combination *ology*.

ITIS-ICITIS Write a disjoined capital *I* thus to express the combinations *itis-icitis*. Write it close to the word to which it belongs.

Assignment 2 — **New vocabulary**. Read and write the words and phrases on page 144 until you can read and write them rapidly. Memorize the standard symbols.

Learning tip: Note that special symbols are used to express metric measures. They represent both the singular and plural. These symbols are used throughout the world.

Assignment 3 – **Reading and writing shorthand**. Read each sentence from shorthand until you can read it as rapidly as you can read from print. Write each sentence in shorthand until you can write each one rapidly and accurately.

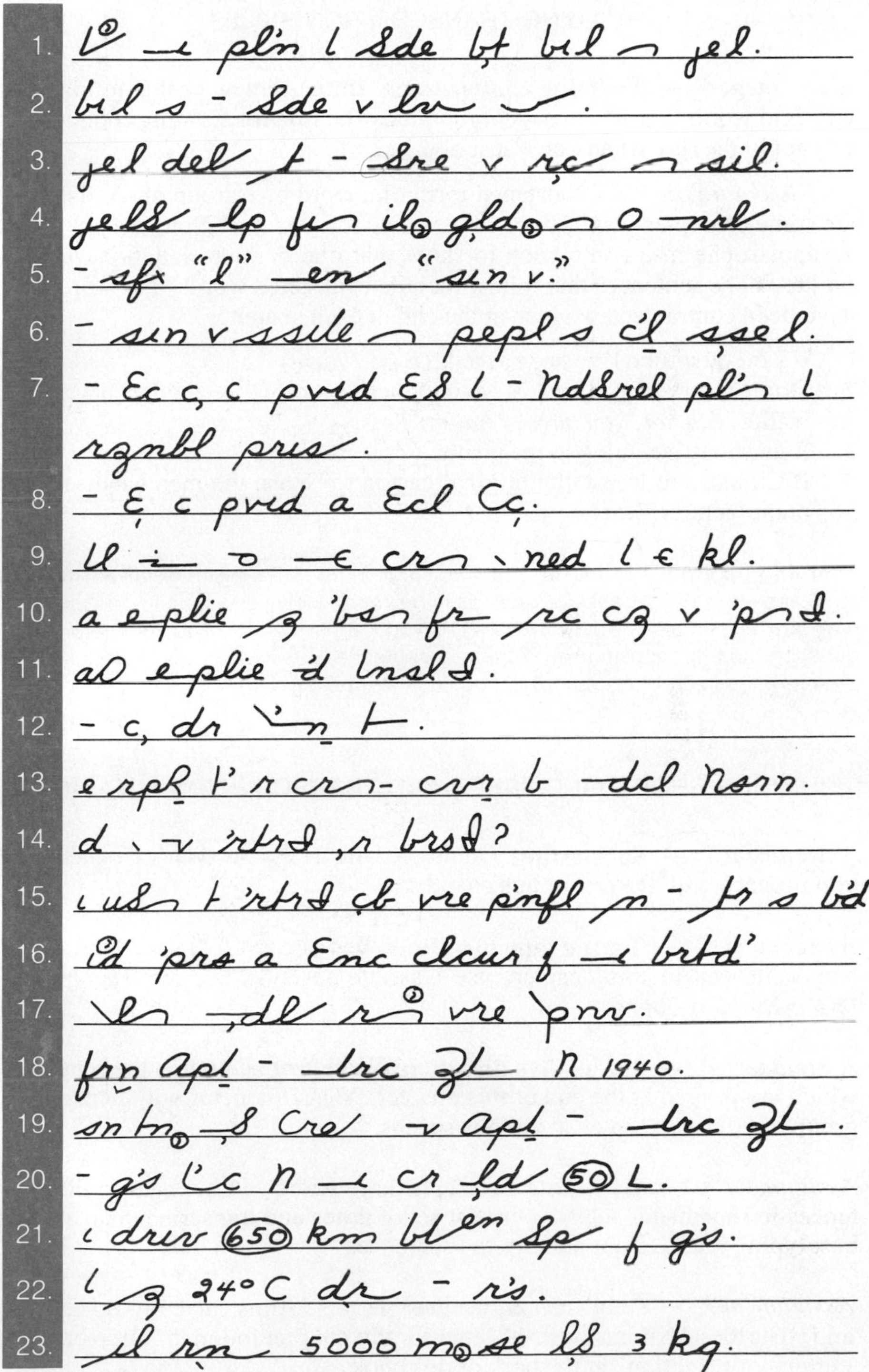

BUILDING TRANSCRIPTION SKILLS

Assignment 4 — **Forming contractions**. In the sentences that follow, you will find words that are *contractions*. Study the rule for forming contractions and apply the rule when you transcribe.

A *contraction* is a shortened form of a word or a group of words. Here are some examples: *can't* for *cannot*, *we've* for *we have*. Note that you insert an apostrophe in a contraction to show that one or more letters have been omitted. The sentences that follow include contracted words. The words that have been contracted are given at the end of each sentence.

1. It's the first time I've been asked. (*it is*, *I have*)
2. Don't worry if you've lost your ticket because I've another one in my wallet. (*do not*, *you have*, *I have*)
3. Everybody's coming to the picnic. (*everybody is*)
4. It's important to use the original carton to return the merchandise to its manufacturer. (*it is*)

Learning tip: Note that both *its* and *it's* appear in the last sentence above. The word *its* is already in the possessive case, as in *his, hers*. How can you tell when to add or omit the apostrophe? Apply this test: If you can substitute *it is* for the word in question, add the apostrophe. In the last sentence, *it is* can be substituted for *it's*; therefore, you add the apostrophe. You cannot substitute *it is* for *its*.

BUILDING SHORTHAND SPEED AND TRANSCRIPTION ACCURACY

Assignment 5 — **Self-testing**. Complete Unit 31 in your *Study Guide* before you proceed with the rest of this chapter.

Assignment 6 — **Taking tape dictation**. To write from dictation the words and sentences in this chapter, use Cassette 15 Side B from *Theory and Speed-Building Tapes*.

Assignment 7 — **Taking live dictation**. Write from dictation the sentences which are printed at the end of this chapter. Your instructor will dictate each group of 20 words to you at various speeds.

Assignment 8 — **Own-note transcription**. After you have taken the sentences in shorthand, select your best set of notes and transcribe them at your best typing rate. Do not number the sentences.

Assignment 9 — **Supplemental business letters.** If instructed to do so, read and write the additional business letter for this chapter found in "Supplemental Letters for Dictation" at the back of this book.

TRANSCRIPT OF SHORTHAND SENTENCES

1. It's my plan to study both biology and geology.
2. Biology is the study of living things. (20)
3. Geology deals with the history of rocks and soil.
4. Geologists help find oil, gold, and other minerals. (40)
5. The suffix "ology" means "science of."
6. The science of society and people is called sociology. (60)
7. The electric company can provide electricity at the industrial plant at reasonable prices. (80)
8. The electrician can provide an electrical connection.
9. Tell him how much current you need at each control. (100)
10. An employee was absent from work because of appendicitis.
11. Another employee had tonsillitis. (120)
12. The company doctor examined them.
13. He reported they are currently covered by medical insurance. (140)
14. Do you have arthritis or bursitis?
15. I understand that arthritis can be very painful when the weather is bad. (160)
16. I'd appreciate an electronic calculator for my birthday.
17. Excellent models aren't very expensive. (180)
18. France adopted the metric system in 1940.
19. Since then, most countries have adopted the metric system. (200)
20. The gas tank in my car holds 50 L.
21. I drive 650 km between stops for gas. (220)
22. It was 24°C during the race.
23. While running 5000 m, she lost 3 kg. (240)

CHAPTER 32

BUSINESS LETTER DICTATION AND TRANSCRIPTION

BUILDING TRANSCRIPTION SKILLS

Assignment 1 — **Spelling review**. Follow the steps outlined in Chapter 12 to check your ability to spell the following words correctly:

1. benefits
2. brief
3. completion
4. connection
5. currently
6. educational
7. effectively
8. electrical
9. expenses
10. filing
11. interested
12. material
13. models
14. necessary
15. nuclear
16. operations
17. regulations
18. system

BUSINESS LETTERS

Assignment 2 — **Letter 1**. Read and write each of the new words and phrases until you can read and write each one rapidly and accurately. Then read and write the shorthand for Letter 1 to build your writing speed.

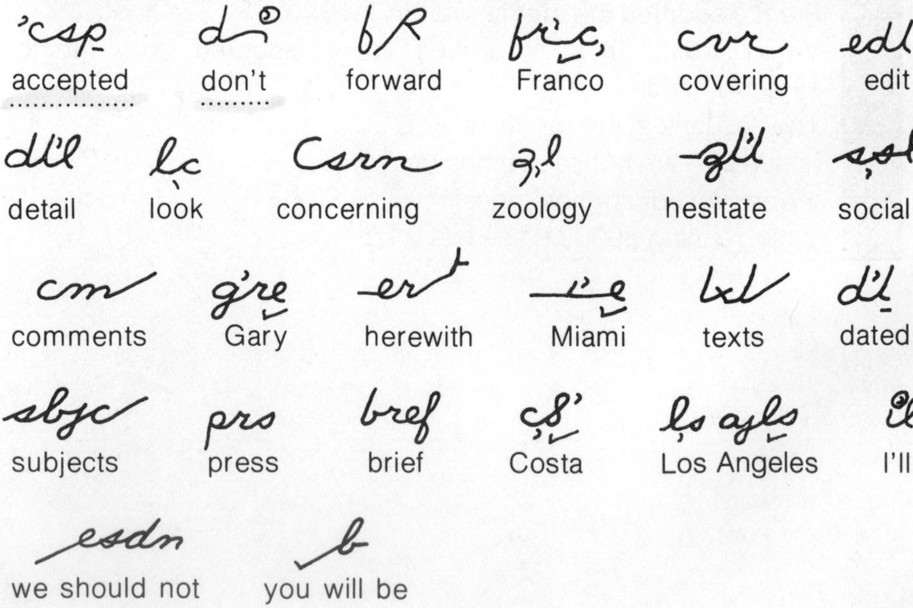

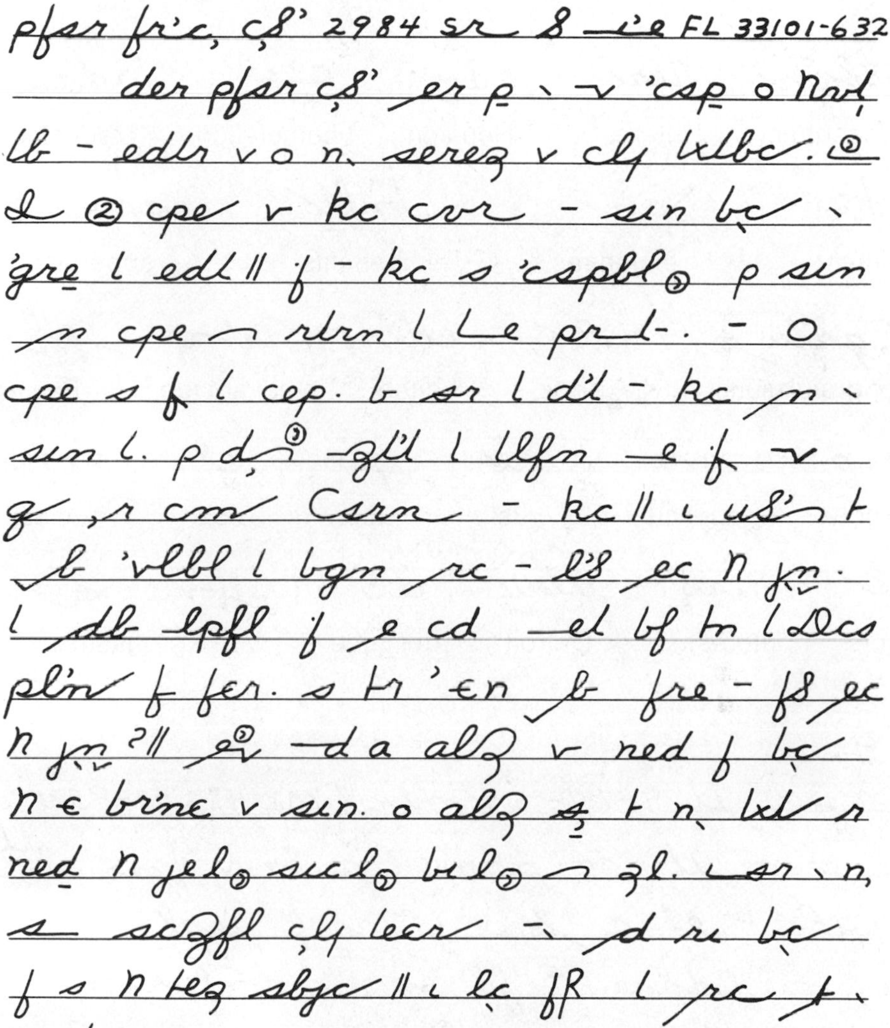

Assignment 3 — Letter 2. Read and write each new word for Letter 2 until you can read and write each one rapidly and accurately. Then read and write the shorthand for Letter 2 to build your writing speed.

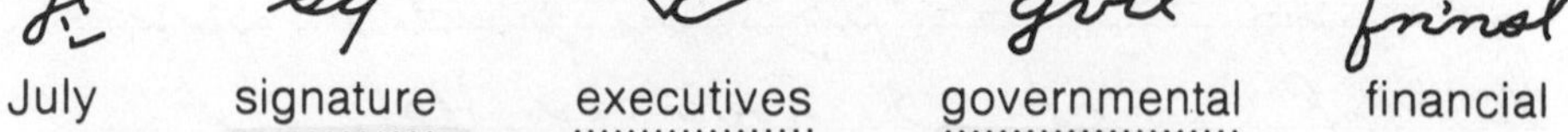

July signature executives governmental financial

subscribers	interest	Houston	completion	reducing	
James	expenses	benefits	supervised		
congratulations	experts	editors	advantage	Paula	
simply	agencies	rush	upon	coal	nuclear
fuels	interested	Detroit	describe	won't	issues

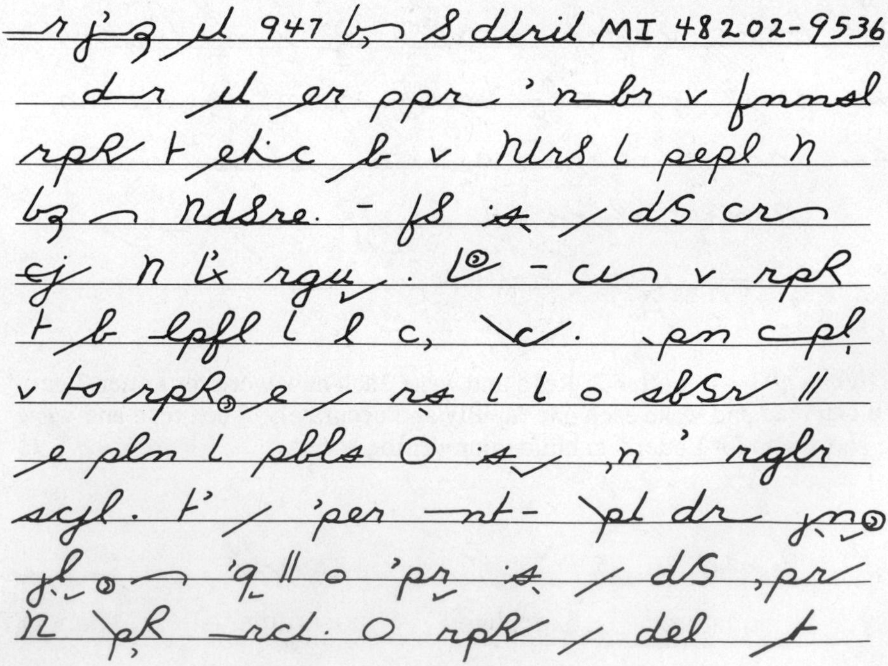

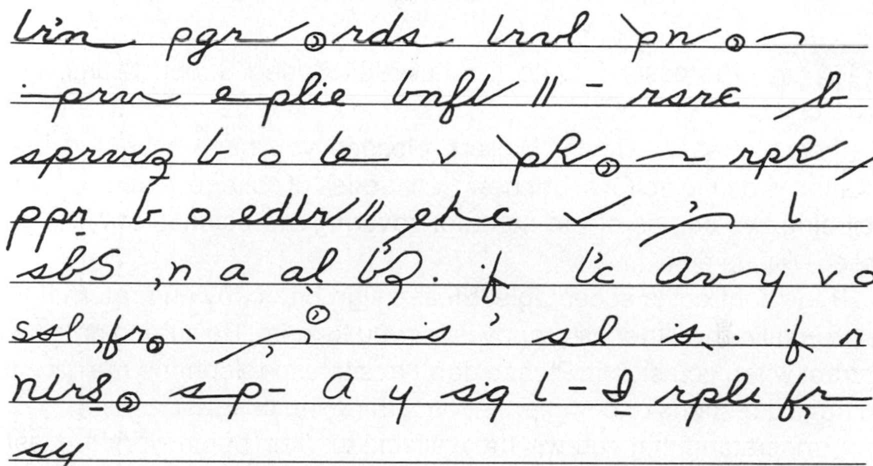

Assignment 4 — **Supplemental business letters.** If instructed to do so, read and write the additional business letter for this chapter found in "Supplemental Letters for Dictation" at the back of this book.

BUILDING SHORTHAND SPEED AND TRANSCRIPTION ACCURACY

Assignment 5 — **Self-testing**. Complete Unit 32 in your *Study Guide* before you proceed with the rest of this chapter.

Assignment 6 — **Taking tape dictation**. To write from dictation the new words and letters in this chapter, use Cassette 16 Side B from *Theory and Speed-Building Tapes*

Assignment 7 — **Taking live dictation**. Write from dictation the letters which are printed at the end of this chapter. Your instructor will dictate to you from these transcripts at various speeds.

Assignment 8 — **Own-note transcription**. Transcribe at your best typing rate an accurate copy of at least one of the letters you took in shorthand in Assignment 7. Type the letter in the form requested by your instructor.

TRANSCRIPTS OF LETTERS 1 AND 2

Letter 1 Professor Franco Costa, 2984 Spring Street, Miami, FL 33101-6321

Dear Professor Costa: We are pleased you have accepted our invitation to be the editor of our new (20) series of college textbooks. I'm enclosing two copies of the contract covering the science books you agreed (40) to edit.

If the contract is acceptable, please sign one copy and return it to me promptly. The other (60) copy is for you to keep. Be sure to date the contract when you sign it. Please don't hesitate to telephone me (80) if you have questions or comments concerning the contract.

I understand that you will be available to (100) begin work the last week in June. It would be helpful if we could meet before then to discuss plans for the future. Is (120) there a chance you will be free the first week in June?

We've made an analysis of the need for books in each branch of (140) science. Our analysis showed that new texts are needed in geology, psychology, biology, and (160) zoology. I am sure you know some successful college teachers who would write books for us in these subjects.

I (180) look forward to working with you on this important project. Sincerely yours, (194)

Letter 2 Mr. James White, 947 Bond Street, Detroit, MI 48202-9536

Dear Mr. White: We are preparing a number of financial reports that we think will be of interest to (20) people in business and industry. The first issue will describe current changes in tax regulations. It's the (40) kind of report that will be helpful to all company executives. Upon completion of this report, we (60) will rush it to our subscribers.

We plan to publish other issues on a regular schedule. They will appear (80) monthly except during June, July, and August.

Our April issue will describe opportunities in the export (100) market. Other reports will deal with training programs, reducing travel expenses, and improving employee (120) benefits.

The research will be supervised by our team of experts, and the reports will be prepared by our (140) editors.

We think you will want to subscribe on an annual basis. If you take advantage of our special (160) offer, you won't miss a single issue. If you are interested, simply add your signature to the enclosed reply (180) form. Sincerely yours, (184)

REVIEWING THE WRITING PRINCIPLES

All the writing principles, abbreviated words, and standard abbreviations you have learned in Chapters 25 through 32 are reviewed on Tape 18 Side B of the *Theory and Speed-Building Tapes*. Take dictation from this tape before completing the Final Examination.

EXAMINATION 8

Remove and complete Examination 8 at the back of your *Study Guide*.

11-26-90

FINAL EXAMINATION

Remove and complete the Final Examination at the back of your *Study Guide*.

APPENDIX A

SUPPLEMENTAL LETTERS FOR DICTATION

There are 34 supplemental letters for dictation practice. There is one letter for each theory chapter beginning with Chapter 6. Beginning with Chapter 8, there are two letters for each business letter chapter. Each letter contains the writing principles introduced up to that chapter. For example, the supplemental letter headed Chapter 6 in this appendix would be used only after study of Chapter 6 is completed. This supplemental dictation material is included with the dictation material for each chapter on *Theory and Speed-Building Tapes*. For example, the supplemental letter for Chapter 6 may be found on Cassette 6, Side A. They may be used as follows:

- As additional class assignments.
- As new material dictation.
- As test letters.

INSTRUCTIONS

1. **Dictation** —Have each letter dictated to you until you can write each letter in shorthand at your best dictation rate.

2. **Transcription** —Transcribe from your own notes in a style directed by your instructor.

Chapter 6 — Supplemental Letter

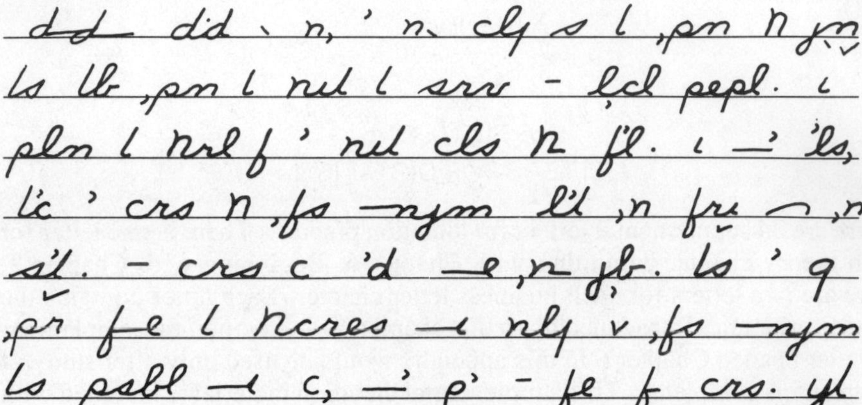

Dear Madam: Did you know a new college is to open in June? It is to be open at night to serve the (20) local people. I plan to enroll for a night class in the fall. I may also take a course in office management (40) late on Friday and on Saturday. The course can aid me on the job. It is a good opportunity for me (60) to increase my knowledge of office management. It is possible my company may pay the fee for the course. (80) Yours truly, (82)

Chapter 7 — Supplemental Letter

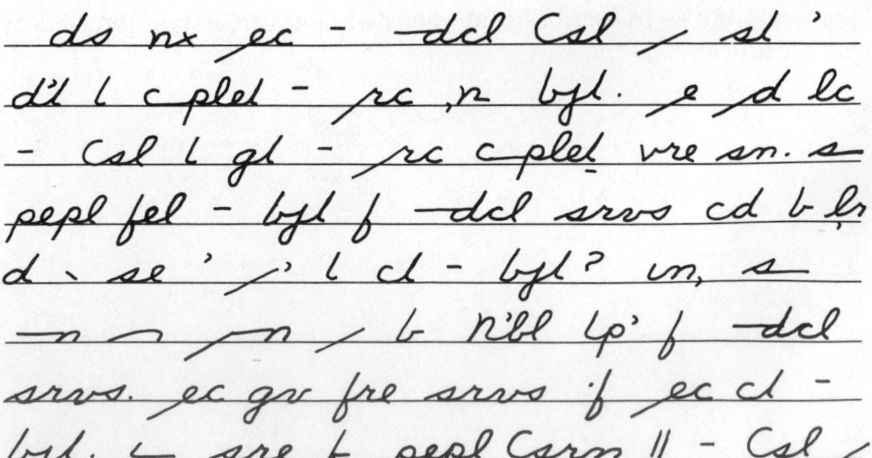

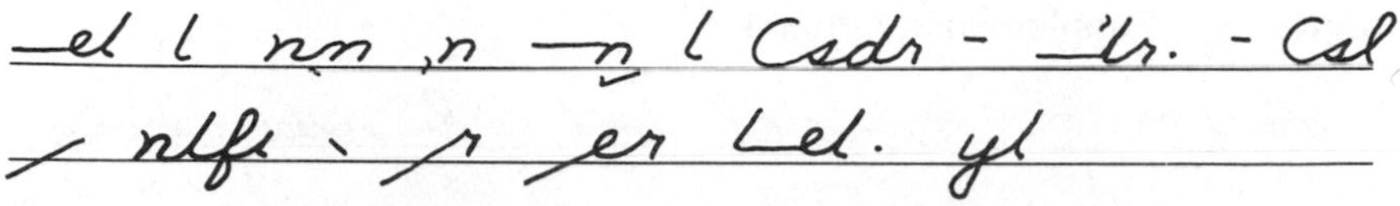

Dear Sir: Next week the medical council will set a date to complete the work on the budget. We would like the council (20) to get the work completed very soon. Some people feel the budget for medical service could be lower. (40) Do you see a way to cut the budget? I know some men and women will be unable to pay for medical (60) service. We can give free service if we can cut the budget. I am sorry for the people concerned.

The council (80) will meet at noon on Monday to consider the matter. The council will notify you where we are to meet. Yours (100) truly, (101)

Chapter 8 — Supplemental Letter 3

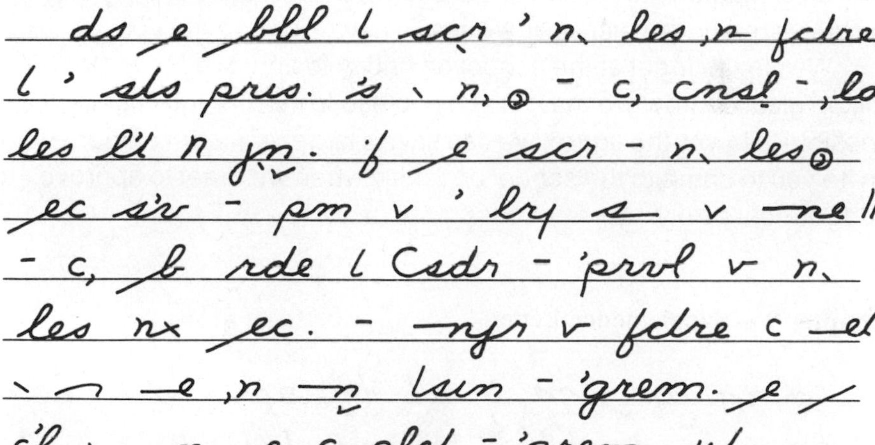

Dear Sir: We will be able to secure a new lease on the factory at a satisfactory price. As you (20) know, the company canceled the old lease late in June. If we secure the new lease, we can save the payment of a (40) large sum of money.

The company will be ready to consider the approval of the new lease next week. The (60) manager of the factory can meet you and me on Monday to sign the agreement. We will call you when we (80) complete the agreement. Yours truly, (87)

Chapter 8 — Supplemental Letter 4

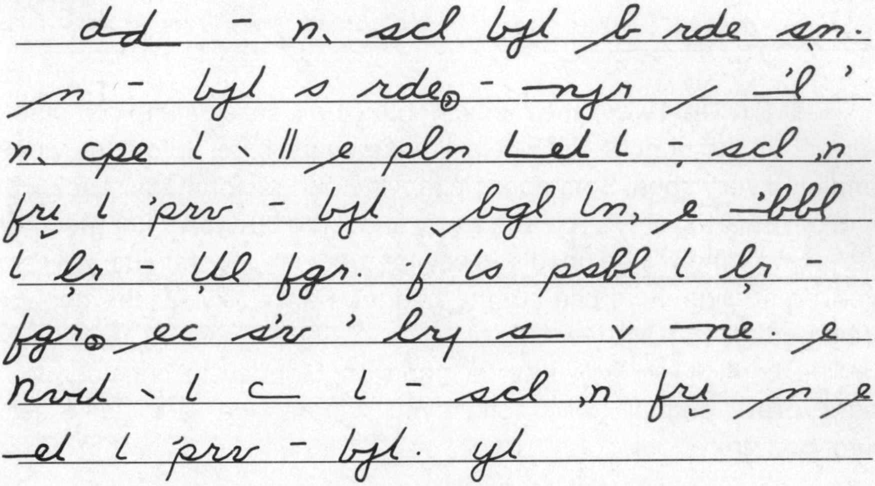

Dear Madam: The new school budget will be ready soon. When the budget is ready, the manager will mail a new (20) copy to you.

We plan to meet at the school on Friday to approve the budget. You will be glad to know we may (40) be able to lower the total figure. If it is possible to lower the figure, we can save a large (60) sum of money. We invite you to come to the school on Friday when we meet to approve the budget. Yours truly, (80)

Chapter 9 — Supplemental Letter

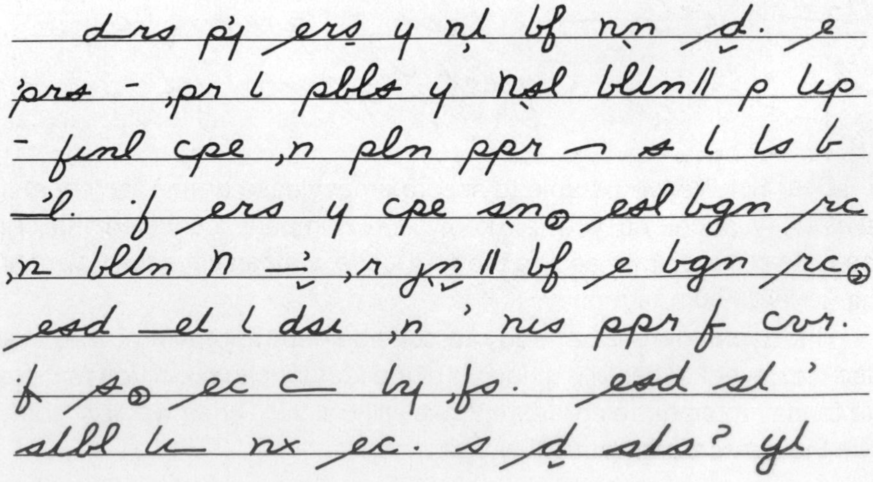

Dear Mrs. Page: We received your note before noon Wednesday. We appreciate the opportunity to publish (20) your unusual bulletin.

Please type the final copy on plain paper and ship it to us by mail. If we (40) receive your copy soon, we shall begin work on the bulletin in May or June.

Before we begin work, we should (60) meet to decide on a nice paper for the cover. If you wish, we can come to your office. We should set a (80) suitable time next week. Is Wednesday satisfactory? Yours truly, (91)

Chapter 10 — Supplemental Letter

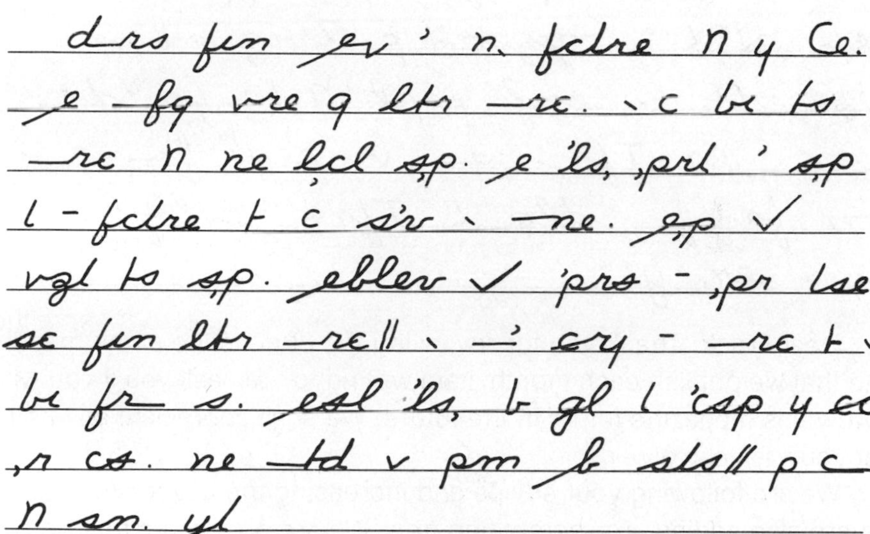

Dear Mrs. Fine: We have a new factory in your county. We manufacture very good leather merchandise. (20) You can buy this merchandise in any local shop. We also operate a shop at the factory that can (40) save you money. We hope you will visit this shop. We believe you will appreciate the opportunity to (60) see such fine leather merchandise.

You may charge the merchandise that you buy from us. We shall also be glad to accept (80) your check or cash. Any method of payment will be satisfactory.

Please come in soon. Yours truly, (99)

Chapter 11 — Supplemental Letter

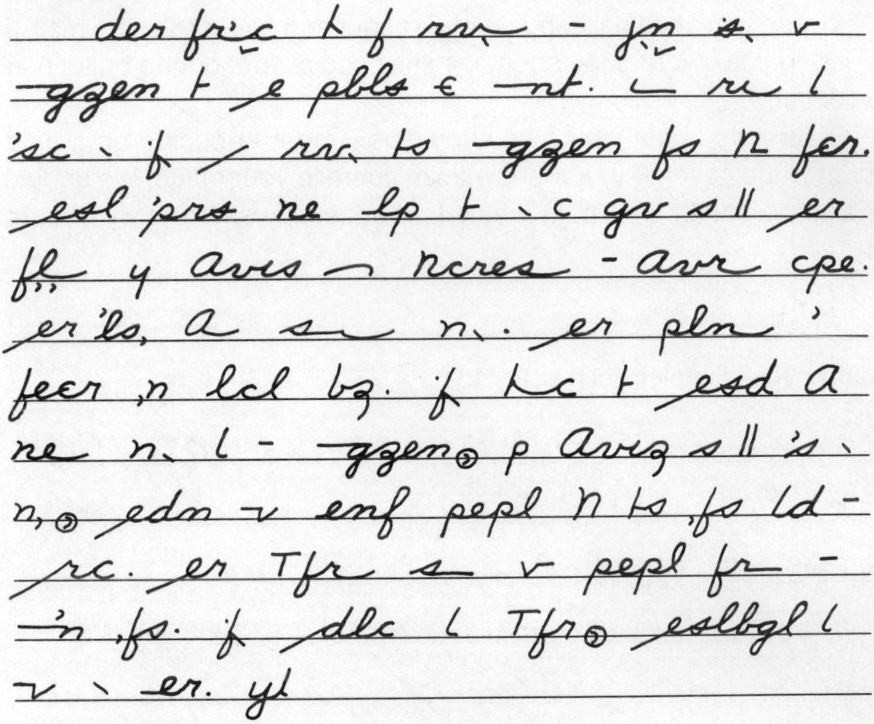

Dear Frank: Thank you for reviewing the June issue of the magazine that we publish each month. I am writing to (20) ask you if you will review this magazine for us in the future. We shall appreciate any help that you (40) can give us.

We are following your advice and increasing the advertising copy. We are also adding (60) something new. We are planning a feature on local business. If you think that we should add anything new to the (80) magazine, please advise us.

As you know, we do not have enough people in this office to do the work. We are (100) transferring some of the people from the main office. If you would like to transfer, we shall be glad to have you here. (120) Yours truly, (122)

Chapter 12 — Supplemental Letter 3

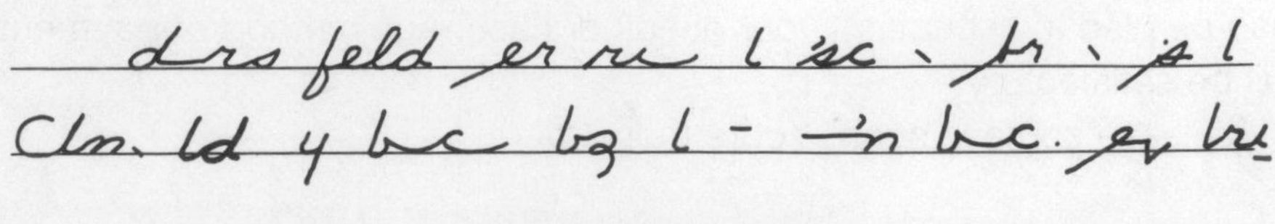

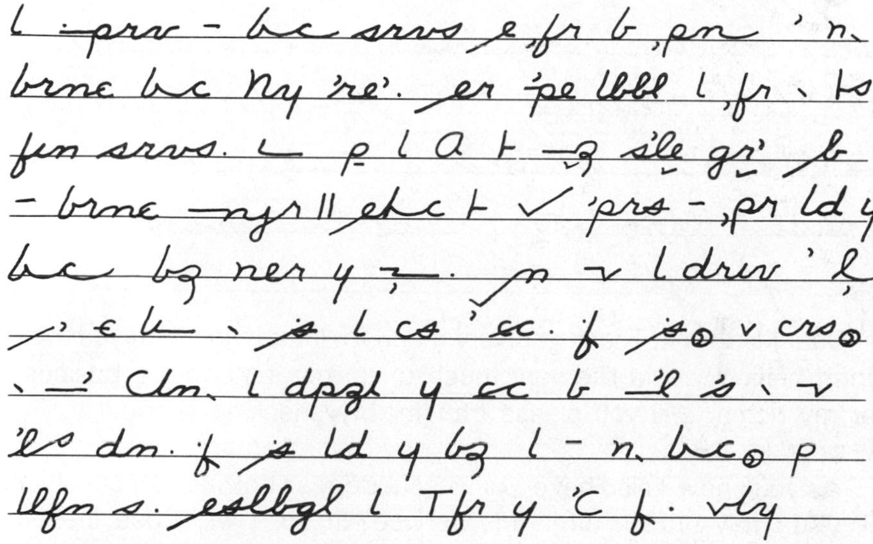

Dear Mrs. Field: We are writing to ask you whether you wish to continue to do your banking business at the (20) main bank. We have tried to improve the banking service we offer by opening a new branch bank in your area (40). We are happy to be able to offer you this fine service. I am pleased to add that Ms. Sally Gray will (60) be the branch manager.

We think that you will appreciate the opportunity to do your banking business (80) near your home. You will not have to drive a long way each time you wish to cash a check. If you wish, of course, you may (100) continue to deposit your check by mail as you have always done. If you wish to do your business at the new bank, (120) please telephone us. We shall be glad to transfer your account for you. Very truly yours, (136)

Chapter 12 — Supplemental Letter 4

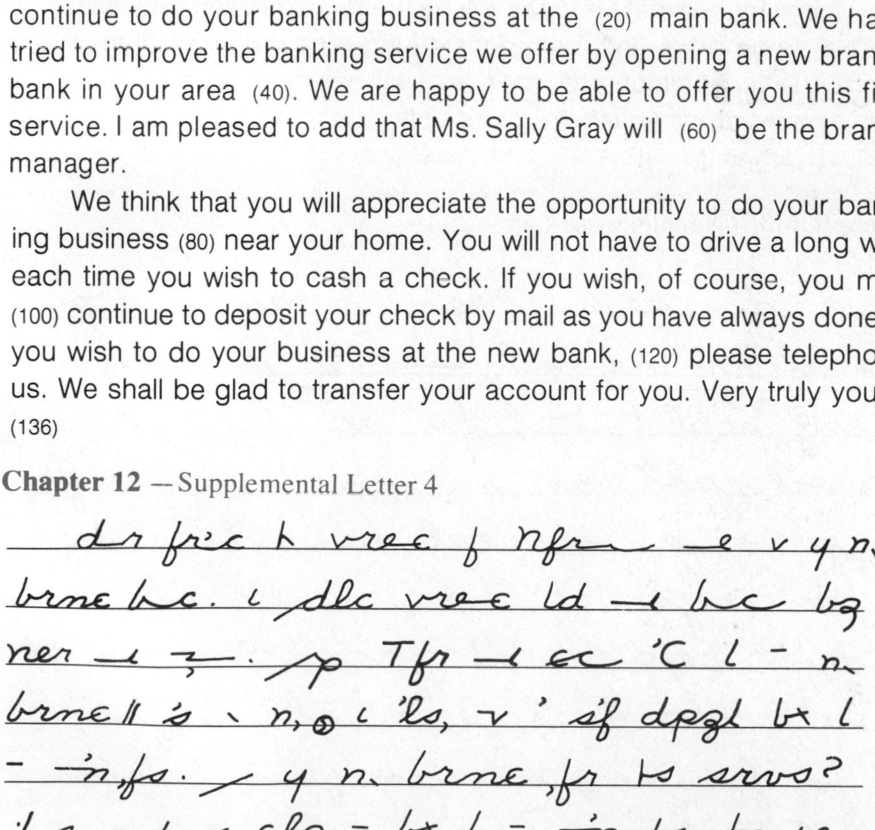

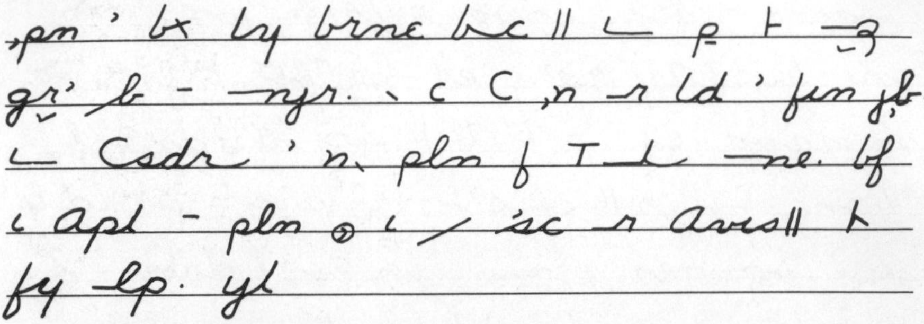

Dear Mr. Frank: Thank you very much for informing me of your new branch bank. I would like very much to do my (20) banking business near my home. Will you please transfer my checking account to the new branch.

As you know, I also have (40) a safe deposit box at the main office. Will your new branch offer this service? If so, I will close the box at (60) the main office. Then I can open a box at your branch bank.

I am pleased that Ms. Gray will be the manager. You (80) can count on her to do a fine job. I am considering a new plan for transmitting money. Before I adopt (100) the plan, I will ask her advice.

Thank you for your help. Yours truly, (112)

Chapter 13 — Supplemental Letter

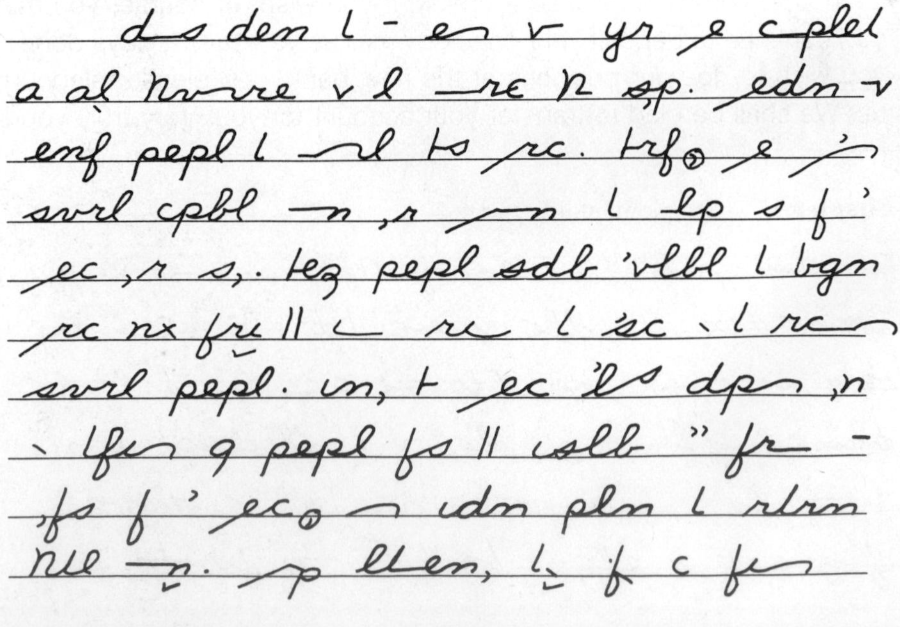

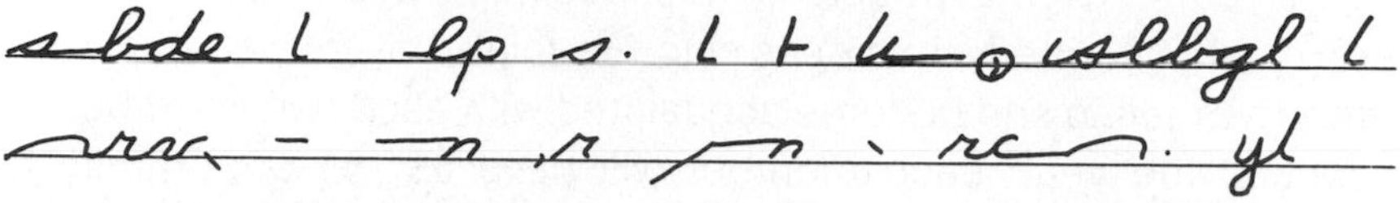

Dear Miss Dean: At the end of the year we complete an annual inventory of all merchandise in the shop. (20) We do not have enough people to handle this work. Therefore, we want several capable men or women to (40) help us for a week or so. These people should be available to begin work next Friday.

I am writing to (60) ask you to recommend several people. I know that we can always depend on you to find good people for (80) us.

I shall be away from the office for a week, and I do not plan to return until Monday. Will you please (100) let me know Tuesday if you can find somebody to help us. At that time, I shall be glad to interview the men (120) or women you recommend. Yours truly, (127)

Chapter 14 — Supplemental Letter

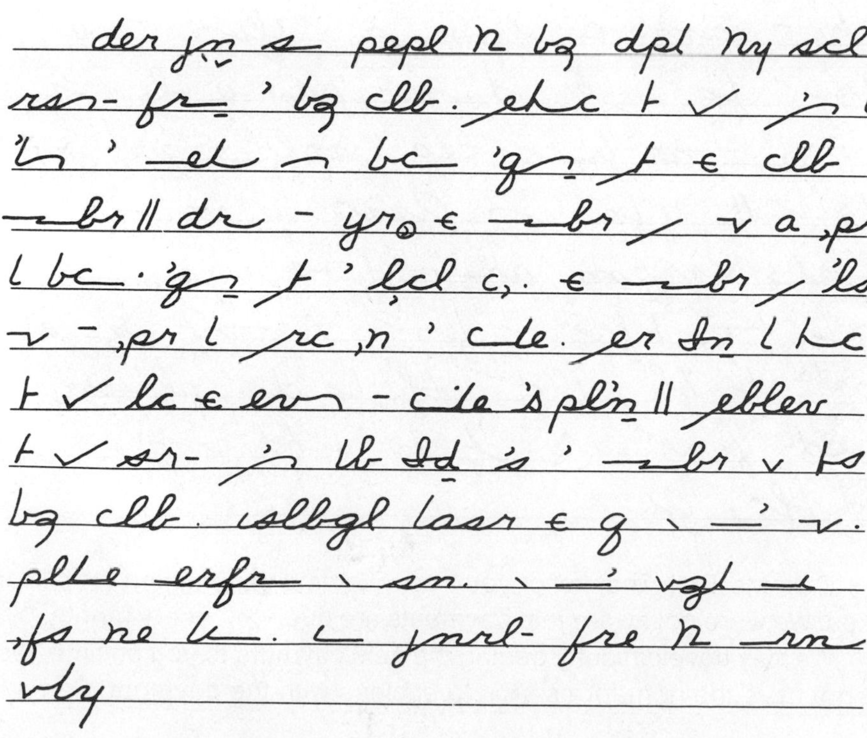

Dear June: Some people in the business department in your school recently formed a business club. We think that you will (20) want to attend a meeting and become acquainted with each club member.

During the year, each member will have an (40) opportunity to become acquainted with a local company. Each member will also have the (60) opportunity to work on a committee. We are inclined to think that you will like each event the committee has (80) planned.

We believe that you will surely want to be included as a member of this business club. I shall be glad (100) to answer each question you may have. Please let me hear from you soon. You may visit my office any time. I am (120) generally free in the morning. Very truly yours, (128)

Chapter 15 – Supplemental Letter

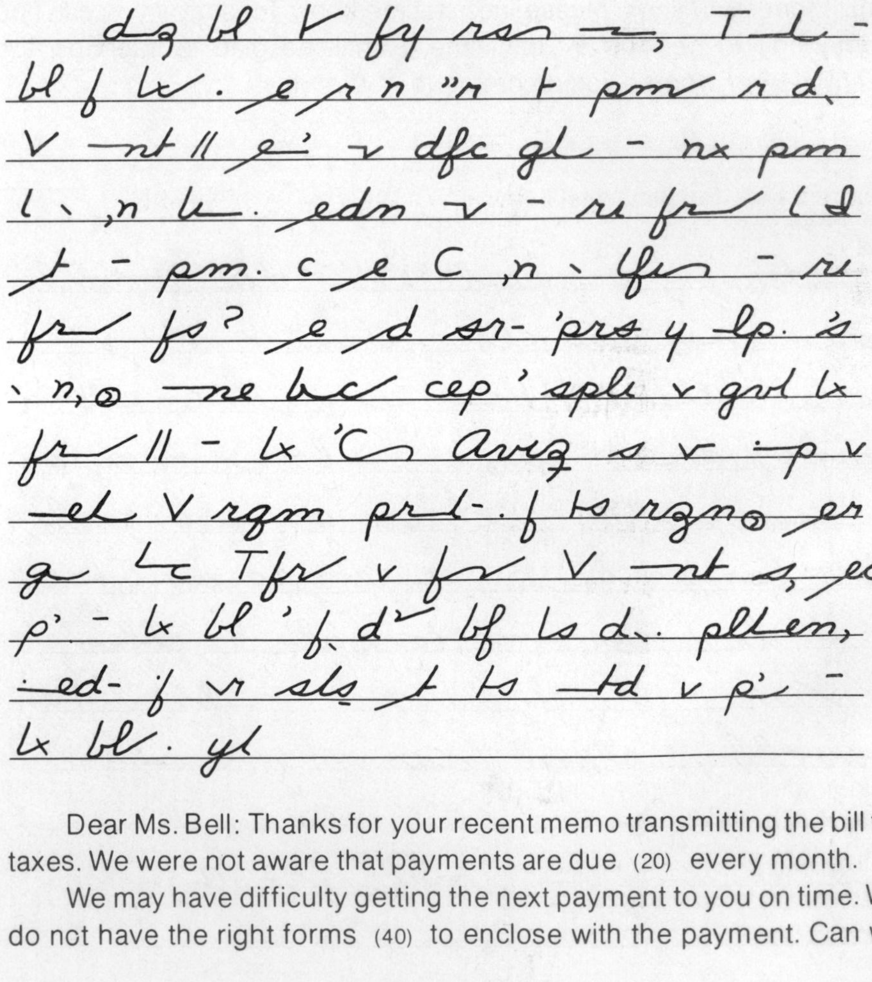

Dear Ms. Bell: Thanks for your recent memo transmitting the bill for taxes. We were not aware that payments are due (20) every month.

We may have difficulty getting the next payment to you on time. We do not have the right forms (40) to enclose with the payment. Can we count on you to find the right forms for us? We would surely appreciate your (60) help. As you know, many banks keep a supply of government tax forms.

The tax accountant advised us of the (80) importance of meeting every requirement promptly. For this reason, we are going to make transfers of funds every (100) month so we can pay the tax bill a few days before it is due. Please let me know immediately if you (120) are satisfied with this method of paying the tax bills. Yours truly, (133)

Chapter 16 — Supplemental Letter 3

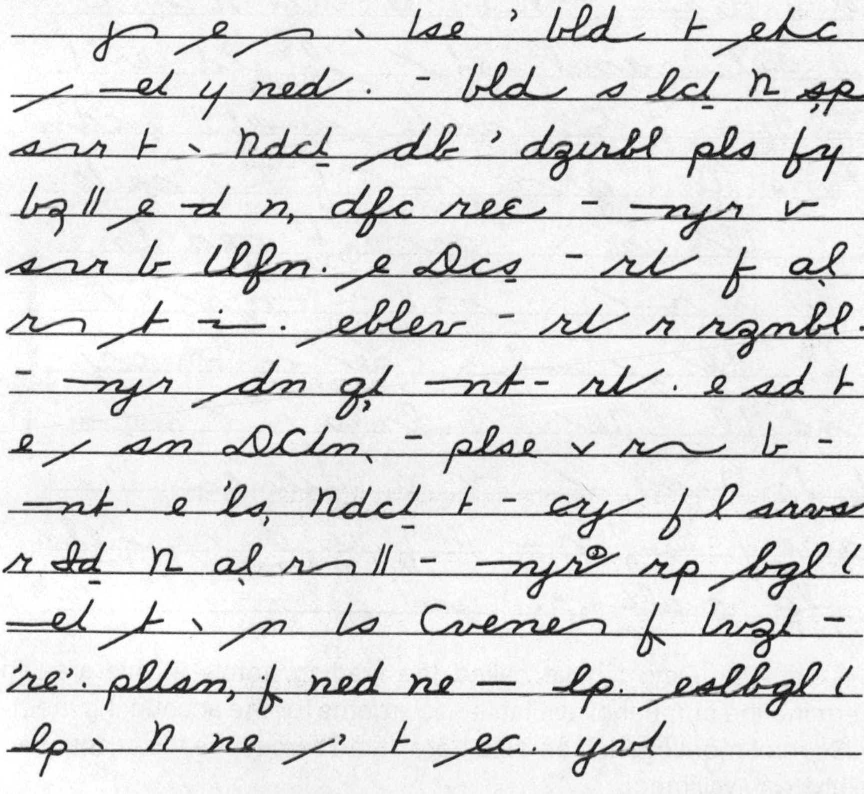

Gentlemen: We want you to see a building that we think will meet your needs. The building is located in the shopping (20) center that you indicated would be a desirable place for your business.

We had no difficulty (40) reaching the manager of the center by telephone. We discussed the rates for the annual rent with him. We (60) believe the rates are reasonable. The manager would not quote monthly rates. He said that he will soon discontinue (80) the policy of renting by the month. He also indicated that the charges for all services are (100) included in the annual rent.

The manager's representative will be glad to meet with you when it is (120) convenient for you to visit the area. Please let us know if you need any more help. We shall be glad to help (140) you in any way that we can. Yours very truly, (150)

Chapter 16 – Supplemental Letter 4

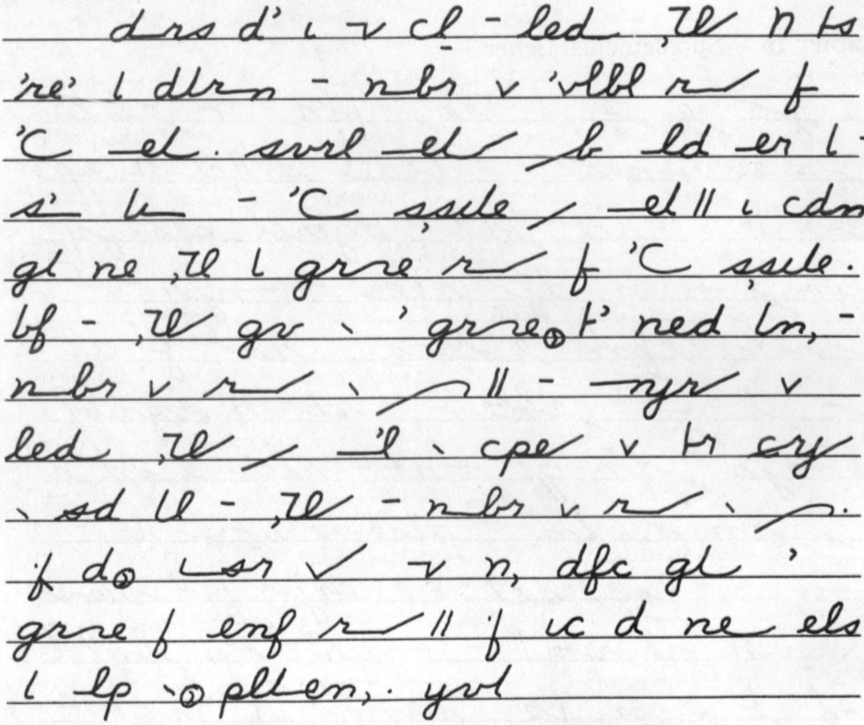

Dear Mrs. Day: I have called the leading hotels in this area to determine the number of available (20) rooms for the accounting meeting. Several meetings will be held here at the same time the accounting society (40) will meet.

I could not get any hotel to guarantee rooms for the accounting society. Before (60) the hotels give you a guarantee, they need to know the number of rooms you want.

The managers of leading hotels (80) will mail you copies of their charges. You should tell the hotels the number of rooms you want. If you do, I am (100) sure you will have no difficulty getting a guarantee for enough rooms.

If I can do anything else to (120) help you, please let me know. Yours very truly, (128)

Chapter 17 — Supplemental Letter

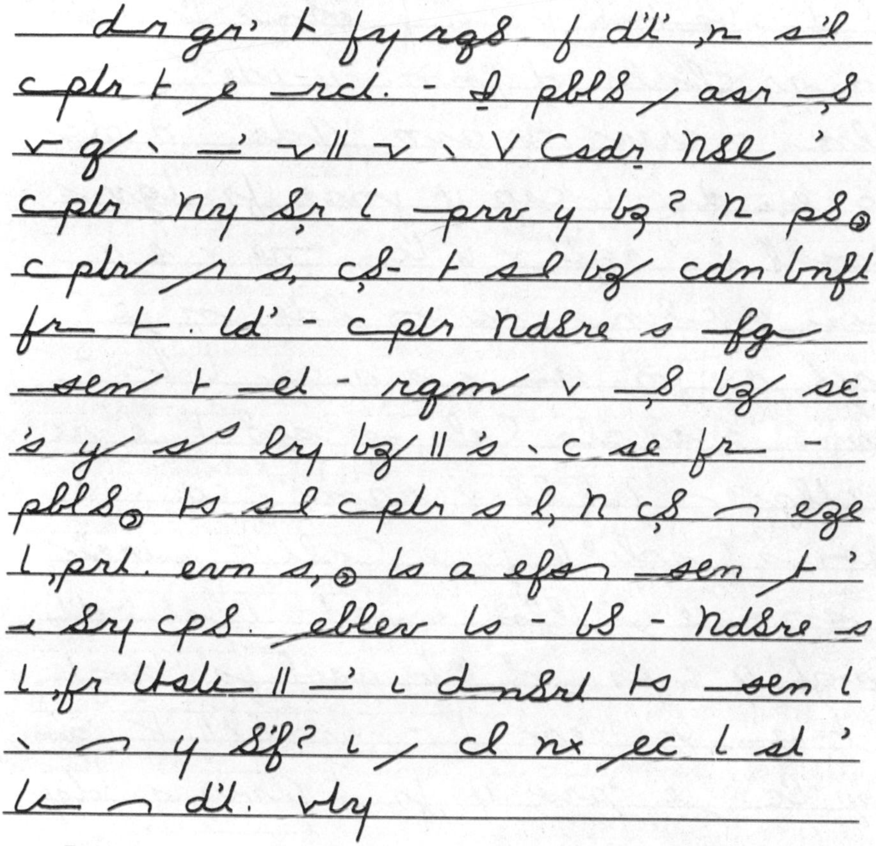

Dear Mr. Gray: Thank you for your request for data on the small computer that we market. The enclosed publicity (20) will answer most of the questions you may have.

Have you ever considered installing a computer (40) in your store to improve your business? In the past, computers were so costly that small businesses could not (60) benefit from them. Today the computer industry is manufacturing machines that meet the requirements (80) of most businesses such as yours as well as large businesses.

As you can see from the publicity, this small (100) computer is low in cost and easy to operate. Even so, it is an efficient machine with a high (120) storage capacity. We believe it is the best the industry has to offer at this time.

May I demonstrate (140) this machine to you and your staff? I will call next week to set a time and a date. Very truly yours, (160)

Chapter 18 — Supplemental Letter

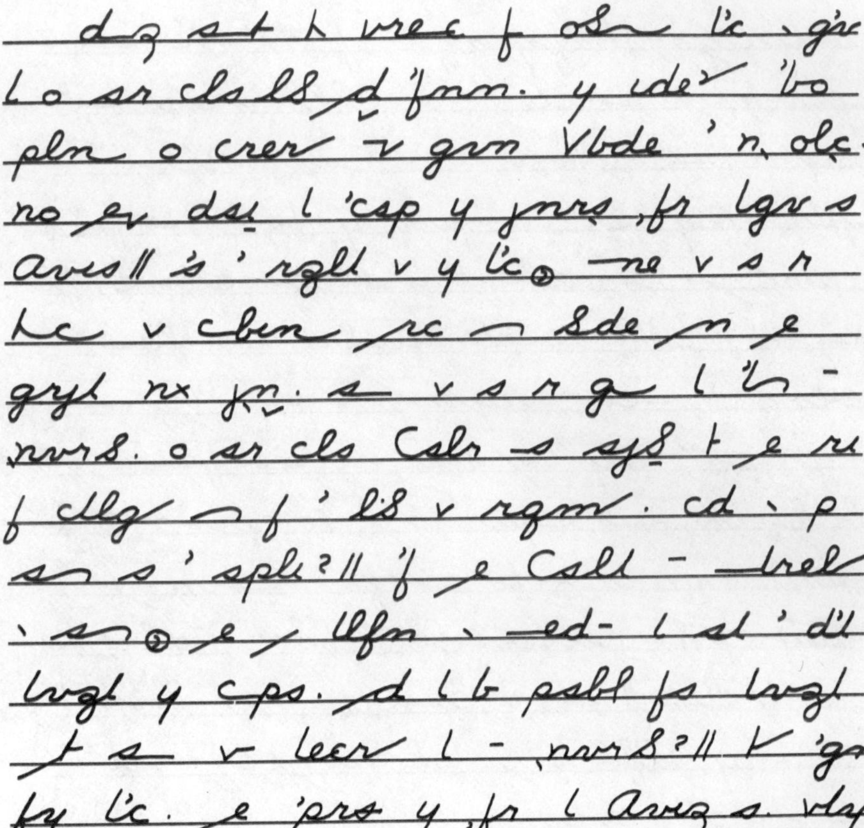

Dear Ms. Smith: Thank you very much for the outstanding talk you gave to our senior class last Wednesday afternoon. Your (20) ideas about planning our careers have given everybody a new outlook. Now we have decided to (40) accept your generous offer to give us advice.

As a result of your talk, many of us are thinking of (60) combining work and study when we graduate next June. Some of us are going to attend the university. (80) Our senior class counselor has suggested that we write for catalogs and for a list of requirements. Could you (100) please send us a supply?

After we consult the materials you send, we will telephone you immediately (120) to set a date to visit your campus. Would it be possible for us to visit with some of the teachers at (140) the university?

Thanks again for your talk. We appreciate your offer to advise us. Very truly yours, (161)

Chapter 19 — Supplemental Letter

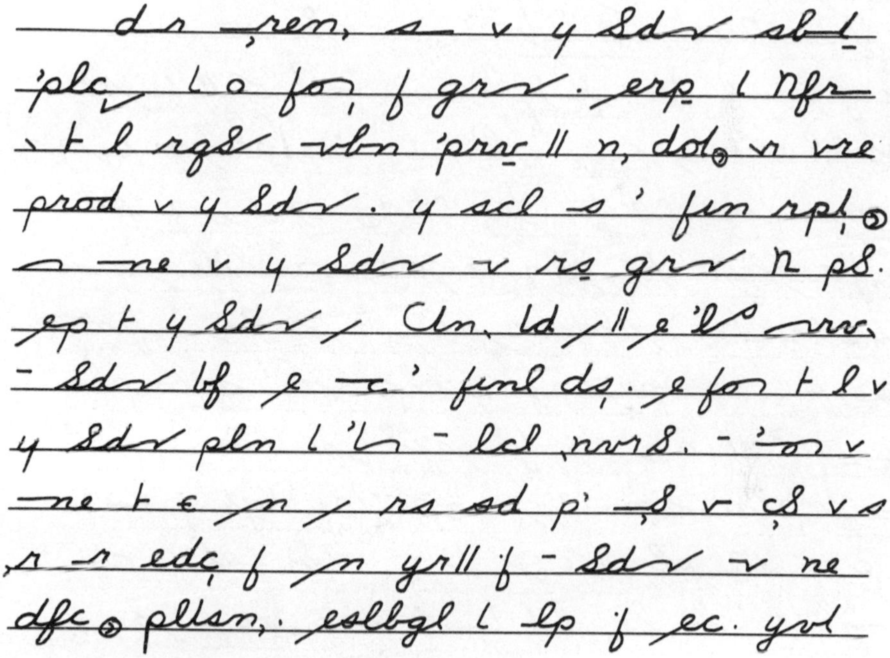

Dear Mr. Moreno: Some of your students submitted applications to our foundation for grants. We are pleased (20) to inform you that all requests have been approved.

No doubt, you are very proud of your students. Your school has a fine (40) reputation, and many of your students have received grants in the past. We hope that your students will continue to (60) do well.

We always interview the students before we make a final decision. We found that all of your (80) students plan to attend the local university. The amount of money that each one will receive should pay most (100) of the cost of his or her education for one year.

If the students have any difficulty, please let us (120) know. We shall be glad to help if we can. Yours very truly, (131)

Chapter 20 — Supplemental Letter 3

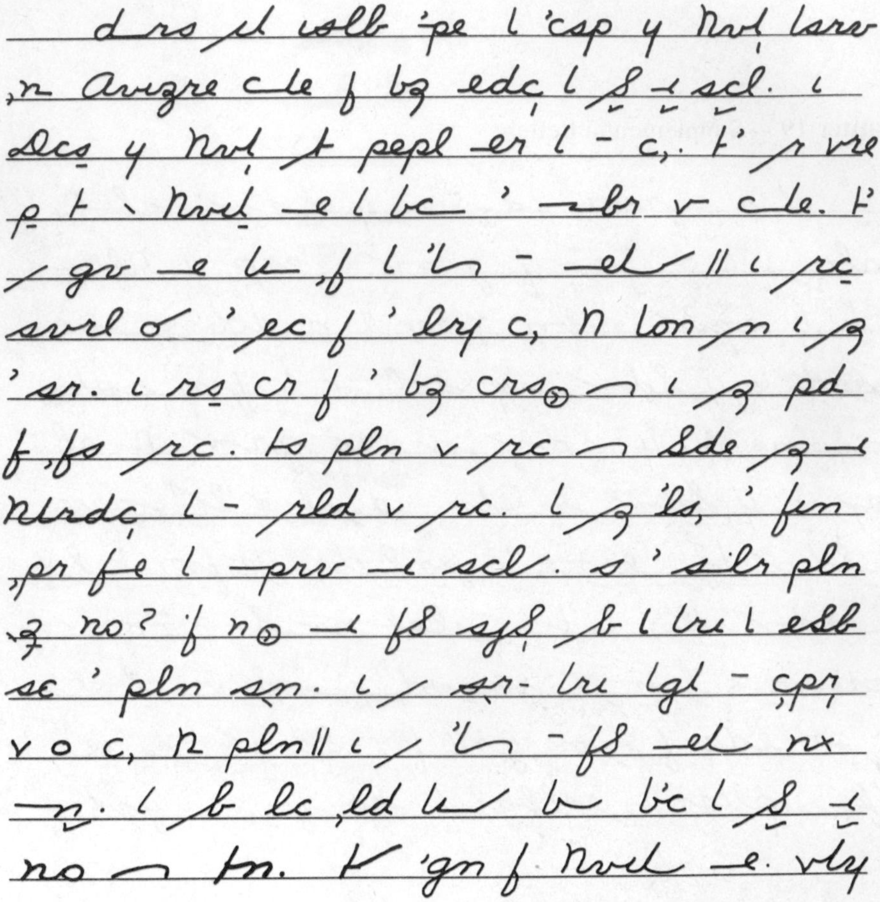

Dear Mrs. White: I shall be happy to accept your invitation to serve on the advisory committee (20) for business education at West High School. I discussed your invitation with people here at the company (40). They were very pleased that you invited me to become a member of the committee. They will give me time off (60) to attend the meetings.

I worked several hours a week for a large company in town when I was a senior (80). I received credit for a business course, and I was paid for the office work. This plan of work and study was my (100) introduction to the world of work. It was also a fine opportunity for me to improve my skills. Is (120) a similar plan used now? If not, my first suggestion will be to try to establish such a plan soon. I will (140) surely try to get the cooperation of our company in the plan.

I will attend the first meeting next (160) Monday. It will be like old times being back to West High now and then. Thanks again for inviting me. Very truly (180) yours, (181)

Chapter 20 — Supplemental Letter 4

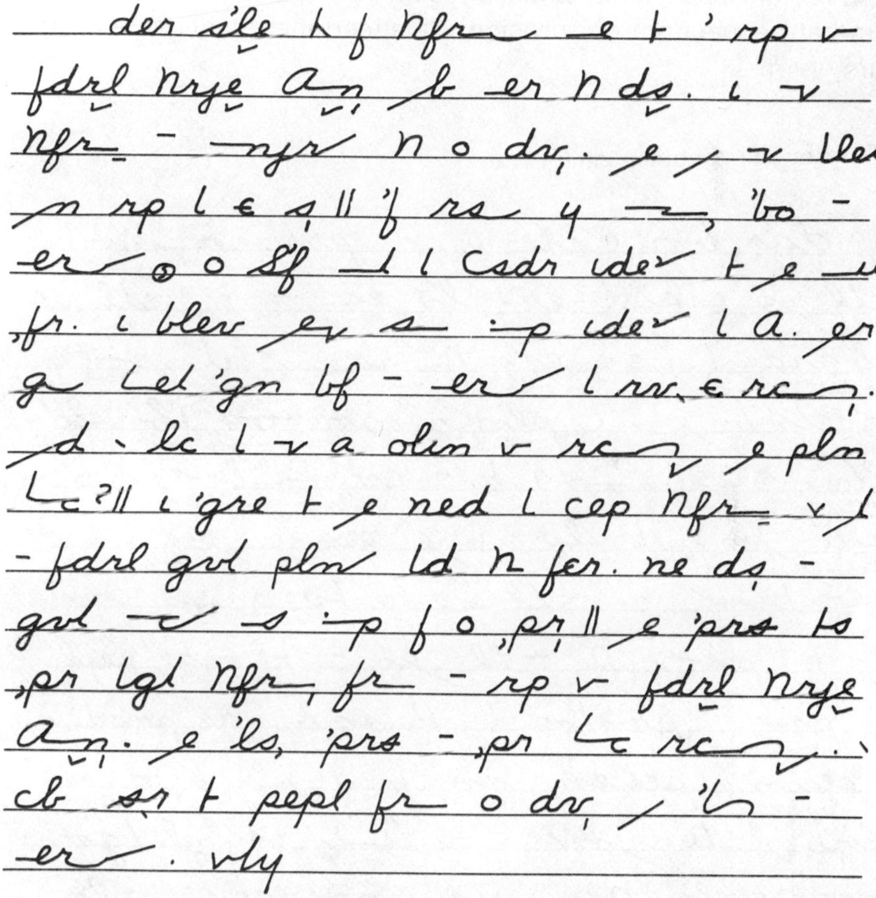

Dear Sally: Thank you for informing me that a representative of the Federal Energy Administration (20) will be here in December. I have informed the managers in our division. We will have at least one (40) representative at each session.

After receiving your memo about the hearings, our staff met to consider (60) ideas that we might offer. I believe we have some important ideas to add. We are going (80) to meet again before the hearings to review each recommendation. Would you like to have an outline of (100) the recommendations we plan to make?

I agree that we need to keep informed of what the federal government (120) plans to do in the future. Any decision the government makes has importance for our operation.

We (140) appreciate this opportunity to get information from the representative of the Federal (160) Energy Administration. We also appreciate the opportunity to make recommendations. (180) You can be sure that people from our division will attend the hearings. Very truly yours, (197)

Chapter 21 — Supplemental Letter

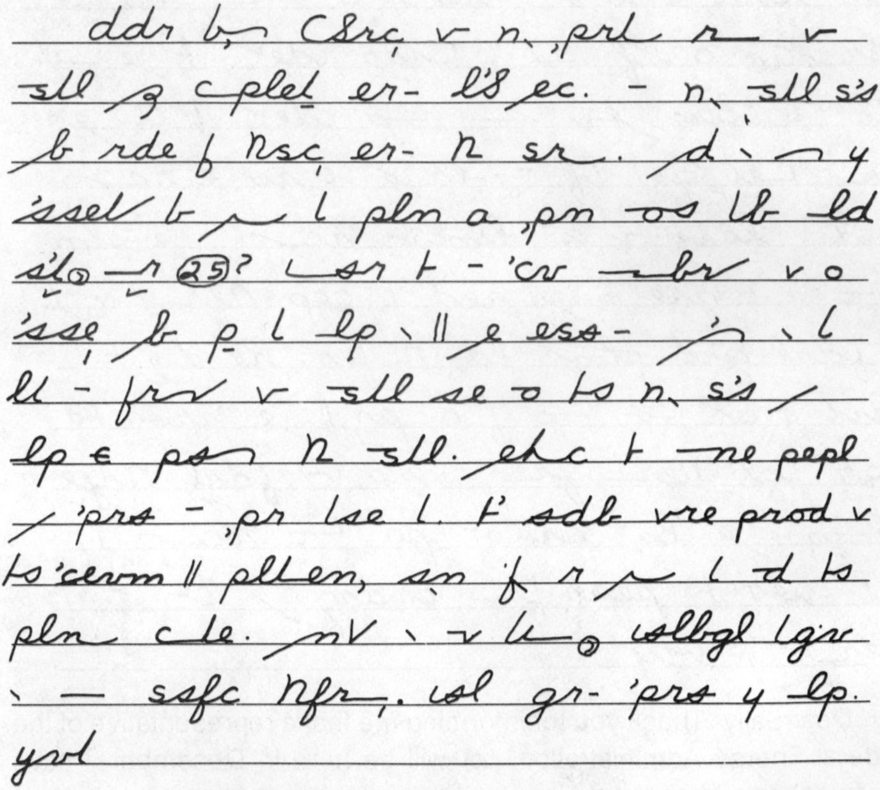

Dear Dr. Bond: Construction of the new operating room of the hospital was completed early last week. (20) The new hospital space will be ready for inspection early in the spring. Would you and your associates be (40) willing to plan an open house to be held Saturday, March 25? I am sure that the active members of (60) our association will be pleased to help you.

We especially want you to let the friends of the hospital (80) see how this new space will help each patient in the hospital. We think that many people will appreciate the (100) opportunity to see it. They should be very proud of this achievement.

Please let me know soon if you are willing (120) to head this planning committee. Whenever you have time, I shall be glad to give you more specific information. (140) I shall greatly appreciate your help. Yours very truly, (152)

Chapter 22 — Supplemental Letter

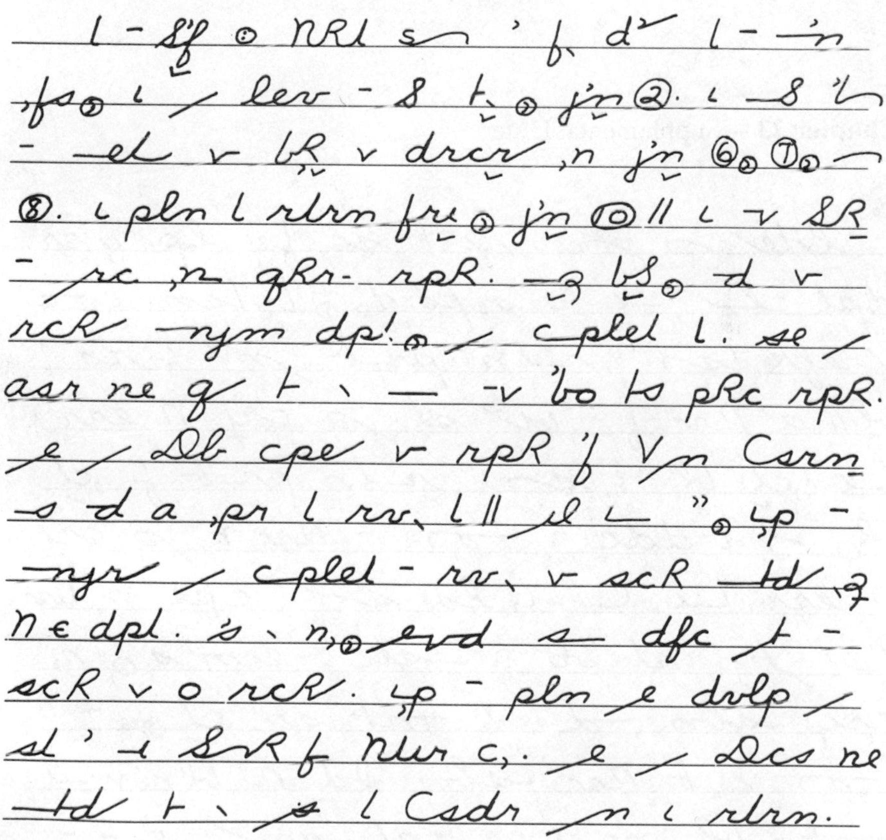

To the Staff: In order to spend a few days at the main office, I will leave the city Thursday, January 2. I (20) must attend the meeting of the Board of Directors on January 6, 7, and 8. I plan to return (40) Friday, January 10.

I have started the work on the quarterly report. Ms. Doot, head of the Records Management (60) Department, will complete it. She will answer any questions that you may have about this particular (80) report. We will distribute copies of the report after everyone concerned has had an opportunity to (100) review it.

While I am away, I hope the managers will complete the review of the security methods (120) used in each department. As you know, we have had some difficulty with the security of our records. I (140) hope the plan we develop will set a high standard for the entire company. We will discuss any methods that (160) you wish to consider when I return. (170)

Chapter 23 — Supplemental Letter

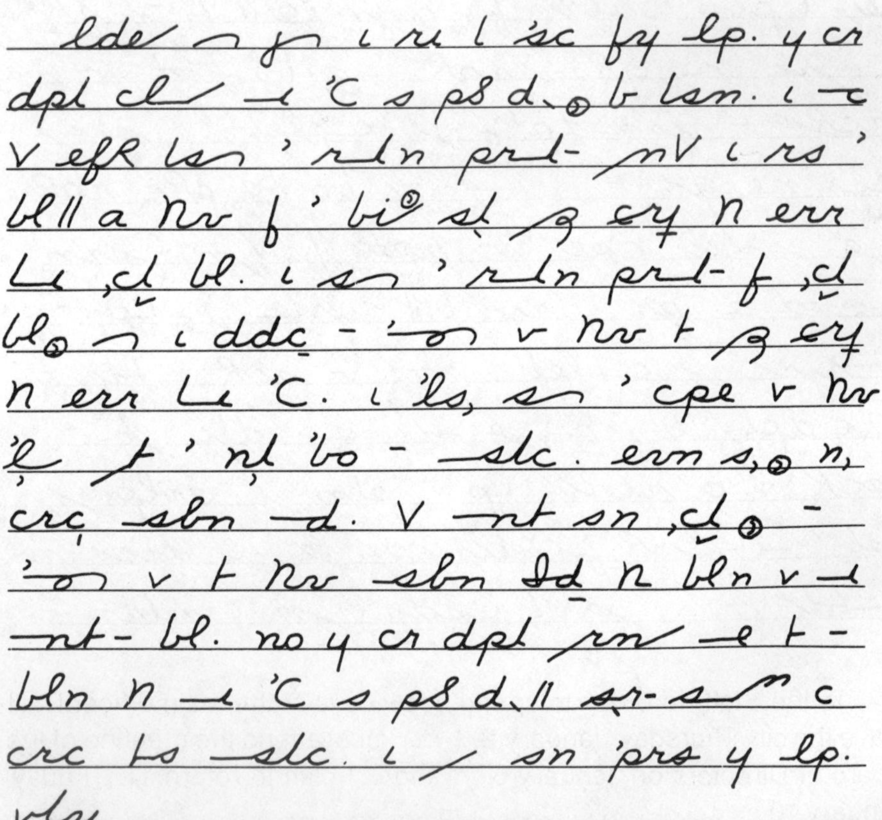

Ladies and Gentlemen: I write to ask for your help. Your credit department claims my account is past due, but it (20) is not. I make every effort to send a remittance promptly whenever I receive a bill.

An invoice for (40) a boy's suit was charged in error to my October bill. I sent a remittance promptly for the October bill, (60) and I deducted the amount of the invoice that was charged in error to my account. I also sent a (80) copy of the invoice along with a note about the mistake. Even so, no correction has been made. Every month (100) since October, the amount of that invoice has been included in the balance of my monthly bill. Now your (120) credit department warns me that the balance in my account is past due.

Surely someone can correct this mistake. I (140) will sincerely appreciate your help. Very truly yours, (151)

Chapter 24 – Supplemental Letter 3

_r r' _,ren,⊙ 're' eplim,fs⊙ 415 crc
S⊙ _ne'pls MN 55403-9001
d r _,ren, e / vre p l lrn t y
pln _sbn 'prv l ,rq a eplim,fs f
i scl Sd n 're'. _sr - pln /
bnfl bt Sd _ eplir ll 's, n,⊙
e epli _ne y_ pepl n pRol _ P.
i SR _i ,n bz crer n ts /'. i bg'n
t ' sr jb 's sc l - d bir f sR.
no _ rsnbl f eplim,fs f nler Sr.
svrl v o dpl d 'ls, bg'n tr bz crer
's p'Rol_ rcr ll ,p y ,fs b n ,pr er-
n sr. e / ned _ne pRol_ pepl l
lp t o ssl sr sl. e / 'ls, ned 'f.

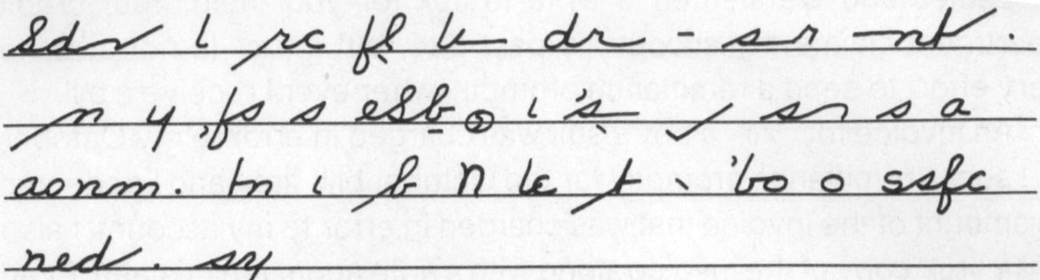

Mr. Ray Moreno, Area Employment Office, 415 Church Street, Minneapolis, MN 55403-9001

Dear Mr. Moreno: We were very pleased to learn that your plan has been approved to organize an employment (20) office for high school students in the area. I am sure the plan will benefit both students and employers. (40)

As you know, we employ many young people in part-time positions. I started my own business career in this (60) way. I began with a summer job as secretary to the head buyer for sportswear. Now I am responsible (80) for the employment office for the entire store. Several of our department heads also began their (100) business careers as part-time workers.

I hope your office will be in operation early in the spring. We will need (120) many part-time people to help with our special spring sale. We will also need a few students to work full time (140) during the summer months. When your office is established, I assume you will send us an announcement. Then I will be (160) in touch with you about our specific needs. Sincerely yours, (170)

Chapter 24 — Supplemental Letter 4

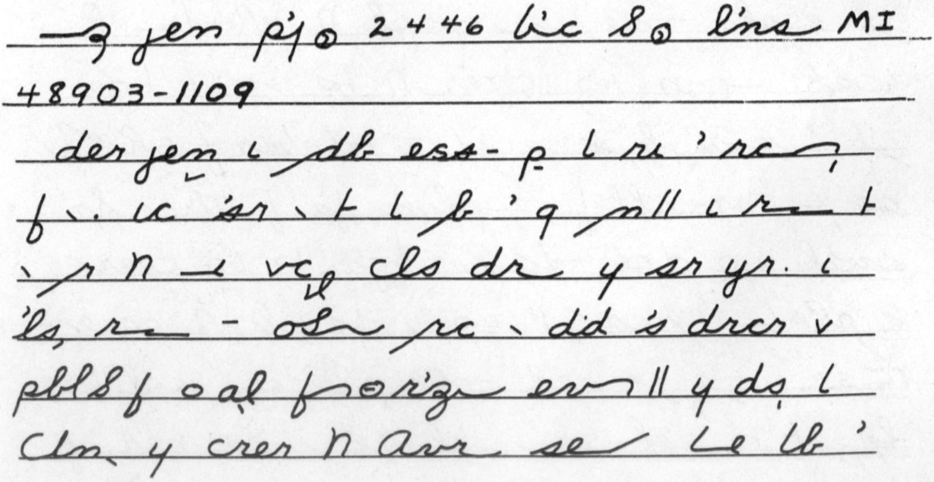

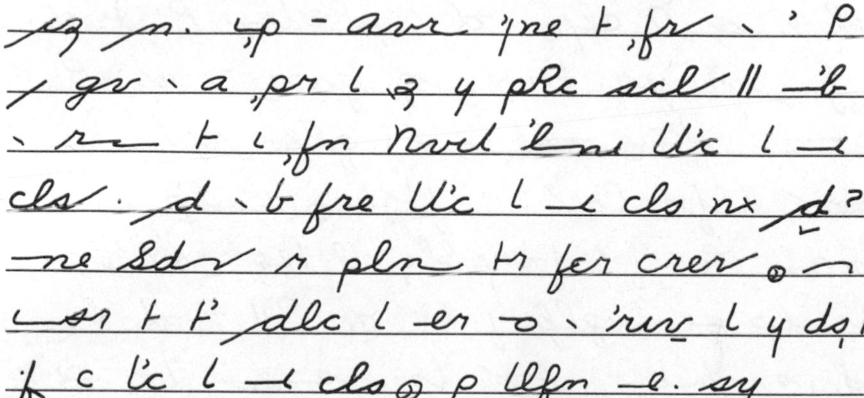

Ms. Jean Page, 2446 Bank Street, Lansing, MI 48903-1109

Dear Jean: I would be especially pleased to write a recommendation for you. I can assure you that it will (20) be a good one.

I remember that you were in my vocational class during your senior year. I also (40) remember the outstanding work you did as director of publicity for our annual fund-raising event. (60)

Your decision to continue your career in advertising seems to me to be a wise one. I hope the (80) advertising agency that offers you a position will give you an opportunity to use your (100) particular skills.

Maybe you remember that I often invite alumni to talk to my classes. Would you be (120) free to talk to my class next Wednesday? Many students are planning their future careers, and I am sure that they would (140) like to hear how you arrived at your decision.

If you can talk to my class, please telephone me. Sincerely yours, (160)

Chapter 25 — Supplemental Letter

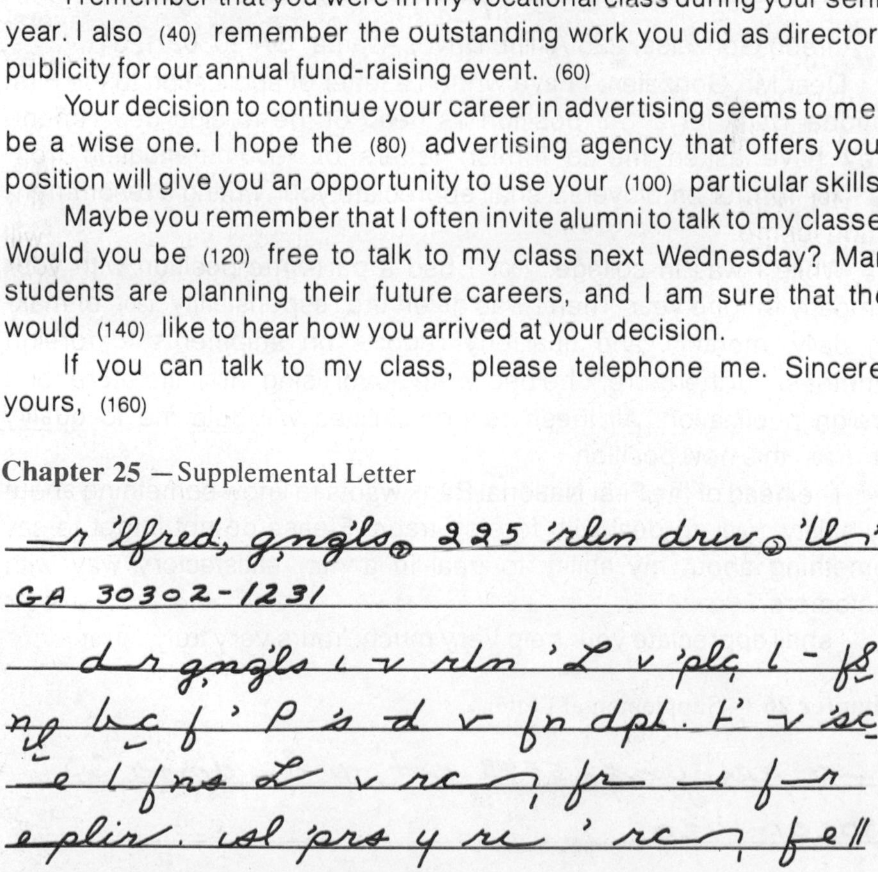

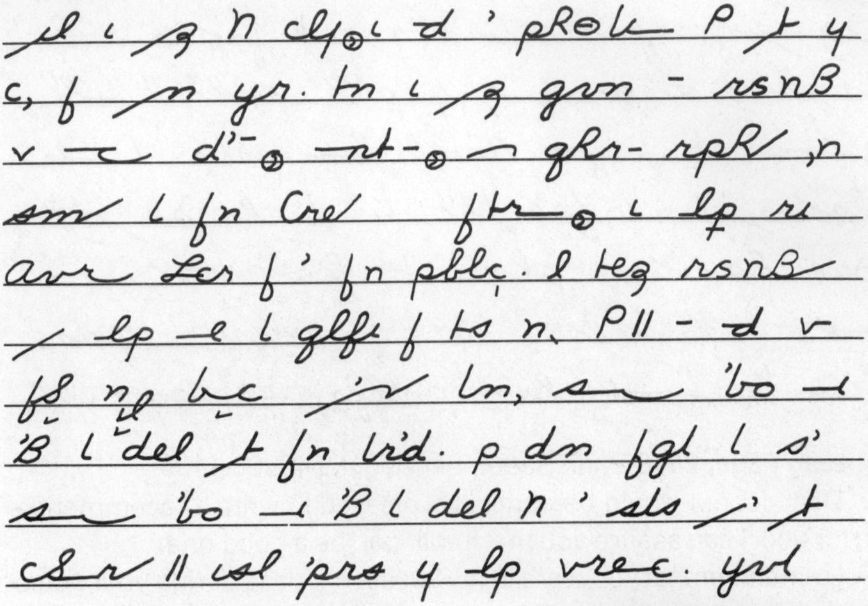

Mr. Alfredo Gonzales, 225 Airline Drive, Atlanta, GA 30302-1231

Dear Mr. Gonzales: I have written a letter of application to the First National Bank for a (20) position as head of the foreign department. They have asked me to furnish letters of recommendation from my (40) former employers. I shall appreciate your writing a recommendation for me.

While I was in college, (60) I had a part-time position with your company for one year. Then I was given the responsibility (80) of making daily, monthly, and quarterly reports on shipments to foreign countries. Furthermore, I helped write advertising (100) literature for a foreign publication. All these responsibilities will help me to qualify for (120) this new position.

The head of the First National Bank wants to know something about my ability (140) to deal with foreign trade. Please do not forget to say something about my ability to deal in a (160) satisfactory way with customers.

I shall appreciate your help very much. Yours very truly, (178)

Chapter 26 — Supplemental Letter

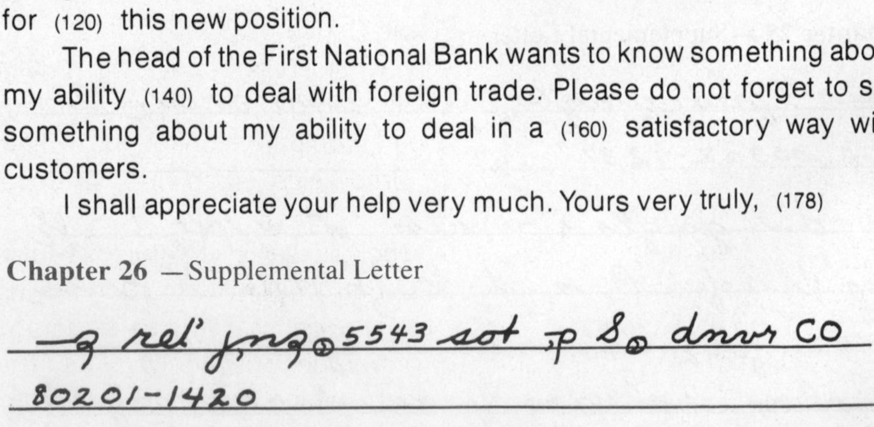

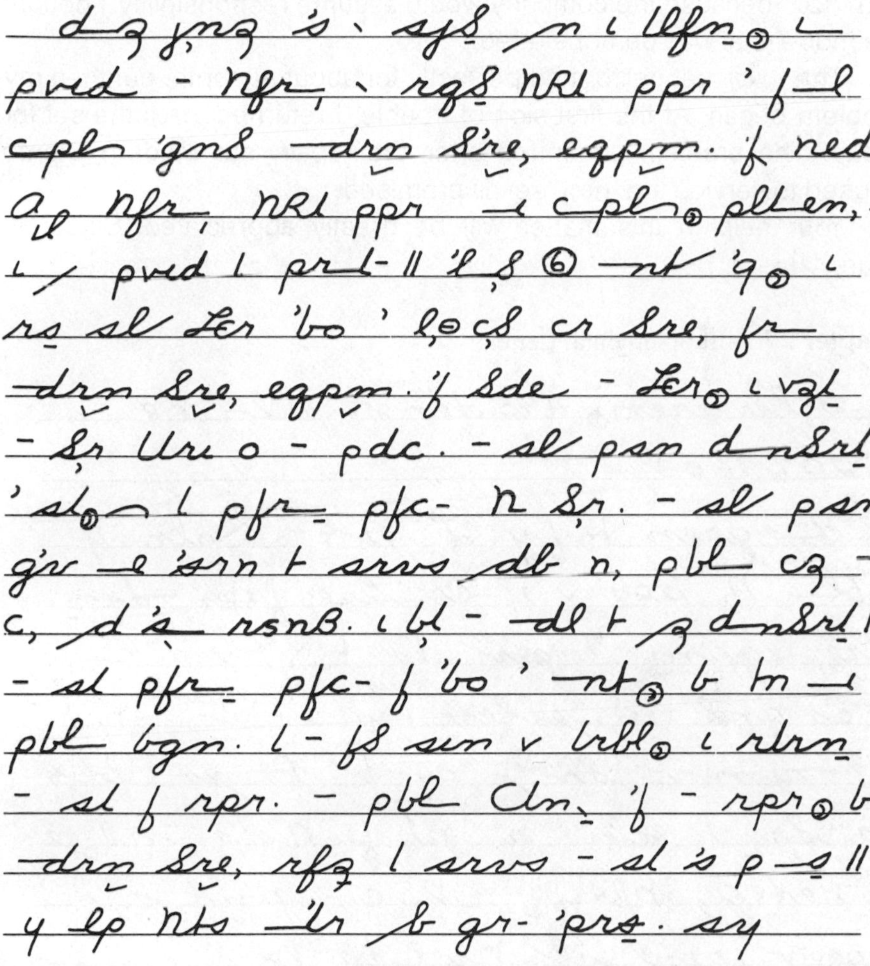

Ms. Rita Jones, 5543 South Hope Street, Denver, CO 80201-1420

Dear Ms. Jones: As you suggested when I telephoned, I am providing the information you requested in (20) order to prepare a formal complaint against Modern Stereo Equipment. If you need additional (40) information in order to prepare my complaint, please let me know. I will provide it promptly.

Almost six months ago, (60) I received sales literature about a low-cost car stereo from Modern Stereo Equipment. After (80) studying the literature, I visited the store to try out the product. The sales person demonstrated (100) a set, and it performed perfectly in the store. The sales person gave me assurance that service would be no problem (120) because the company would assume responsibility. I bought the model that was demonstrated.

The (140) set performed perfectly for about a month, but then my problem began. At the first sign of trouble, I returned (160) the set for repair. The problem continued after the repair, but Modern Stereo refused to service the (180) set as promised.

Your help in this matter will be greatly appreciated. Sincerely yours, (196)

Chapter 27 — Supplemental Letter

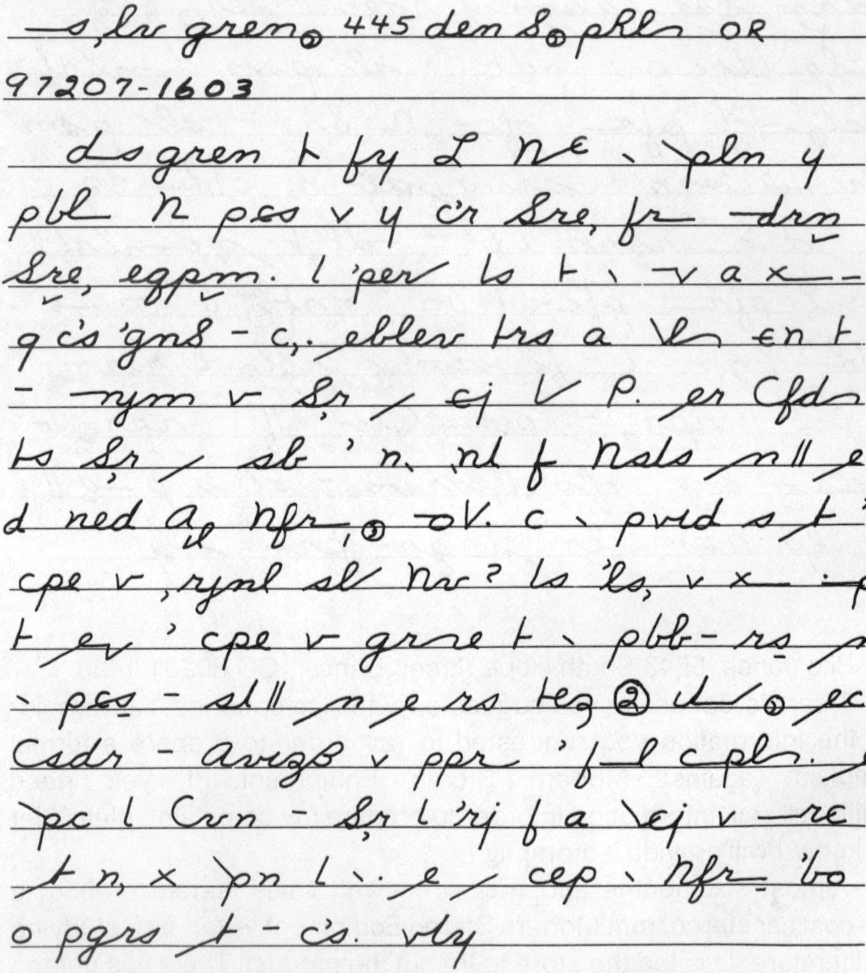

Miss Olive Green, 445 Dean Street, Portland, OR 97207-1603

Dear Miss Green: Thank you for your letter in which you explain your problem in the purchase of your car stereo from (20) Modern Stereo Equipment. It appears to us that you have an extremely good case against the company. (40) We believe there is an excellent chance that the management of the store will change its position. We are confident (60) this store will substitute a new unit for the unsatisfactory one.

We do need additional (80) information, however. Can you provide us with a copy of the original sales invoice? It is also (100) of extreme importance that we have a copy of the guarantee that you probably received when you purchased (120) the set.

When we receive these two items, we can consider the advisability of preparing a formal (140) complaint. We expect to convince the store to arrange for an exchange of merchandise with no extra expense (160) to you. We will keep you informed about our progress with the case. Very truly yours, (175)

Chapter 28 — Supplemental Letter 3

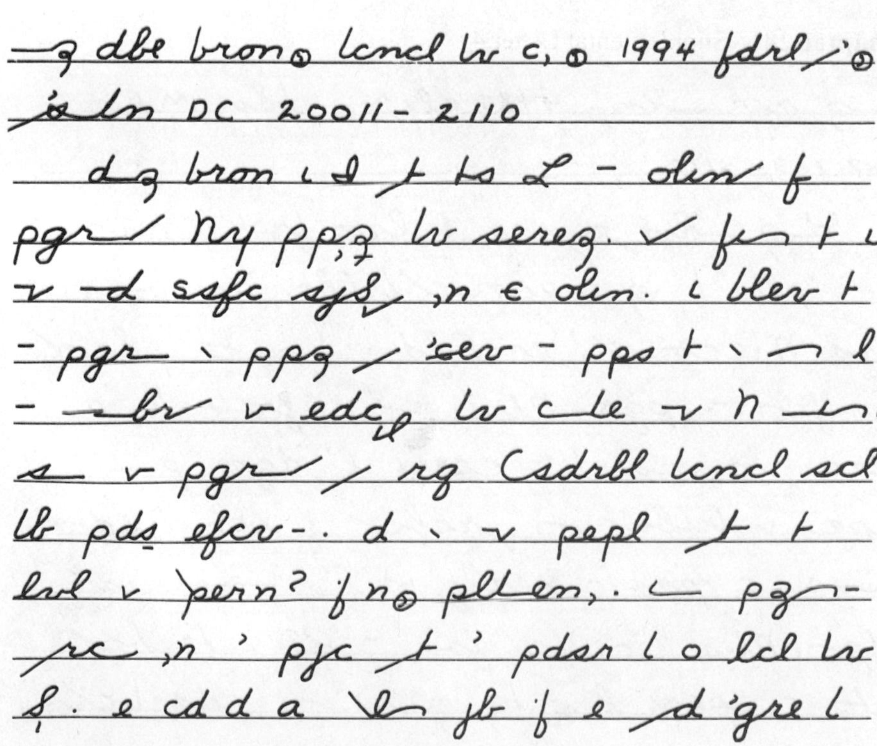

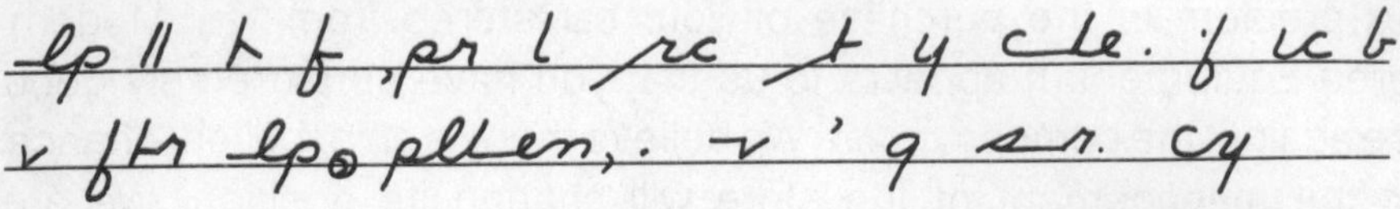

Ms. Debby Brown, Technical Television Company, 1994 Federal Way, Washington, DC 20011-2110

Dear Ms. Brown: I enclose with this letter the outlines for the programs in your proposed television series. You (20) will find that I have made specific suggestions on each outline. I believe that the program you propose will (40) achieve the purpose that you and all the members of the educational television committee have in mind. (60)

Some of the programs will require considerable technical skill to be produced effectively. Do you have (80) people with that level of experience? If not, please let me know. I am presently working on a project (100) with a producer at our local television station. He could do an excellent job if he would agree (120) to help.

Thank you for the opportunity to work with your committee. If I can be of further help, please let (140) me know. Have a good summer. Cordially yours, (148)

Chapter 28 — Supplemental Letter 4

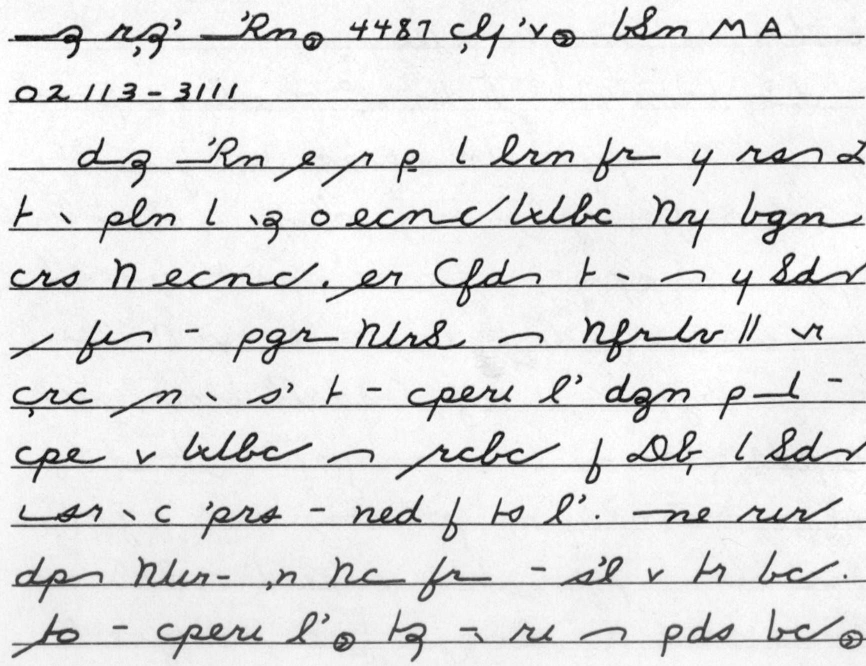

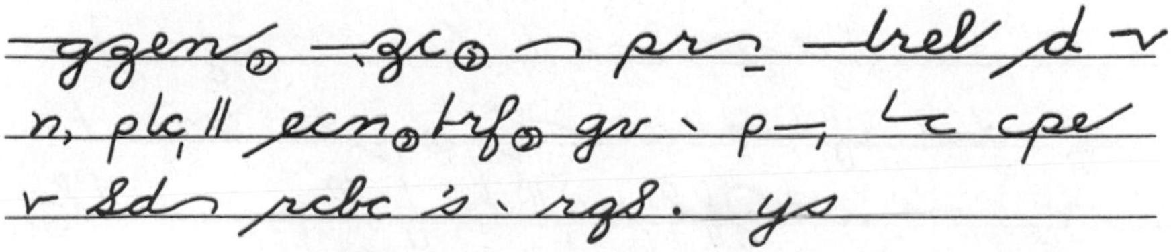

Ms. Rosa Martin, 4487 College Avenue, Boston, MA 02113-3111

Dear Ms. Martin: We were pleased to learn from your recent letter that you plan to use our economics textbook in (20) your beginning course in economics. We are confident that you and your students will find the program interesting (40) and informative.

You are correct when you say that the copyright law does not permit the copying of (60) textbooks and workbooks for distribution to students. I am sure you can appreciate the need for this law. Many (80) writers depend entirely on income from the sale of their books. Without the copyright law, those who write and (100) produce books, magazines, music, and printed materials would have no protection.

We cannot, therefore, give you (120) permission to make copies of the student workbook as you request. Yours sincerely, (135)

Chapter 29 — Supplemental Letter

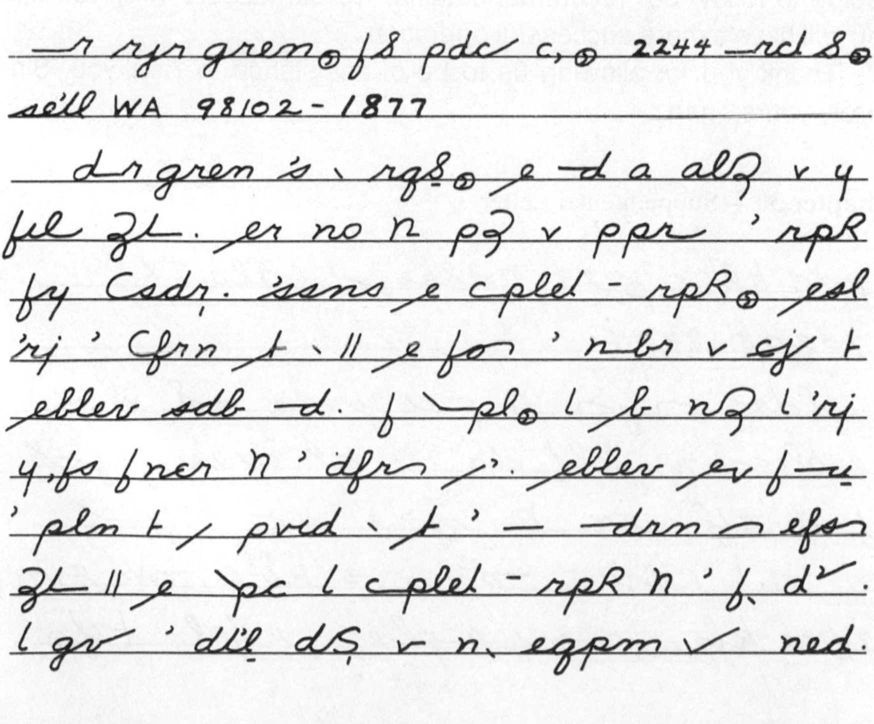

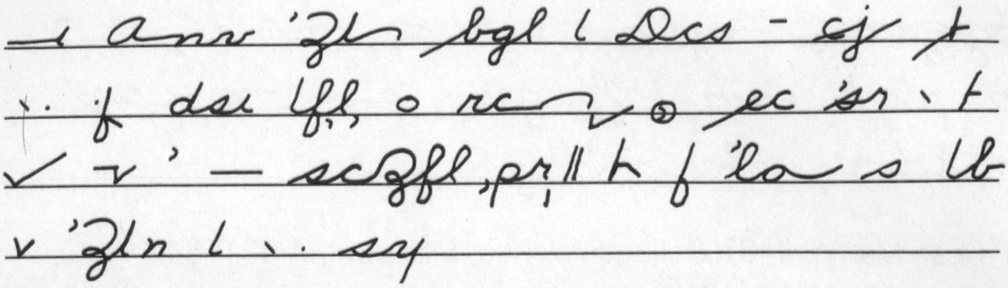

Mr. Roger Green, Forest Products Company, 2244 Market Street, Seattle, WA 98102-1877

Dear Mr. Green: As you requested, we made an analysis of your filing system. We are now in the process (20) of preparing a report for your consideration. As soon as we complete the report, we shall arrange (40) a conference with you.

We found a number of changes that we believe should be made. For example, it will be (60) necessary to arrange your office furniture in a different way. We believe we have formulated (80) a plan that will provide you with a more modern and efficient system.

We expect to complete the report in a (100) few days. It gives a detailed description of the new equipment you will need. My administrative (120) assistant will be glad to discuss the changes with you. If you decide to follow our recommendations, we can assure (140) you that you will have a more successful operation.

Thank you for allowing us to be of assistance to (160) you. Sincerely yours, (164)

Chapter 30 — Supplemental Letter

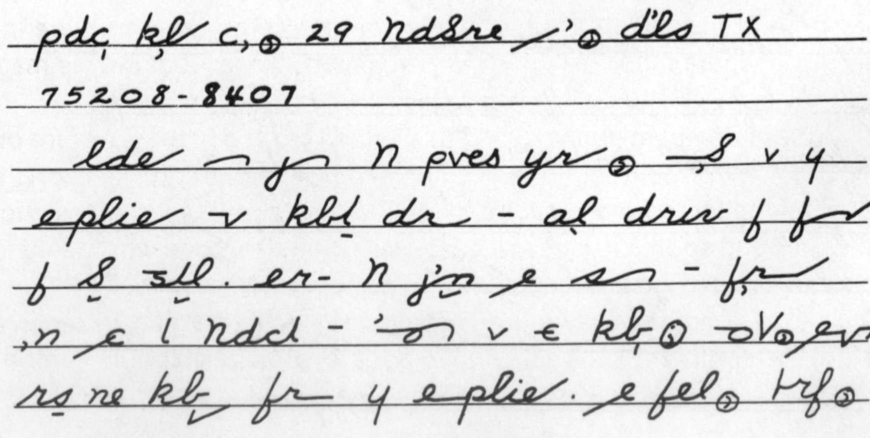

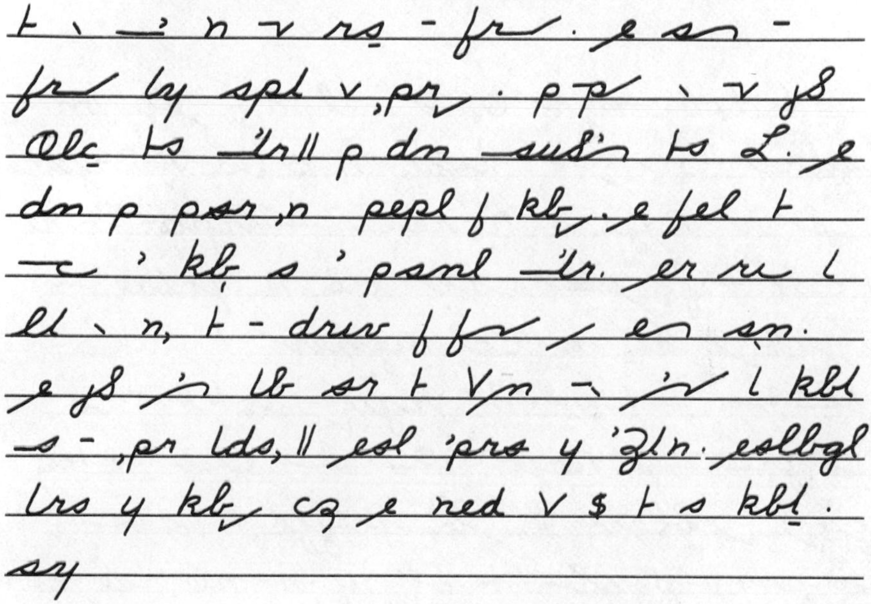

Production Controls Company, 29 Industry Way, Dallas, TX 75208-8407

Ladies and Gentlemen: In previous years, most of your employees have contributed during the annual (20) drive for funds for City Hospital. Early in January we sent the forms on which to indicate the amount (40) of each contribution; however, we have not received any contributions from your employees. We feel, (60) therefore, that you may not have received the forms. We sent the forms to your superintendent of operations. Perhaps (80) you have just overlooked this matter.

Please do not misunderstand this letter. We do not put pressure on people (100) for contributions. We feel that making a contribution is a personal matter. We are writing to (120) let you know that the drive for funds will end soon. We just want to be sure that everyone who wants to contribute has (140) the opportunity to do so.

We shall appreciate your assistance. We shall be glad to receive your (160) contributions because we need every dollar that is contributed. Sincerely yours, (175)

ter 31 — Supplemental Memorandum

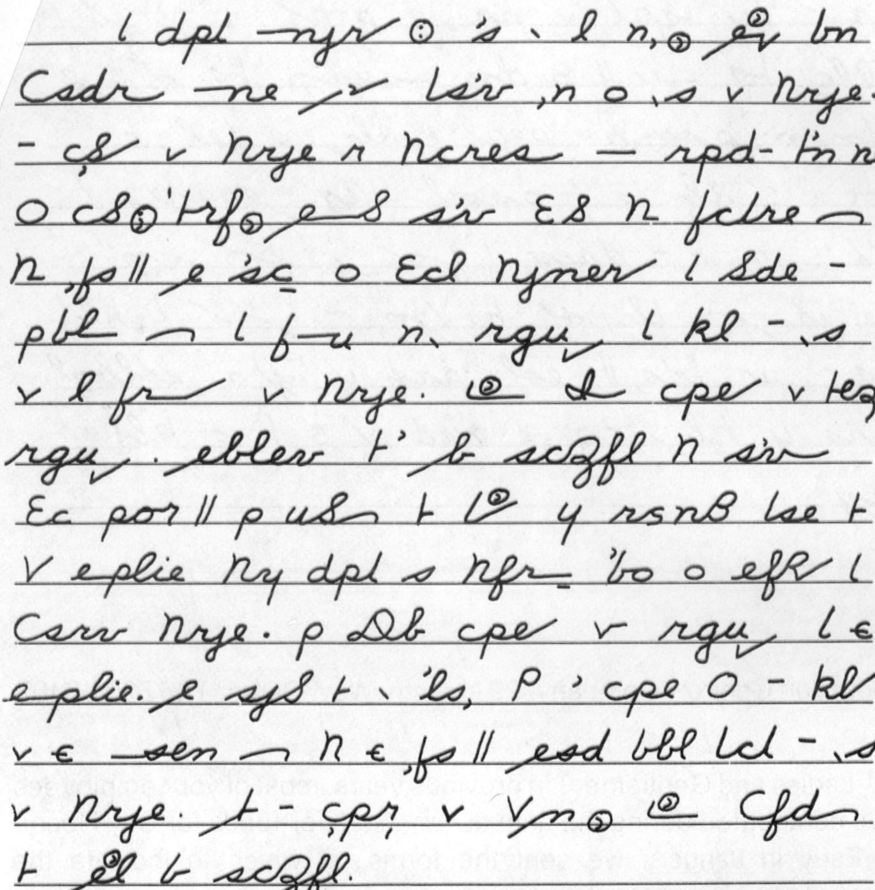

To Department Managers: As you all know, we've been considering many ways to save on our use of energy. (20) The costs of energy are increasing more rapidly than any other cost; therefore, we must save electricity (40) in the factory and in the office.

We asked our electrical engineers to study the problem (60) and to formulate new regulations to control the use of all forms of energy. I'm enclosing copies (80) of these regulations. We believe they will be successful in saving electric power.

Please understand that (100) it's your responsibility to see that every employee in your department is informed about our efforts (120) to conserve energy. Please distribute copies of the regulations to each employee. We suggest that (140) you also post a copy over the controls of each machine and in each office.

We should be able to cut (160) the use of energy. With the cooperation of everyone, I'm confident that we'll be successful. (179)

Chapter 32 — Supplemental Letter 3

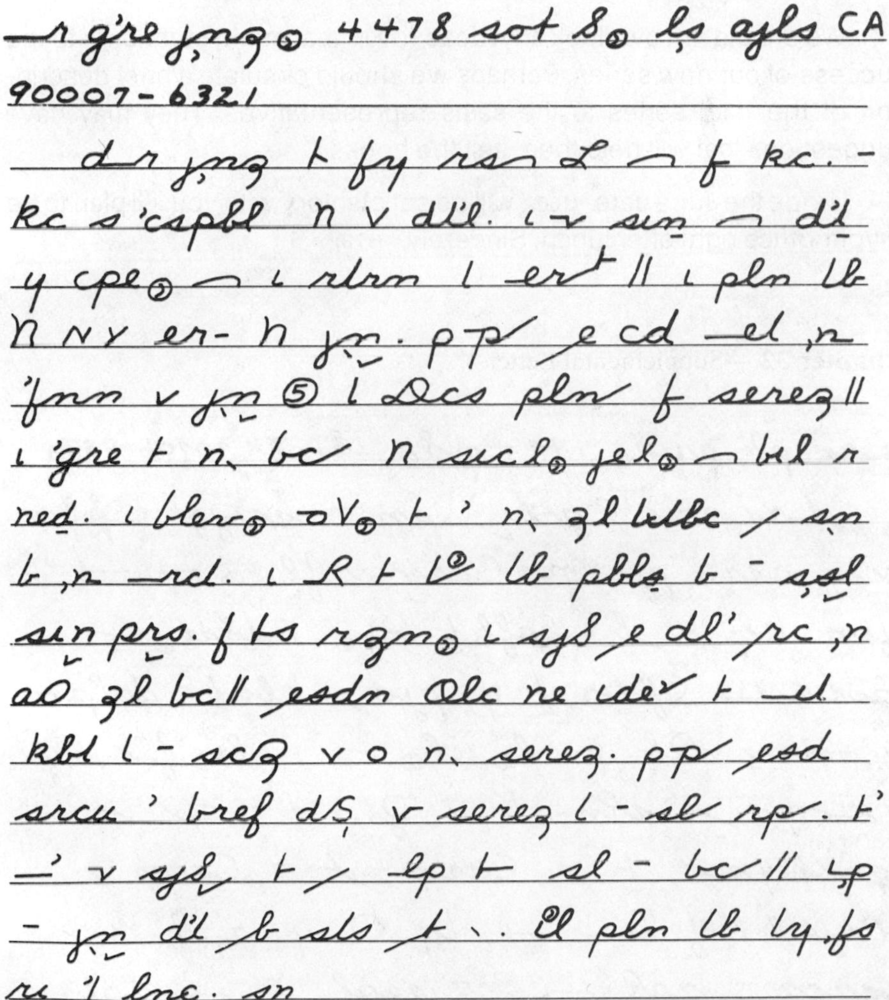

Mr. Gary Jones, 4478 South Street, Los Angeles, CA 90007-6321

Dear Mr. Jones: Thank you for your recent letter and for the contract. The contract is acceptable in every (20) detail. I have signed and dated your copy, and I return it herewith.

lan to be in New York early in (40) June. Perhaps we could meet afternoon of June 5 to discuss plans for the series.

agree that new books (60) in psychology, geology, and biology needed. I believe, however, that a new zoology (80) textbook will n be on the market. I heard that it's to be published by the Social ience Press. For this (100) reason, I suggest we delay work on other zoology book.

We should not overlook any ideas (120) that might contribute to the success of our new series. Perhaps we should circulate a brief description of the (140) series to the sales representatives. They may have suggestions that will help them sell the books.

I hope the June date (160) will be satisfactory with you. I'll plan to be at your office right after lunch. Sincerely, (178)

Chapter 32 — Supplemental Letter 4

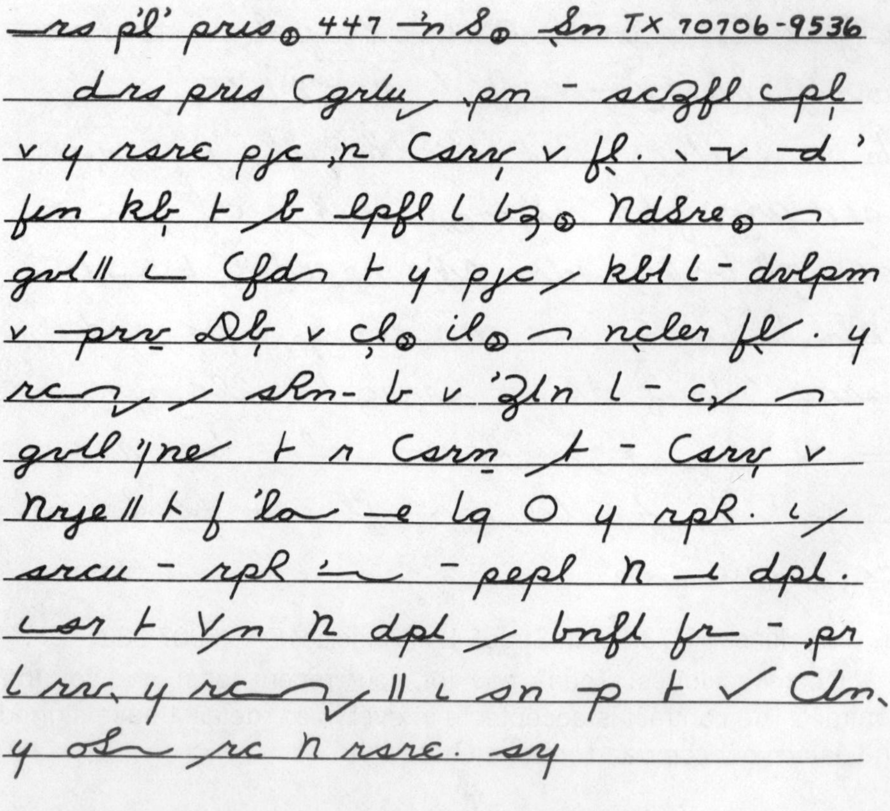

Mrs. Paula Price, 447 Main Street, Houston, TX 70706-9536

Dear Mrs. Price: Congratulations upon the successful completion of your research project on the (20) conservation of fuel. You have made a fine contribution that will be helpful to business, industry, and government. (40)

I am confident that your project will contribute to the development of improved distribution of (60) coal, oil, and nuclear fuels. Your recommendations will certainly be of assistance to the companies (80) and governmental agencies that are concerned with the conservation of energy.

Thank you for allowing (100) me to go over your report. I will circulate the report among the people in my department. I am (120) sure that everyone in the department will benefit from the opportunity to review your recommendations (140).

I sincerely hope that you will continue your outstanding work in research. Sincerely yours, (157)

APPENDIX B

Abbreviations and Symbols

States, Districts, and Territories

Canadian Provinces and Territories

Summary of Writing Principles—Eight Sentences

Letter Sample—Block Style

List of Phrases

STANDARD ABBREVIATIONS

approximate (approx.)	'prx	manufacture (mfg.)	—fq
avenue (ave.)	'v	memorandum (memo)	—,
certificate (cert.)	sR	Mr.	—r
Company (Co.)(company)	c,	Mrs.	—rs
credit (cr)	cr	Ms.	—z
debit (dr)	dr	purchase order (P.O.)	p,
department (dept.)	dpl	regard (re)	re
doctor (Dr.)	dr	represent (rep.)	rp
estimate (est.)	e8	representative (rep.)	rp
et cetera (etc.)	elc	secretary (sec.)	sc
executive (exec.)	\c	senior (Sr.)	sr
gentlemen (gent.)	jn	signature (sig.)	sig
government (govt.)	gvl	stenographer (steno)	Sn,
Incorporated (Inc.)	nc	street (St.)	S
invoice (inv.)	nv	substitute (sub.)	sb
junior (Jr.)	jr	superintendent (supt.)	spl
laboratory (lab.)	l'b	television (TV)	tv
Limited (Ltd.)	lld	year (yr.)	yr

STANDARD SYMBOLS*

Celsius	C	dollar	$
centimeter/centimetre	cm	dollars	$
degree	°	gram	g

*The metric symbols represent both singular and plural forms of the terms.

kilogram	kg	meter/metre	m
kilometer/kilometre	km	milligram	mg
liter/litre	L	millimeter/millimetre	mm

ABBREVIATED WORDS

about	'bo	correspondence	crs	importance	—p
accept	'csp	difficult	dfc	important	—p
acknowledge	'c	difficulty	dfc	inquire	Nq
administer	a—n	distribute	Db	is	s
advertise	avr	do	d	it	l
after	'f	each	€	like	lc
all	l	establish	esb	merchandise	—r€
am	—	extra	x	more	—
and	⌒	extreme	x—	necessary	nz
any	ne	first	fs	next	nx
appreciate	'pr	for	f	not	n
are	r	glad	gl	of	v
as	's	go	g	opportunity	,pr
at	l	good	g	order	R
be	b	great	gr	organization	,rg
because	cz	has	's	organize	,rg
business	bz	have	⌐v	our	o
but	b	he	e	out	o
by/bye	b	his	s	particular	pRc
can	c	hour	o	please	p
correspond	crs	immediate	-ed	practical	prc

principal	prin	satisfactory	sls	that	t (crossed)
principle	prin	satisfy	sls	the	—
put	p	ship	s (crossed)	to	t
quantity	q'n	short	s (crossed)	us	s
question	q	side	si	well	/
receive	rs	sincere	sn	will	/
remember	r—	sincerely	sn	write	ri
require	rq	suggest	sjs	you	`
right	ri	thank	t (crossed)	your	y

ABBREVIATIONS FOR DAYS AND MONTHS

Sunday (Sun.)	sn	January (Jan.)	jn
Monday (Mon.)	—n	February (Feb.)	fb
Tuesday (Tue.)	t	March (Mar.)	—r
Wednesday (Wed.)	d	April (Apr.)	'pr
Thursday (Thu.)	t (crossed)	May	—
Friday (Fri.)	fri	June	jn
Saturday (Sat.)	st	July (Jul.)	jl
		August (Aug.)	'g
		September (Sep.)	sp
		October (Oct.)	'ct
		November (Nov.)	nv
		December (Dec.)	ds

STATES, DISTRICTS, AND TERRITORIES

Alabama	AL	Montana	MT
Alaska	AK	Nebraska	NE
Arizona	AZ	Nevada	NV
Arkansas	AR	New Hampshire	NH
California	CA	New Jersey	NJ
Colorado	CO	New Mexico	NM
Connecticut	CT	New York	NY
Delaware	DE	North Carolina	NC
District of Columbia	DC	North Dakota	ND
Florida	FL	Ohio	OH
Georgia	GA	Oklahoma	OK
Guam	GU	Oregon	OR
Hawaii	HI	Pennsylvania	PA
Idaho	ID	Puerto Rico	PR
Illinois	IL	Rhode Island	RI
Indiana	IN	South Carolina	SC
Iowa	IA	South Dakota	SD
Kansas	KS	Tennessee	TN
Kentucky	KY	Texas	TX
Louisiana	LA	Utah	UT
Maine	ME	Vermont	VT
Maryland	MD	Virginia	VA
Massachusetts	MA	Virgin Islands	VI
Michigan	MI	Washington	WA
Minnesota	MN	West Virginia	WV
Mississippi	MS	Wisconsin	WI
Missouri	MO	Wyoming	WY

CANADIAN PROVINCES AND TERRITORIES

Alberta	AB	Nova Scotia	NS
British Columbia	BC	Ontario	ON
Labrador	LB	Prince Edward Island	PE
Manitoba	MB	Quebec	PQ
New Brunswick	NB	Saskatchewan	SK
Newfoundland	NF	Yukon Territory	YT
Northwest Territories	NT		

SUMMARY OF WRITING PRINCIPLES

Sound or Sound Combination	Expressed by		Illustrations		Text Chapter
a	'		paper	p'pr	2
ad (p)[1]	a		adverse	avrs	11
an (p)	a		answer	asr	13
awa (p)	"		await	"l	7
ax-ex-ox (p)	\		axle	\l	27
be-de-re (p)	b-d-r		belief	blef	9
bility (s)[2]	B		ability	'B	25
c (hard)	c		case	c's	3
c (soft)	s		face	f's	3
cess-cis-sess-sis-sus-sys	3		basis	b'3	29
ch	€		chase	€'s	10
sity-city (s)	S	(d)[3]	publicity	pblS	17
con-coun-count(p)	C		confer	Cfr	7
contr (p)	k		control	kl	30
ct (ending)	c		fact	f'c	21
dis-des (p)	D		discuss	Dcs	13
ed (past tense)	–		asked	'sc̲	6
e (long)	e		feel	fel	1
e (short)			fell	fl	1
electr (p)	E		electric	Ec	31

[1](p) = prefix
[2](s) = suffix
[3](d) = disjoined

SUMMARY OF WRITING PRINCIPLES

Sound or Sound Combination	Expressed by		Illustrations		Text Chapter
in-en-un (p)	n		envy	nve	6
incl-enclose (p)	I		include	Id	14
ever-every (p) or (s)	V	(d)	everybody	V b,de	15
for-fore-fer-fur (p)	f	(d)	forget	fgl	25
g (soft)-j	j		edge	ej	6
h	–		her	–r	9
i (long)	ı		sign	sin	1
i (short)	·		did	did	2
itis-icitis (s)	I	(d)	appendicitis	'pnI	31
ing-thing (s)	‿		seeing se‿	nothing n‿	11
instr (p)	N	(d)	instrument	Nm	21
k	c		keep	cp	3
letter-liter (p)	L		literal	Ll	25
ly (s)	-	(d)	nearly	ner-	14
m	—		mine	—in	5
ment	m		comment	cm	5
nce-nse	n	(d)	science	sin	23
nd-nt	⌒		center	s⌒r	13
ng	‿		rang	r‿	11
nge	j		range	rj	27
o	,		old	,ld	3
oi-oy	i		join	jin	23
ology (s)	l	(d)	psychology	sicl	31
oo	`		room	r—	5

SUMMARY OF WRITING PRINCIPLES

Sound or Sound Combination	Expressed by		Illustrations		Text Chapter
over-other (p) or (s)	O		another	aO	30
ou-ow	o		now	no	18
out (p) or (s)	o		outcome	oc	18
pre-pri pro-per-pur (p)	p	(d)	person	psn	26
position-post (p) or (s)	P		postpone	Ppn	23
qu	q		quick	qc	14
rd-rt	R		toward	tR	22
rity (s)	R	(d)	clarity	clR	22
s (hard)-z	z		reason	rzn	10
s (added to root word)	/		runs rn/ days d/		15
scribe-script (s)	S		inscribe	nS	29
self (p) or (s)	s	(d)	myself	m s	18
sh	sh		she	she	9
sion-tion (s)	|	(d)	edition	ed|	19
sp	s		speak	sec	21
st	st		test	tst	17
t	l		settle	stl	2
th	th		they	th	10
trans (p)	T	(d)	transfer	Tfr	11
u	`		duty	d`e	5
ulate (s)	u		regulate	rgu	29
under	U		undertake	Utc	30

SUMMARY OF WRITING PRINCIPLES

Sound or Sound Combination	Expressed by	Illustrations	Text Chapter
w		work 	7
wh		when 	7

SUMMARY OF WRITING PRINCIPLES

The following eight sentences contain all of the writing principles in Forkner Shorthand.

Chapters 1—4

Eve gave the press a big photo of the bike race.

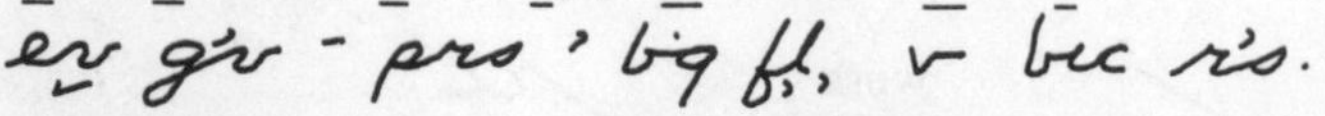

Sound of long *e*	Sound of *a*	Sound of hard *c* and *k*
Sound of short *e*	Sound of *t*	Sounds of *o*
Sound of long *i*	Sound of short *i*	Sound of soft *c*

Chapters 5—8

Are you aware the general may not approve the payment when due unless

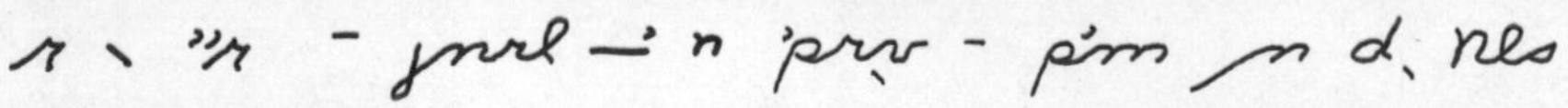

he is consulted?

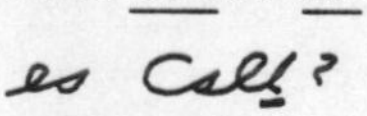

Sounds of *u-oo*	Sound of soft *g* and *j*	Sound of *w-wh*
Sound of *m*	Prefixes *in-en-un*	*awa-away*
Syllable *ment*	*d* or *ed* added to a root word	Prefixes *con-coun-count*

Chapters 9—12

She advised her children to transfer the deposit this evening.

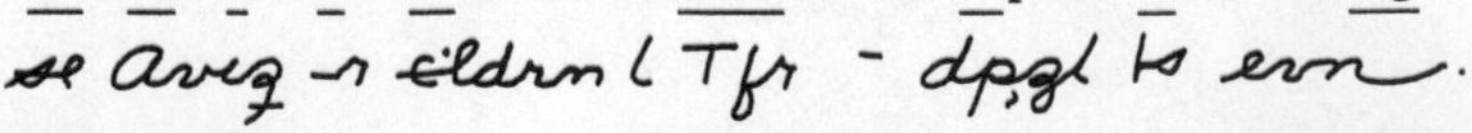

Sound of *h*	Sound of *ch*	Sounds of *ng-ing-thing*
Sound of *sh*	Sound of *th*	Prefix *ad-add*
Prefixes *be-de-re*	Sound of hard *s* and *z*	Prefix *trans*

Chapters 13—16

Everybody left the annual school display quickly, including my friends.

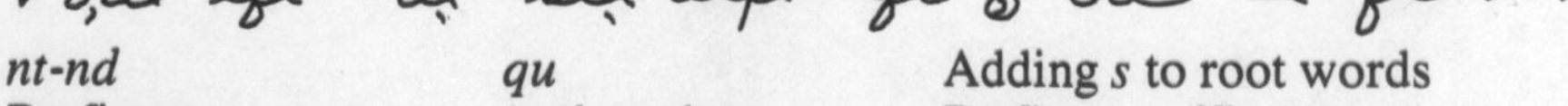

nt-nd	*qu*	Adding *s* to root words
Prefix *an*	*incl-enclose*	Prefix or suffix *ever-every*
Prefixes *dis-des*	*ly*	

SUMMARY OF WRITING PRINCIPLES

Chapters 17—20

The booklet outlines information and publicity on the self-service store

- bcll olin nfr, - pbl8 ,n ssrvs S,

downtown.

donton.

st
sity-city
Sound of *ou-ow*
Prefix or suffix *out*
Prefix or suffix *self*
Sound of *"shun"*

Chapters 21—24

The director instructed the employee to postpone the report at the special

- drcr nc - eplie l Ppn - rpRl - sel

conference on security.

Cfrn ,n scR.

sp
ct
instr
rt-rd
rity
Sound of *oi-oy*
nce-nse
post-position

Chapters 25—28

I forgot to explain that I prefer a change in letterhead design to give greater

l fgl l xpln t l pfr , cj n Ld dgen lgv grr

flexibility.

flxB.

Prefixes *for-fore-fer-fur*
bility
letter-liter
Prefixes *pre-pri-pro-per-pur*
Prefixes *ax-ex-ox*
nge

SUMMARY OF WRITING PRINCIPLES

Chapters 29—32

They undertake, with some success, to regulate, overcome, or control the

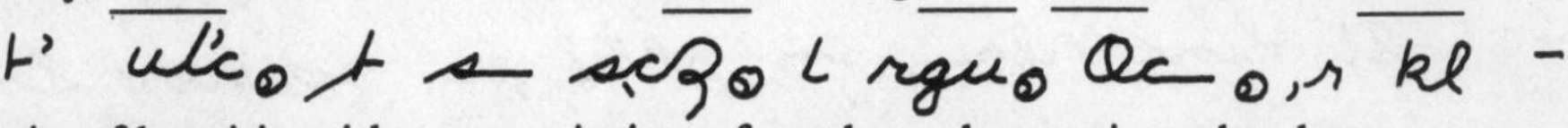

pain of bursitis with a prescription of modern electronic technology.

Syllables *sys-sess-sus-sis-cess-cis*	*contr*	*electr*
ulate	*over-other*	*ology*
scribe-script	*under*	*itis-icitis*

World Wide Travel 1200 Avenue of the Americas, New York, NY 10036 (212) 867-6600

(Current date)

Mr. William French
375 Banks Street
Lansing, MI 48924-1140

Dear Mr. French

There are many acceptable styles for business letters. This is an example of the block style.

Punctuation styles also vary in business letters. This letter has open punctuation. With this style, you omit punctuation at the ends of lines in the address, after the salutation, and after the complimentary close.

You begin the date at the left margin two spaces below the last line of the printed letterhead. Then type the name and address at least four spaces below the date. With short letters, add more space between the date and the name and address so that the letter is well placed.

Now type the salutation at the left margin two spaces below the address. The first paragraph begins at the left margin two spaces below the salutation. Double space between paragraphs.

Begin the complimentary close at the left margin two spaces below the last paragraph. Then place the typed signature of the dictator four spaces below the complimentary close. Add the title of the dictator on the next line if required.

The secretary's identifying initials are typed two spaces below the typed signature or title of the dictator. Some employers prefer to have the dictator's initials typed before those of the secretary. In this case, the two sets of initials are separated by a colon.

Yours truly

Kenneth R. Nelson

Kenneth R. Nelson

krn:js

Tokyo • Sao Paulo • London • New York

LIST OF PHRASES

and the	—	15	he said	esd	2
any time	nele	14	hear from	erfr	14
as soon as	ssns	5	I am	—	6
at least	lles	20	I am sure	—sr	13
at this	lts	20	I can	ic	2
at your	ly	12	I cannot	icn	3
at this time	ltsle	17	I did	idd	3
as well as	s s	17	I do not	idn	7
can be	cb	12	I hope	ip	9
could be	cdb	12	I know	in,	3
could not	cdn	7	I shall	isl	12
did not	ddn	7	I shall be	islb	13
does not	dzn	10	I shall be glad	islbgl	13
for me	fe	6	if you	f	5
for the	f	2	in order to	nRl	22
for you	f	8	in the	n	6
for your	fy	13	in this	nts	22
for us	fs	8	in your	ny	14
had been	dbn	18	in which	nc	27
has been	sbn	23	it is	ls	2
have not	vn	16	it is not	lsn	5
he can	ec	2	let me know	len,	8
he did not	eddn	4	let us know	lsn,	20
he is	es	11	may be	—b	10

Numbers following phrases indicate chapters in which the phrase is introduced.

may be able	—bbl	5	to go	lg	2
must be	—Sb	16	to know	ln,	8
of the	v—	2	to let us	lls	21
on the	,n	3	to make	l—c	15
please let me	pll—	14	to meet	l—el	5
please let me know	pll—n,	10	to pay	lp'	3
please let us know	pllsn,	16	to plan	lpln	2
should be	sdb	9	to receive	lrs	20
should not	sdn	9	to see	lse	9
some time	sl—	12	to send	ls—	13
thank you	^	11	to serve	lsrv	20
there are	trr	20	to settle	lsll	2
there is	trs	25	to sign	lsin	3
this is	tss	20	to talk	ltc	6
to answer	lasr	14	to take	ltc	6
to be	lb	2	to tell	ltl	8
to be able	lbbl	12	to this	lts	20
to bring	lbr—	11	to try	ltri	21
to buy	lbi	8	to us	ls	27
to call	lcl	25	to visit	lvzl	10
to come	lc—	12	to your	ly	6
to do	ld	11	very much	vre—c	16
to find	lfi—	13	was not	zn	30
to follow	lfl,	26	we are	er	7
to get	lgl	20	we are pleased	erp	19
to give	lgv	2	we believe	eblev	9

Numbers following phrases indicate chapters in which the phrase is introduced.

we can	7
we do not	10
we feel	8
we have	10
we have had	22
we have been	12
we have not	30
we hope	10
we may	13
we may not be able	28
we must	17
we plan	28
we received	9
we shall	9
we shall be glad	11
we should	9
we should like	12
we should not	32
we think	11
will be	10
will be glad	16
will not be	22
will you	10
will you please	10
would like	8
would be	7
would have	12
you are	8
you will	10
you will be	32
you will be able	8
you will not	12

Numbers following phrases indicate chapters in which the phrase is introduced.